A Realist Approach for
Qualitative
Research

J. Michael Shirley PhD
Teaching & Learning Assoc.
2042 Level Grove Rd.
Cornelia, GA 30531

This book is dedicated to the memory of Matthew B. Miles and A. Michael Huberman. Pioneers of realism in qualitative research, their book on qualitative data analysis was not only enormously influential in general but was instrumental in shaping my own thinking about the relevance of realism for qualitative research. In addition, they were personally very supportive and helpful to me as I began developing my ideas. They left us much too soon.

A Realist Approach for
Qualitative
Research

Joseph A. Maxwell
George Mason University

Los Angeles | London | New Delhi
Singapore | Washington DC

Los Angeles | London | New Delhi
Singapore | Washington DC

FOR INFORMATION:

SAGE Publications, Inc.
2455 Teller Road
Thousand Oaks, California 91320
E-mail: order@sagepub.com

SAGE Publications Ltd.
1 Oliver's Yard
55 City Road
London EC1Y 1SP
United Kingdom

SAGE Publications India Pvt. Ltd.
B 1/I 1 Mohan Cooperative Industrial Area
Mathura Road, New Delhi 110 044
India

SAGE Publications Asia-Pacific Pte. Ltd.
33 Pekin Street #02-01
Far East Square
Singapore 048763

Acquisitions Editor: Vicki Knight
Editorial Assistant: Kalie Koscielak
Production Editor: Catherine M. Chilton
Copy Editor: Mark Bast
Typesetter: Hurix Systems Pvt. Ltd.
Proofreader: Annette R. Van Deusen
Indexer: Jennifer Pairan
Cover Designer: Candice Harman
Marketing Manager: Helen Salmon
Permissions: Adele Hutchinson

Copyright © 2012 by SAGE Publications, Inc.

Printed in the United States of America

Library of Congress Cataloging-in-Publication Data

Maxwell, Joseph Alex, 1941-
  A realist approach for qualitative research / Joseph Maxwell.
    p. cm.
  Includes bibliographical references and index.
  ISBN 978-0-7619-2923-9 (pbk. : alk. paper)
1. Qualitative research. 2. Social sciences—Research.
3. Research—Methodology. I. Title.
  H62.M324 2012
  001.4'2—dc23
                              2011021356

This book is printed on acid-free paper.

11 12 13 14 15 10 9 8 7 6 5 4 3 2 1

Contents

Preface: The Value of Realism for Qualitative Research   vii

Acknowledgments   x

About the Author   xiii

Part I. A Realist Stance for Qualitative Research   **1**

Chapter 1.   What Is Realism, and Why Should
Qualitative Researchers Care?   3
Chapter 2.   Meaning and Culture Are Real   15
Chapter 3.   Causation Is Real   33
Chapter 4.   Diversity Is Real   49

Part II. Realism and Qualitative Methods   **69**

Chapter 5.   The Realities of Research Design   71
Chapter 6.   Research Relationships and Data Collection   93
Chapter 7.   Real and Virtual Relationships in Qualitative
Data Analysis (with Barbara Miller)   109
Chapter 8.   Understanding, Validity, and Evidence   127

Part III. Applications of Realism in Qualitative Research   **149**

Chapter 9.   Explaining Plains Indian Social Organization   151
Chapter 10. Meaning and Diversity in Inuit
Kinship and Culture   165

Conclusion   181

References   183

Author Index   205

Subject Index   211

Preface

The Value of Realism for Qualitative Research

This book is an argument for the value of a realist philosophical perspective—specifically, what I will call "critical realism"—for qualitative researchers. Chapter 1 provides a detailed explanation of critical realism; here, I want to simply summarize two important characteristics of this perspective, and how I see these as relevant to qualitative research.

The first, and most central, characteristic of critical realism relates to the distinction between ontology and epistemology. Ontology refers to what actually exists—the nature of reality. Epistemology, in contrast, refers to how we gain knowledge of what exists—how we can know anything. Critical realism combines a realist ontology (the belief that there is a real world that exists independently of our beliefs and constructions) with a constructivist epistemology (the belief that our *knowledge* of this world is inevitably our own construction, created from a specific vantage point, and that there is no possibility of our achieving a purely "objective" account that is independent of all particular perspectives). All knowledge is thus "theory-laden," but this does not contradict the existence of a real world to which this knowledge refers.

As I argue in Chapter 1, in our everyday lives most of us implicitly accept both of these propositions. We believe that the earth was round and revolved around the sun long before humans understood this, and most of us believe that global warming is occurring, with potentially serious consequences for humanity, regardless of how many people deny it. We also believe that our knowledge about these things is never complete or infallible, but is always partial and subject to revision. Critical realism simply makes both propositions explicit, and tries to develop their implications for what we do and how we assess our understanding of things.

Second, critical realists in the social sciences treat the ideas and meanings held by individuals—their concepts, beliefs, feelings, intentions, and so on—as equally real to physical objects and processes. Critical realists see these two aspects of reality not as inherently independent and separate realms, but as interacting in social life and mutually influencing one another. Again, this is something most of us accept in our everyday lives. We believe that the meanings people attach to things have consequences for their actions and for the physical world; for example, most of us think that changing people's understanding of the causes of global warming can help to reduce our production of greenhouse gases and thus mitigate the rise in temperature. We also believe that physical events, such as the melting of the Arctic icepack, can influence people's beliefs.

Such views have gained substantial acceptance in philosophy, as I document in Chapter 1, and have been explicitly endorsed by some qualitative researchers (e.g., Hammersley, 1992a; House, 1991; Huberman & Miles, 1985), and implicitly by many others. However, the dominant view in published statements on this issue is that qualitative research requires a thoroughgoing constructivist and relativist ontology *and* epistemology that holds that reality is itself a social construction, and has no existence outside of this construction (e.g., Denzin & Lincoln, 2005a; Guba & Lincoln, 1989).

Thus, in their chapter in the second edition of the *SAGE Handbook of Qualitative Research*, Smith and Deemer (2000; see also Smith, 2008b) challenged my realist approach to validity in qualitative research (Maxwell, 1992), asserting that the ontological concept of a reality independent of our theories and constructions can serve no useful function in qualitative research, since there is no way to employ this that will avoid the constraints of a relativist epistemology. They concluded that "Maxwell is unable to show us how to get reality to do some serious work" (p. 883).

This book is in part a belated response to this challenge. What I want to do in this book is to show how realism can do some serious and important work for qualitative researchers. I believe that taking a realist ontology seriously, and systematically and critically applying this to a number of theoretical and methodological issues in qualitative research, can both provide a stronger justification for what qualitative researchers do, and significantly contribute to and reshape some of our theories and practices.

My goal in making this case is not to critique constructivism or relativism, or to show why realism is superior. An incident may help to illustrate my approach. Some years ago, at a meeting of the Society for the Social Study of Science, I ran into an old friend and former mentor, the philosopher Bill Wimsatt. As we were catching up with each other, I asked him what he was working on these days. He said, "I'm trying to come up with a version of realism that constructivists can't refute." My immediate response was, "I'm trying to come up with a version of realism that constructivists are willing to accept."

Bill replied, "That's what I meant," but the difference between the two approaches is important. Philosophical arguments rarely persuade anyone but philosophers, and in any case there is already an extensive literature, pro and con, on the philosophical implications of realism. My purpose in this book, in contrast to this literature, is informed by two basic principles derived from research on the diffusion of innovations (Rogers, 2003): that for people to adopt an innovation, they must see it as helping them to meet a perceived need of theirs, and must also see it as compatible with their other important beliefs and practices. Here, I hope to make the case that critical realism can meet both of these criteria, at least for many qualitative researchers. I argue that realism helps to resolve some serious philosophical, theoretical, methodological, and political problems that qualitative researchers face, and that it is quite compatible with the actual "logic-in-use" of much qualitative research.

I am not arguing that critical realism is the "correct" paradigm for qualitative research; I am in fact skeptical of the entire concept of "paradigm" as this term is used in the social sciences (Maxwell & Mittapalli, 2010), for reasons suggested in Chapters 2 and 4. The constructivist epistemology of critical realism implies that *no* position or theory can claim to be a complete, accurate representation of any phenomenon, including research itself, and that we should view every theory from both the "believing" and "doubting" perspectives (Elbow, 1986), looking both for what insights and advantages it provides, and for where its blind spots and distortions are (Maxwell, 2010a). However, I think that realism can be a *useful* perspective for qualitative researchers, one that provides insights and strategies that other perspectives ignore or misrepresent, and that can make important contributions to the "paradigm dialog" in the social sciences.

This book has three parts. Part I describes critical realism and addresses three issues for which a critical realist approach has important implications—specifically, for how we conceptualize meaning and culture, causation, and diversity. I claim that all of these phenomena are "real" in the sense that our concepts and theories about these point to, and attempt to capture something about, some aspect of reality. Part II applies critical realist ideas and approaches to the design and methods of qualitative research, including research design itself, research relationships, data collection and analysis, and quality, validity, or trustworthiness. Finally, Part III presents two in-depth case studies of qualitative research projects that I conducted, describing the ways in which realist (and other) perspectives informed my research and the consequences these had for my methods and conclusions.

I believe that a realist perspective can both provide new and productive ways of thinking about the phenomena we study and the methods we use, and help us to defend qualitative research against the criticisms that are often leveled against it by proponents of "science-based" research (Maxwell, 2004b).

Acknowledgments

Chapter 1 incorporates material from "Realism as a stance for mixed method research" (Maxwell & Mittapalli, 2010) and from "The value of realism for qualitative research" (Maxwell, 2007).

An earlier version of Chapter 2 was published as "A realist/postmodern concept of culture" (Maxwell, 1999).

Chapter 3 draws on several previous publications, including "Causal explanation, qualitative research, and scientific inquiry in education" (Maxwell, 2004a); "Using qualitative methods for causal explanation" (Maxwell, 2004c); and "The value of a realist understanding of causality for qualitative research" (Maxwell, 2008), as well as "The importance of qualitative research for causal explanation in education" (Maxwell, 2011).

Earlier versions of parts of Chapter 4 were presented as "Rethinking homogeneity and diversity" (Maxwell, 1993); as an invited address at the Fourth Puerto Rican Congress of Research in Education, San Juan, PR, February 1995, subsequently published as "Diversity and methodology in a changing world" (Maxwell, 1996a); and "Rethinking diversity and community" (Maxwell, 1996b).

Parts of Chapter 5 and 6 are adapted from the second edition of my book *Qualitative research design: An interactive approach* (Maxwell, 2005).

A substantial part of Chapter 7 was previously published as "Categorizing and connecting strategies in qualitative data analysis" (Maxwell & Miller, 2008).

Chapter 8 is drawn substantially, with major revisions, from "Understanding and validity in qualitative research" (Maxwell, 1992), and from "Evidence: A critical realist perspective for qualitative research" (Maxwell, 2009).

Chapter 9 is based in part on "The evolution of Plains Indian kin terminologies: A non-reflectionist account" (Maxwell, 1978) and "Kinship and social organization" (Maxwell & Eggan, 2001).

Chapter 10 is based in part on "Biology and social organization in the kin terminology of an Inuit community" (Maxwell, 1995).

Far too many people have had an influence on this book for me to thank them all here, but I want to single out a few for special recognition:

Bill Wimsatt, who informed and sharpened my thinking about philosophy, biology, and systems theory when I was a doctoral student at Chicago, and who introduced me to Donald Campbell's work.

Fred Erickson, with whom I have intermittently discussed causality in qualitative research for over 25 years, and who encouraged me to continue working on this.

Scott Bauer, David Brazer, Becky Fox, and Julie Kidd, the other members of my writing group, who provided valuable feedback on early drafts of a number of chapters.

Kavita Mittapalli, with whom I collaborated on several papers on realism and qualitative or mixed-method research, and who broadened my understanding of realist approaches in other disciplines.

Marjee Chmiel, my current graduate research assistant, who not only did a lot of the scut work of finding and summarizing sources and cleaning up citations and references, but provided insightful feedback on drafts.

A series of editors at SAGE Publications during the long gestation of this book, particularly C. Deborah Laughton, who encouraged the initial proposal and shepherded it to approval, and Vicki Knight, who guided and chided the work to completion.

My wife, Lynn Konnerth, and my daughters Dora and Ellen, who graciously tolerated my extended time in the basement at my computer.

My debt to Matt Miles and Michael Huberman is too great to simply mention here; I have dedicated this book to their memory.

SAGE Publications would like to thank the following reviewers:

Jan Buhrmann
Illinois College

John Heeren
*California State University,
San Bernardino*

Janet S. Jedlicka
University of North Dakota

Thomas M. Kersen
Jackson State University

Marianna L. Litovich
Wesleyan University

Sam Porter
Queen's University Belfast

Adah L. Ward Randolph
Ohio University

About the Author

Joseph A. Maxwell is a professor in the College of Education and Human Development at George Mason University, where he teaches courses on research design and methods. He is the author of *Qualitative Research Design: An Interactive Approach* (second edition, Sage, 2005), as well as papers on qualitative methodology, mixed-method research, sociocultural theory, and medical education. He has also worked in applied settings. He has given seminars and workshops on teaching qualitative research methods and on using qualitative and mixed methods, and has been an invited speaker at conferences and universities in the United States, Puerto Rico, Europe, and China. He has a Ph.D. in anthropology from the University of Chicago.

Part I

A Realist Stance for Qualitative Research

Introduction

Part I of this book presents a perspective on those aspects of contemporary realist thinking, in both philosophy and the social sciences, that I see as particularly relevant to qualitative research.

Chapter 1 provides an overview of what I am calling "critical realism." This term is often used (particularly outside the US) for one specific version of realism, that associated with the work of Roy Bhaskar (e.g., 1978, 1986, 1989, 2011). However, the term has a long history in philosophy, with diverse definitions, and was first used in the sense I am employing here (the combination of ontological realism and epistemological constructivism) by Donald Campbell (1974). Many other philosophers and social scientists have presented similar views, but with no agreement on a term for this position, so I'm using "critical realism" as a convenient cover term for this range of views.

Chapters 2–4 present a realist perspective on four key concepts that are particularly relevant to qualitative research. Chapter 2 argues that meaning and culture are real; Chapter 3, that causation is real; and Chapter 4, that diversity is real.

Realist social scientists (e.g., Sayer, 1992) have tended to assume that meaning, and mental phenomena in general, are real, rather than being simply theoretical abstractions or social constructions. However, they haven't presented a systematic philosophical justification for this claim. Such a justification has been advanced by some realist philosophers, and in Chapter 2, I develop this justification and its implications for qualitative research. I then apply this to the concept of culture, arguing that culture, being meaningful/mental, is also real, but is a property of groups rather than individuals. This concept implies that culture is not necessarily learned or socially transmitted, and that the mental characteristics of individuals that constitute culture are socially distributed, rather than inherently shared. The latter view has been repeatedly advanced by anthropologists, but has rarely been taken seriously outside of this discipline.

In Chapter 3, I present a realist understanding of causation, as an alternative to the traditional positivist or "regularity" understanding that dominated philosophy until recently and is the basis for almost all quantitative research. The latter view of causation has understandably been rejected by almost all qualitative researchers, and as a result, many qualitative researchers have abandoned the concept of causation entirely, despite using language in presenting their research that implies causation. Only recently has a robust realist conception of causation been developed in philosophy, although this conception has so far had little influence on qualitative research. I present this alternative view of causation, which is quite compatible with qualitative methods and goals, and develop its implications.

In Chapter 4, I argue, following the implications of my analysis of culture in Chapter 2, that diversity is a real phenomenon. This position is opposed to the view (prominent in quantitative research) that regularities and general patterns are the primary reality, with diversity being simply error or "noise" that interferes with identification of "main effects" or "true values." This position has important implications for our understanding of social solidarity and community, which have generally been held to result from shared beliefs, norms, or values. I present an alternative understanding of community, one that sees diversity as inherent in communities and as a possible source of solidarity, rather than being intrinsically problematic and destructive of solidarity. This understanding has important implications for qualitative methodology, which I discuss. The fundamental importance of diversity is also a central theme of postmodernism, and I attempt to combine postmodern insights into, and commitments to, diversity with a realist conception of diversity.

1

What Is Realism, and Why Should Qualitative Researchers Care?

Realism

Philosophic realism in general is defined by Phillips (1987, p. 205) as "the view that entities exist independently of being perceived, or independently of our theories about them." Schwandt adds that "scientific realism is the view that theories refer to real features of the world. 'Reality' here refers to whatever it is in the universe (i.e., forces, structures, and so on) that causes the phenomena we perceive with our senses" (1997, p. 133).

Such views were ignored or disparaged during much of the twentieth century, both by positivists and by constructivists and other antipositivists. However, they have emerged as a serious position in current philosophical discussion (Boyd, 2010; Devitt, 2005; Niiniluoto, 2002; Putnam, 1987, 1990, 1999; Salmon, 2005). In the philosophy of science, including the philosophy of the social sciences, realism has been an important, and arguably the dominant, approach for over 30 years (Baert, 1998, pp. 189–190; Hammersley, 1998, p. 3; Suppe, 1977, p. 618); realism has been prominent in other areas of philosophy as well (Miller, 2010).

There are ongoing philosophical debates over realism that remain unresolved, and realist philosophers themselves disagree about many of these issues; one advocate of realist views claimed that "scientific realism is a majority position whose advocates are so divided as to appear a minority" (Leplin, 1984, p. 1). However, equally serious issues confront alternative positions, and the idea that there is a real world with which we interact, and to which our concepts and theories refer, has proved to be a resilient and powerful one that has attracted increased philosophical attention following the demise of positivism.

In the social sciences, the most prominent manifestation of realism is the "critical realist" tradition usually associated with the work of Roy Bhaskar (1978, 1989, 2011; Archer, Bhaskar, Collier, Lawson, & Norrie, 1998; Manicas, 2006; Sayer, 1992, 2000). However, Bhaskar's work, particularly his more recent development of critical realism as an emancipatory perspective, which he called "dialectical critical realism," departed in significant ways from the position I take here, and has been criticized by others in the "critical realist" tradition (e.g., Pawson, 2006[1]; http://en.wikipedia.org/wiki/Roy_Bhaskar, accessed 11/2/2009). I have therefore not adopted Bhaskar's views in general, although I find his basic positions (particularly on the importance of distinguishing ontology from epistemology) compatible with the stance that I present here.

My position draws substantially from other versions of realism that I see as compatible with the key ideas of the critical realist tradition, and that provide additional insights and alternative perspectives for using realism in qualitative research. These include the work of the social scientist Donald Campbell (1988) and the philosophers Cartwright (1999, 2007), Davidson (1980, 1993, 1997), Haack (1998, 2003), Little (1991, 1995/1998, 2010), McGinn (1999), Putnam (1990, 1999), Salmon (1984, 1989, 1998, 2005), and Wimsatt (2007); the physicist Barad (2007); the linguist Lakoff (1987; Lakoff & Johnson, 1999); the evaluation researchers Pawson and Tilley (1997; Pawson, 2006) and Henry, Julnes, and Mark (1998; Mark, Henry, & Julnes, 2000); and the qualitative researchers Huberman and Miles (1985; Miles & Huberman 1994) and Hammersley (1992a, 1998, 2002, 2009).

A wide range of terms have been used for such versions of realism, including "critical" realism (Archer et al., 1998; Bhaskar, 1989; Campbell, 1974, 1988; Cook & Campbell, 1979), "experiential" realism (Lakoff, 1987), "constructive" (and, later, "perspectival") realism (Giere, 1999), "subtle" realism (Hammersley, 1992a), "emergent" realism (Henry, Julnes, & Mark, 1998; Mark, Henry, & Julnes, 2000), "natural" realism (Putnam, 1999), "innocent" realism (Haack, 1998, 2003), and "agential" realism (Barad, 2007); Wimsatt (2007) didn't give his approach to realism a formal name, but used the phrase

---

[1] Pawson (2006) aligned himself with Campbell's rather than Bhaskar's version of critical realism:

> It is the "critical" element that causes the confusion. . . . Campbell is a critical realist in a quite, quite different sense from Bhaskar and his emancipatory colleagues. For Bhaskarians criticism is warranted on the basis of the analyst's privileged understanding of the oppressive aspects of the social condition and those responsible for it. For Campbell, criticism is something that scientists apply to each other. (p. 20)

"multi-perspectival realism" (p. 12) to describe this. I will use the term "critical realism" in a broad sense to include all of these versions of realism.[2]

A distinctive feature of all of these forms of realism is that they deny that we can have any "objective" or certain knowledge of the world, and accept the possibility of alternative valid accounts of any phenomenon. All theories about the world are seen as grounded in a particular perspective and worldview, and all knowledge is partial, incomplete, and fallible. Lakoff states this distinction between "objectivist" and "realist" views as follows:

> Scientific objectivism claims that there is only one fully correct way in which reality can be divided up into objects, properties, and relations. . . . Scientific realism, on the other hand, assumes that "the world is the way it is," while acknowledging that there can be more than one scientifically correct way of understanding reality in terms of conceptual schemes with different objects and categories of objects. (1987, p. 265)

As Frazer and Lacey put it, "Even if one is a realist at the ontological level, one *could* be an epistemological interpretivist . . . our knowledge of the real world is inevitably interpretive and provisional rather than straightforwardly representational" (1993, p. 182).

Critical realists thus retain an ontological realism (there is a real world that exists independently of our perceptions, theories, and constructions) while accepting a form of epistemological constructivism and relativism (our *understanding* of this world is inevitably a construction from our own perspectives and standpoint). The different forms of realism referenced here agree that there is no possibility of attaining a single, "correct" understanding of the world, what Putnam (1999) describes as a "God's eye view" that is independent of any particular viewpoint.

This position has achieved widespread, if often implicit, acceptance as an alternative both to naïve realism and to radical constructivist views that deny the existence of any reality apart from our constructions. Shadish, Cook, and

---

[2] Bhaskar did not initially use the term "critical realism" for his position, calling his philosophical views "transcendental realism" and his extension of these to the social sciences "critical naturalism." The phrase "critical realism," used previously by other philosophers with different meanings (Groff, 2007, p. 4), was first suggested by others in the Bhaskarian tradition, and then adopted by Bhaskar (http://en.wikipedia.org/wiki/Roy_Bhaskar). It isn't clear whether this suggestion was influenced by Donald Campbell's earlier use, in presenting his theory of what he called "evolutionary epistemology," of the phrase "critical realism" (e.g., 1974/1988, p. 432; Cook & Campbell, 1979, pp. 28–30) to refer to the linking of ontological realism and epistemological relativism (1988, pp. 440–450), a position that is central to Bhaskar's views. Since Campbell's use has historical priority, I will use the term "critical realism" in a broad sense to include a range of positions incorporating this view, including Bhaskar's.

Campbell (2002) argued that "all scientists are epistemological constructivists and relativists" in the sense that they believe that *both* the ontological world and the worlds of ideology, values, etc. play a role in the construction of scientific knowledge (p. 29). Conversely, Schwandt, in his *SAGE Dictionary of Qualitative Inquiry* (2007), stated that

> on a daily basis, most of us probably behave as garden-variety empirical realists—that is, we act as if the objects in the world (things, events, structures, people, meanings, etc.) exist as independent in some way from our experience with them. We also regard society, institutions, feelings, intelligence, poverty, disability, and so on as being just as real as the toes on our feet and the sun in the sky. (p. 256)

Such views have frequently been presented as a commonsense basis for social research. For example, the anthropologist Karl Barth, in a classic work on the rituals and cosmologies of several indigenous New Guinea communities (1987), stated that

> Like most of us, I assume that there is a real world out there—but that our representations of that world are constructions. People create and apply these constructions in a struggle to grasp the world, relate to it, and manipulate it through concepts, knowledge, and acts. In the process, reality impinges; and the events that occur consequently are not predicated on the cultural system of representations employed by the people, although they may largely be interpretable within it. A people's way of life is thus not a closed system, contained within their own cultural constructions. That part of the real world on which we as anthropologists need to focus is composed of this widest compass: a natural world, a human population with all its collective and statistical social features, and a set of cultural ideas in terms of which these people try to understand and cope with themselves and their habitat. (p. 87)

The integration of ontological realism and epistemological constructivism or interpretivism has also been given explicit philosophical defenses, for the physical as well as social sciences (Barad, 2007; Keller, 1992; Lenk, 2003).

Given the wide acceptance of realist views in philosophy, including the philosophy of the social sciences, and the presence of a commonsense realist ontology in much qualitative research, it is puzzling that realism has not had a more direct influence on qualitative research. Despite the early advocacy of an explicitly realist approach to qualitative research by Huberman and Miles (1985; Miles & Huberman, 1994) and others (Hammersley, 1992a; Maxwell, 1990a, 1990b, 1992), critical realism has been largely unnoticed by most qualitative researchers. When it *has* been noticed, it has generally been seen as simply positivism or foundationalism in another guise (Denzin & Lincoln, 2005a; Mark et al., 2000, p. 166).

Example 1.1

A particularly detailed and sophisticated statement of the sort of realism I adopt here (although focused specifically on the physical sciences) was presented by the physicist and historian of science Evelyn Fox Keller (1992), with the assumption that this viewpoint is so widely shared that it needs no explicit defense. She stated,

> I begin with a few philosophical platitudes about the nature of scientific knowledge upon which I *think* we can agree, but which, in any case, will serve to define my own point of departure. First,
>
> - Scientific theories neither mirror nor correspond to reality.
> - Like all theories, they are models, in Geertz's (1973) terms, both models of and models for, but especially, they are models *for*; scientific theories represent in order to intervene, if only in search of confirmation. And the world in which they aim to intervene is, first and foremost, the world of material (that is, physical) reality. For this reason, I prefer to call them tools. From the first experiment to the latest technology, they facilitate our actions in and on that world, enabling us not to mirror, but to bump against, to perturb, to transform that material reality. In this sense scientific theories are tools for changing the world.
> - Such theories, or stories, are invented, crafted, or constructed by human subjects, interacting both with other human subjects and with nonhuman subjects/objects.
> - But even granted that they are constructed, and even abandoning the hope for a one-to-one correspondence with the real, the effectiveness of these tools in changing the world has something to do with the relation between theory and reality. To the extent that scientific theories do in fact "work"—that is, lead to action on things and people that, in extreme cases (for example, nuclear weaponry), appear to be independent of any belief system—they must be said to possess a kind of "adequacy" in relation to a world that is not itself constituted symbolically—a world we might designate as "residual reality."
> - I take this world of "residual reality" to be vastly larger than any possible representation we might construct. Accordingly, different perspectives, different languages will lead to theories that not only attach to the real in different ways (that is, carve the world at different joints), but they will attach to different parts of the real—and perhaps even differently to the same parts. (pp. 73–74)

However, critical realism is strikingly different from positivism in many of its premises and implications (Baert, 1998, pp. 192–193; Maxwell, 1990a, 1990b). There are several features, besides its joining of ontological realism and epistemological constructivism, that distinguish most contemporary realist approaches from positivism and empiricism. The most important of these is that realists reject the view of theoretical concepts that was one of the defining characteristics of positivism (Feyerabend, 1981, pp. 176–202; Norris, 1983; Phillips, 1987, p. 40). Positivists argued that theoretical terms and concepts were simply logical constructions based on, and defined by, observational data, "fictions" that were useful in making predictions but which had no claim to any "reality." This view, generally termed "instrumentalism," although largely discredited in philosophy, is still influential in psychology and the social sciences (Salmon, 1984, pp. 5–7). Realists, in contrast, see theoretical terms as referring to (although, as the Keller quote given earlier makes clear, not "reflecting") actual features and properties of a real world (Devitt, 2005).

Two aspects of this rejection of theoretical instrumentalism are particularly important for qualitative research. First, most critical realists hold that mental states and attributes (including meanings and intentions), although not directly observable, are part of the real world, a position denied by both logical positivism and constructivism. For realists, mental and physical entities are equally real, although they are conceptualized by means of different concepts and frameworks (Putnam, 1999). I discuss this aspect of realism in more detail in Chapter 2.

Second, critical realists endorse the concept of "cause" in both the natural and social sciences, a concept that was one of the main targets of both positivism and its antipositivist critics. While many positivists, from Bertrand Russell (1912/1913) to Fred Kerlinger (1979), argued that causality was a metaphysical notion that should have no role in science, and others simply "operationalized" the concept to the observed association between variables (as described in Chapter 3), most realists see causality as a real phenomenon, an *explanatory* concept that is intrinsic to either the nature of the world (Strawson, 1989) or to our understanding of it (Putnam, 1990; Salmon, 1984). As Putnam put it,

> whether causation "really exists" or not, it certainly exists in our "life world." . . . The world of ordinary language (the world in which we actually live) is full of causes and effects. It is only when we insist that the world of ordinary language (or the Lebenswelt) is defective . . . and look for a "true" world . . . that we end up feeling forced to choose between the picture of "a physical universe with a built-in structure" and "a physical universe with a structure imposed by the mind." (1990, p. 89)

For this reason, critical realists reject the theory of causality that is characteristic of contemporary empiricist successors to positivism and is dominant in quantitative research (e.g., Mulaik, 2009, pp. 63–87; Murnane & Willett, 2010, pp. 26–38). This view, usually referred to as the "regularity" theory of causation, holds that causality consists simply of regular associations between events or variables, patterns in our data, and denies that we can know anything about supposed "hidden" mechanisms that produce these regularities. For critical realists, in contrast, the concept of "mechanism" (in the social sciences, "process" is the usual term) is central to explanation, and these mechanisms and processes are seen as real phenomena, rather than simply as abstract models. I discuss the realist understanding of causality in detail in Chapter 3.

A major concern of constructivists has been that invoking the term "reality" implies that there is one ultimately correct description of that reality. Putnam argued that this assumption ignores William James's insight

> that "description" is never a mere copying and that we constantly add to the ways in which language can be responsible to reality. And this is the insight that we must not throw away in our haste to recoil from James's unwise talk of our (partly) "making up" the world. . . . The notion that our words and life are constrained by a reality not of our own invention plays a deep role in our lives and is to be respected. The source of the puzzlement lies in the common philosophical error of supposing that the term "reality" must refer to a single superthing instead of looking at the ways in which we endlessly renegotiate— and are *forced* to renegotiate—our notion of reality as our language and our life develop. (1999, p. 9; cf. Johnson, 2007, p. 40)

Thus, while critical realism rejects the idea of "multiple realities," in the sense of independent and incommensurable worlds that are socially constructed by different individuals or societies, it is quite compatible with the idea that there are different valid *perspectives* on reality. In this, it is also compatible with the classic statement by the anthropological linguist Edward Sapir, that "the worlds that different societies live in are different worlds, not simply the same world with different labels attached" (1929/1958, p. 69). Language doesn't simply put labels on a cross-culturally uniform reality that we all share. The world as we perceive it and therefore live in it is structured by our concepts, which are to a substantial extent expressed in language. Critical realism also holds that these concepts and perspectives, as held by the people we study as well as by ourselves, are *part of* the world that we want to understand, and that our understanding of these perspectives can be more or less correct.

Critical realism is also compatible with some of the assumptions and implications of postmodernism, including the idea that difference is fundamental rather than superficial (discussed in Chapter 4), a skepticism toward "general laws" (e.g., Giere, 1999; Little, 1995/1998, 2010), an antifoundationalist stance, and a relativist epistemology (Maxwell, 1995, 1999). It differs from postmodernism (at least from radical postmodernism) primarily in its realist ontology—a commitment to the existence of a real, though not an "objectively" knowable, world. I present some of the ways in which realism and postmodernism are mutually supporting, particularly with respect to diversity, in Chapter 4.

Such an ecumenical approach is so characteristic of realism that Baert (1998, p. 194) accuses realists of ruling out almost nothing but extreme positivism. It is true that realism is pragmatic in that it does not discard *a priori* those approaches that have shown some ability to increase our understanding of the world. However, the value of realism does not derive simply from its compatibility with different approaches to research, or from its pragmatic orientation to methods; it can perform useful work in social research (Carter & New, 2004; Danermark, Ekstrom, Jakobsen, & Karlsson, 2001). My argument in this book is that critical realism has important implications for the conceptualization and conduct of qualitative research.

Although a substantial amount of qualitative research is implicitly realist in its assumptions and methods, there have been relatively few explicit statements of realist approaches to qualitative research. A particularly clear example of the latter is the work of one of the major contributors to the development of qualitative research, Herbert Blumer, the leading figure in the symbolic interactionist approach to social research (see Hammersley, 1992a). In a classic paper, "The Methodological Position of Symbolic Interactionism" (1969), Blumer asserted that symbolic interactionism is a perspective in empirical social science—"an approach designed to yield verifiable knowledge of human group life and human conduct" (p. 21). He stated,

> I shall begin with the redundant assertion that an empirical science presupposes the existence of an empirical world. Such an empirical world exists as something available for observation, study, and analysis. It *stands over against* the scientific observer, with a character that has to be dug out and established through observation, study, and analysis. . . . "Reality" for empirical science exists only in the empirical world. (pp. 21–22)

However, Blumer combined this ontological realism with an epistemological constructivism (although, since this term was not available to him, he referred to this position as "idealism"). He asserted that

> the empirical necessarily exists always in the form of human pictures and conceptions of it. However, this does not shift "reality," as so many conclude, from the empirical world to the realm of imagery and conception. . . . [This] position is untenable because the empirical world can "talk back" to our pictures of it or assertions about it—talk back in the sense of challenging and resisting, or not bending to, our images or conceptions of it. (p. 22)

Blumer summarized this argument by stating that "fundamentally, empirical science is an enterprise that seeks to develop images and conceptions that can successfully handle and accommodate the resistance offered by the empirical world under study" (pp. 22–23). This view is strikingly similar to the position stated by Keller, cited earlier, and clearly fits my definition of critical realism: ontological realism plus epistemological constructivism.

Another explicit presentation of realism in qualitative research is a paper by Huberman and Miles, "Assessing Local Causality in Qualitative Research" (1985). (This paper was in many ways a philosophical complement to their book *Qualitative Data Analysis* (Miles & Huberman, 1984, 1994), a detailed presentation of qualitative analysis strategies that was implicitly grounded in a realist perspective.) In this paper, they sought to justify the use of qualitative research to discover and validate causal explanations, and discussed the analytic strategies that qualitative researchers can use to accomplish this. However, despite its clear presentation of a realist conception of causality, the paper actually advocated a "middle ground" between realism (which they equated with "neo-positivism") and idealism, and their focus was almost entirely on realism's implications for causal analysis. In their book *Qualitative Data Analysis*, in contrast, the specific discussions of analysis were not explicitly connected to realist issues, and it was only in the second edition of the book that the word "realism" appeared at all.

Some of the work in the British critical realist tradition associated with Bhaskar (particularly Pawson & Tilley, 1997; Sayer, 1992, 2000) focused on methodological issues that have important implications for qualitative research, but these authors did not address qualitative methods specifically. Until recently, the explicit application of realism to qualitative research subsequent to Huberman and Miles's paper consisted mainly of my work (1990a, 1990b, 1992, 1999, 2002, 2004a, 2004c, 2008, 2009) and that of Martyn Hammersley (1992a, 1998, 2002, 2008, 2009); Seale (1999) applied Hammersley's concept of "subtle realism" to issues of quality in qualitative research. More recent discussions of realism and qualitative research are a paper by Manicas (2009) on critical realism and qualitative methods, Porter (2007) on realism and validity, and the entries on Realism (Medill, 2008) and Critical Realism (Clark, 2008) in the *SAGE Encyclopedia of Qualitative Research Methods* (Given, 2008).

Some qualitative researchers (e.g., Denzin & Lincoln, 2000) have dismissed such versions of realism as "quasi-foundationalist" in maintaining an ontological realism while accepting a constructivist epistemology. They assume that such realists still hold a correspondence theory of truth—that statements are true insofar as they reflect or correspond to the actual state of affairs. This ignores not only arguments such as those of Keller and Putnam, quoted earlier, but also the fact that there is disagreement about just what the "correspondence theory of truth" actually involves. The historian Alex Callinicos stated that

> the correspondence theory doesn't require that we pick out particular segments [of the world] to which true sentences correspond, nor that we postulate some kind of isomorphism between language and the world . . . It is the nature of the world which makes sentences true or false. This does not mean that the world and sentences resemble one another. (1995, p. 82)

I see Callinicos's position as very similar to that stated by Keller, and to the views of critical realists in general. The disagreement is only over whether the term "correspondence" is an appropriate way of describing the relationship between language (or theories) and reality.

A few constructivist qualitative researchers have given more explicit attention to critical realism. Denzin and Lincoln (2005a), in their introduction to the third edition of the *Handbook of Qualitative Research*, discussed critical realism as a possible "third stance" distinct from both naïve positivism and poststructuralism. However, they ended up rejecting most of what critical realists advocate, and stated that "we do not think that critical realism will keep the social science ship afloat" (p. 13).

Similarly, Smith and Deemer (2000), in their chapter in the second edition of the *Handbook of Qualitative Research*, devoted considerable space to specifically challenging Hammersley's and my arguments for realism. Noting that the epistemology of critical realism is relativist rather than realist, in that it rejects the possibility of objective knowledge of the world and accepts the existence of multiple legitimate accounts and interpretations, they asserted that combining ontological realism and epistemological relativism is logically contradictory, and (as noted in my Preface) that we cannot employ an ontological concept of a reality that is independent of our theories in a way that can avoid the constraints of a relativist epistemology (cf. Smith, 2004, 2008b; Smith & Hodkinson, 2005).

Smith and Deemer's argument is one application of what Lincoln and Guba called the "ontological/epistemological collapse," folding the two into one another so that they become simply reflections of each other (Lincoln & Guba, 2000, pp. 175–176). Lincoln argued that "the naturalistic/constructivist paradigm effectively brought about the irrelevance of the distinction between ontology and epistemology" (1995, p. 286). Smith and Deemer likewise treated ontology as necessarily a reflection of epistemology, so that it has no independent contribution to make to qualitative research.

Critical realists, in contrast, explicitly reject this collapse of the distinction between ontology and epistemology (Bhaskar, 1989, p. 185; Campbell, 1988, p. 447); Scott (2000, p. 3) referred to this conflation of ontology with epistemology as the "epistemic fallacy." As Norris stated, "where the anti-realist goes wrong, the realist will claim, is in confusing ontological with epistemological issues" (2002, pp. 3–4). Not only is ontological realism compatible with epistemological constructivism, but ontology has important implications for research that are independent of those of epistemology. However, similarly to Abbott (2001, 2004) and Seale (1999), I see epistemological and ontological perspectives, not as a set of "foundational" premises that govern or justify qualitative research, but as *resources* for doing qualitative research (Maxwell & Mittapalli, 2010).[3]

Thus, one of the major implications of realism for qualitative research, and for the social sciences generally, is that it relegitimates *ontological* questions about the phenomena we study (Lawson, 2003; Tilly, 2008). If our concepts refer to real phenomena, rather than being abstractions from sense data or purely our own constructions, it is important to ask, to what phenomena or domains of phenomena do particular concepts refer, and what is the nature of these phenomena? For example, Tilly (2008) placed primary emphasis on ontology, rather than epistemology, in his discussion of social processes, and stated that "social analysts frequently arrive at false conclusions by assuming the existence of fundamental entities such as social systems without doing the work required to establish the presence of those entities" (pp. 5–6).

In the remainder of this book, therefore, I want to present some of the most important implications of a realist ontology for qualitative research. I argue that realism *can* do useful work for qualitative methodology and practice if it is taken seriously and its implications systematically developed. I do so mainly by describing some specific applications of critical realism to qualitative research, showing how a realist perspective can provide new and useful ways of approaching problems and can generate important insights into social phenomena. As stated earlier, I am not arguing that realism is the "correct" philosophical stance for qualitative research, only that it brings a valuable perspective to the discussion of what kinds of claims and understandings qualitative research can produce.

---

[3] Similarly, the sociologist of science Karin Knorr-Cetina, in her book *Epistemic Cultures* (1999), stated that

> For me, ontology . . . refers to a potentially empirical investigation into the kinds of entities, the forms of being, or the structure of existence in an area. It is an interest that prompts one to look at the way the empirical universe happens to be configured into entities and properties. By not fixing an ontology from the start—by not committing oneself to the thought that the modern world is populated by rational actors, as in rational choice approaches, or by liberal actors, as in political theory, or by systems, as in systems theory—one can see the configuration of several ontologies side by side and investigate their relationship. (p. 253)

2

Meaning and Culture Are Real

In this chapter, I present a critical realist understanding of "meaning" and of mental phenomena in general, one that assumes that mental properties and processes are just as real as physical ones, although they are understood using a different language and conceptual framework. I then use this analysis to critique the traditional concept of culture, arguing that this concept contains questionable assumptions that undermine some of its value for qualitative research. In doing so, I propose a realist concept of culture that I think can provide a more useful way of conceptualizing cultural phenomena. While none of the challenges that I make to the traditional view of culture are new, I think that all of them are strengthened, and some are significantly reframed, by a realist perspective.

A Critical Realist Approach to Meaning and Mind

Meaning is generally understood to be a mental rather than a physical phenomenon ("meaning" and "mind" both derive from the same Indo-European root); in linguistics, "meaning" is what is intended by the speaker or understood by the hearer. Thus, from an ontological perspective, the nature of meaning depends on the nature of mind and its relationship to the physical world—what has been termed the "mind-body problem." This issue has been the subject of longstanding disagreements within philosophy. To oversimplify somewhat, the most prominent historical approaches to this problem have been either versions of dualism (mind and the physical world, including the body, are separate, independent, and irreducible entities with nothing in common) or physicalism (everything that actually exists is physical, and mental phenomena will eventually be reduced to physical—e.g., neurological—entities and processes).

Realist philosophers and social scientists have developed a third approach to this problem, arguing that mental and physical entities are interacting parts of a single real world, but that mental phenomena are not thereby reducible to physical ones. The meanings, thoughts, beliefs, emotions, values, and intentions of individuals are neither abstractions from behavior nor reducible to neurological or other physical phenomena.

A central motivation for this position is that critical realists see "mental" phenomena as inextricably involved in the causal processes that produce behavior and social phenomena, and as essential to causal explanation in the social sciences (e.g., House, 1991, p. 6; Huberman and Miles, 1985, p. 354). (I provide a more detailed account of "causality" in Chapter 3; here, my focus is mainly on meaning, rather than causality.) Thus, Bhaskar (1989) stated that

> two crude philosophical distinctions, between mind and body and reasons and causes, have done untold damage here. . . . reasons, and social forms generally, must be causes [as well as effects]. . . . we have to see the natural and social dimensions of existence as in continuous dynamic causal interaction. (p. 6)

The major philosophical dilemma for such an argument, despite its resonance with our everyday practices and understandings, has been in explaining how the mind and physical world can interact. Dualists have had to resort to such explanations as that the interaction requires God's intervention, or that the two simply operate in complete parallel with no actual interaction (http://en.wikipedia. org/wiki/Philosophy_of_mind). Physicalists, on the other hand, hold that causal interaction implies that mental phenomena must be ultimately physical.

In this chapter, I draw primarily on the work of the philosopher Hilary Putnam (1990, 1999), who argued for the legitimacy of both "mental" and "physical" ways of making sense of the world, and for a distinction between mental and physical *perspectives* or languages, both referring to reality, but from different conceptual standpoints. Putnam rejected both dualism and reductionist physicalism, arguing that reductionist physicalism is incoherent (1999, p. 82 ff.) and that abandoning physicalism does not entail dualism (1999, p. 132). His view was that the question of "psychophysical correlation," the relationship between mind and body, is based on an incorrect assumption:

> I have argued that the very picture that is presupposed by the question is wrong, that is to say, the picture of our psychological characteristics as "internal states" that . . . must either be "correlated" or "uncorrelated" with what goes on inside (literally "inside") our bodies. I have argued that our psychological characteristics are, as a rule, individuated in ways that are context sensitive and extremely complex, involving external factors (the nature of the objects we perceive, think about, and act on), social factors, and the projections we find it natural and unnatural to make. (1999, p. 132)

In abandoning both physicalism and dualism, Putnam argued only that there is what William James called a "double aspect" to our understanding of the world, a view that Putnam traces to Kant. He summarized his position by stating that "the metaphysical realignment I propose involves an acquiescence in a plurality of conceptual resources, of different and mutually irreducible vocabularies . . . coupled with a return not to dualism but to the 'naturalism of the common man.'" (1999, p. 38). Similarly to Lakoff and Johnson (1999; Johnson, 2007), he agreed that our minds are embodied, but insisted that this embodiment doesn't require that we must somehow be able to reduce the vocabulary of ordinary psychological talk to chemistry, physics, neurology, or computer science (1999, pp 148–149).[1]

Putnam's position is thus compatible with realism, but not with reductionism or behaviorism. It provides a philosophical justification for our everyday use of mental terms to describe people's thoughts, intentions, and emotions, without either reducing them to neurophysiology or interpreting them as referring to behavior or behavioral dispositions. The "mental" framework pertains to phenomena that might, in principle, also be conceptualized in physical terms, but it provides a useful perspective on these phenomena that physical theories currently lack, and for which the latter may never be able to substitute.[2]

---

[1] This does not mean that critical realists reject the results of neurological research on the brain structures and processes that are related to thought, or feel that such research is pointless. Putnam (1999) stated that

> not one word of the argumentation in this book should be construed as opposing serious research into the physical basis of our mental life. Indeed, some of the best work into that basis has been done by scientists who are well aware of the difference between finding physical processes that subserve thought, feeling, memory, perception, and so on, and reductionist claims (whether the latter take the form of insisting that thought, feeling, etc. are "identical" with brain processes or they take the "eliminative materialist" form of regarding the whole of ordinary mentalistic vocabulary as so much bosh). Not only does rejecting reductionist pictures not entail abandoning serious scientific research, but, in fact, it is those pictures that often lead researchers to misconceive the empirical problems. (p. 174)

[2] Thus, another realist philosopher, Paul Feyerabend, argued that

> the choice of an idiom for the description of mental events cannot be decided by considerations of testability and "cognitive content" alone. It may well be that a materialistic language (if it ever gets off the ground) is richer in cognitive content than commonsense and contains physiological knowledge that did not exist when the common idioms arose and were shaped by the demands of a complex and demanding life. . . . But it will be much poorer in other respects. For example, it will lack the associations which now connect mental events with emotions, our relations to others, and which are the basis of the arts and the humanities. We therefore have to make a choice: do we want scientific efficiency, or do we want a rich human life of the kind now known to us and described by our artists? The choice concerns the *quality of our lives*—it is a *moral* choice. (1981, p. 162; emphasis in original)

The mental perspective does not only apply to humans. It is implicit in the approach of early ethologists such as Portmann (1961) and Tinbergen (1961), who used concepts such as "image" and "mood" to represent the minds of animals. Its value for understanding the behavior of nonhuman animals has subsequently been impressively documented by biologists such as de Waal (1990, 2007), for chimpanzees, and Heinrich (1999), for ravens. Shettleworth (2010), in a highly regarded textbook on animal cognition, evolution, and behavior, began her preface to the book by stating that "the study of the animal mind is one of the most exciting areas in the cognitive sciences" (p. v), and provided an encyclopedic review of animal cognition that is fundamentally based on "mental" concepts such as recognition, intention, insight, planning, understanding, and the attribution of mental states to others. This discussion was informed by neurological findings but is in no way reducible to the latter. There has been a similar flourishing of interest in animal minds in philosophy (e.g., Johnson, 2007; Lurz, 2009), with strong arguments that even the behavior of invertebrates can be productively understood in terms of their concepts and intentional states (Carruthers, 2009; Tetzlaff & Rey, 2009).[3]

The general applicability of such a "mentalistic" perspective, even to entities that are well understood in physical terms, is shown by Boulding's discussion (1956, pp. 20–22) of the value system and image of the outside world that a thermostat possesses. Bateson similarly argued that "we can assert that *any* ongoing ensemble of events and objects which has the appropriate complexity of causal circuits and the appropriate energy relations will surely show mental characteristics" (1971, p. 315).

The importance of these arguments is that the use of "meaning" or other mental concepts, in theory or description, commits one neither to the existence of mysterious nonmaterial entities—the "ghost in the machine" (Ryle, 1949, pp. 15–16)—nor to an ultimate reliance on introspection and subjectivism. Concepts, meanings, and intentions are as real as rocks; they are just not as accessible to direct observation and description as rocks. In this, they are like quarks, black holes, the meteor impact that supposedly killed off the dinosaurs, or William Shakespeare: we have no way of directly observing them, and our claims about them are based on a variety of sorts of indirect evidence (including verbal behavior). Statements about entities that belong to this "mental" framework are in principle as testable by scientific methods as statements about any other hypothesized or inferred entities that are not subject to direct observation, with the added advantage that through introspection we can sometimes gain additional information about mental processes.

---

[3] This work challenges the view of some qualitative researchers (e.g., Howe, 2011) that "interpretive" research and understanding are applicable only to humans.

Putnam therefore argued that "mental" statements about someone's beliefs, reasons, motives, and so on can be valid explanations of that person's actions (1999, p. 149). While there has been much philosophical debate over the legitimacy of seeing mental phenomena as causes of behavior (Heil & Mele, 1993), the work of Davidson[4] (1980, 1993, 1997) and McGinn (1991), as well as Putnam, has given this position considerable philosophical credibility. Individuals' meanings have *consequences*; how individuals act is influenced by how they think about and make sense of what is going on, a key premise of the "symbolic interactionist" approach to social research (Blumer, 1969), discussed in Chapter 1. This view of intentions, beliefs, and meanings as causes is fundamental to our commonsense explanations of actions, as well as to psychology as a science (Davidson, 1997, p. 111), and has been affirmed not only by critical realists but by many other philosophers (e.g., MacIntyre, 1967; Robb & Heil, 2003) and social scientists (e.g., Menzel, 1978).[5]

---

[4] Although Davidson is the philosopher usually cited for the argument that reasons are causes, both he and many of his critics accepted the view that causal explanation requires causal laws, although Davidson (1975) saw these laws as individual rather than general. The view of reasons as causes becomes less problematic when this dependence of causality on laws is abandoned (Giere, 1999; Putnam, 1999, pp. 73–91, p. 200 fn. 11, 14; Sayer, 1992, pp. 126–127).

[5] Howe (2011) has recently proposed a different analysis of "meaning" causality in qualitative research, accepting the validity of this concept, but arguing that causation for intentional phenomena (I-causation) is different in kind from that for natural phenomena (N-causation). While I endorse his recognition of causation in human interactions, and his position that qualitative and quantitative methods can both be used for intentional and physical phenomena, I have two main points of disagreement with his conclusions.

First, his analysis in terms of two kinds of phenomena still leaves as mysterious the *interaction* between the two, an interaction that is intrinsic to our everyday understanding of causation. Howe acknowledges this problem (p. 169), but states that it is too complicated to deal with in the paper in question, and provides only a few examples that don't really clarify the nature of the interaction. This interaction between "mental" and "physical" aspects is widely (if usually implicitly) acknowledged in the study of nonhuman animals, and I see no reason to believe that humans are uniquely different from chimps, dolphins, dogs, or ravens in the kinds of causal processes that operate in their lives. Rather than seeing the "intentional/mental" and physical as different kinds of *phenomena*, I see these as different *conceptual frameworks*, or languages (Putnam, 1999) for making sense of a single complex reality, as described earlier.

Second, Howe still seems to implicitly rely on a regularity understanding of causality, for both natural and intentional phenomena. Thus, he describes both types of causation as "establishing and accounting for *ordered patterns* of human behavior" (p. 166). Although Howe acknowledges that for N-causation there is a realist/process alternative to the regularity view, he makes no mention of this in his discussion of intentional causation, and never addresses the possibility of causal explanations of singular events, as opposed to regularities.

The neglect of mental phenomena, or the attempt to deal with these solely within a behavioral, variable-oriented framework, is one of the main limitations that qualitative researchers identify in quantitative research, and this is one of the main arguments that qualitative researchers have made for adopting a constructivist or interpretivist stance, since these approaches inherently recognize the importance of the mental realm. However, the types of realism that I discuss here treat both mental and physical phenomena as real. Seeing meanings, beliefs, values, and so on as part of reality supports an interpretivist approach to understanding mental and social phenomena without entailing a radical constructivism that denies the existence, or causal relevance for mind, of a physical world.

Critical realism thus provides a clear argument for accepting a causal role for meanings, and does not assume a forced choice between realism, on the one hand, and interpretivism or constructivism, on the other. This point is often misunderstood or missed, because there is a widespread view that realism is the doctrine that "the world is independent of the mental" (Callinicos, 1995, p. 82), or that realism applies only to *physical* entities and that "mental" phenomena are outside its reach. For example, Hawthorn argued that

> the more cautious agree that what we say about the world is internal to our scheme and so indeterminate. But they nevertheless insist that there are contents of the world, roughly speaking, those contents of the world that are not the contents of consciousness, for which realism is true. (1987, p. 271)

This view seeks to partition the world into one domain in which realism is valid, and a separate domain in which constructivism or relativism can still be maintained. However, the types of realism that I discuss here do not attempt such a separation; they hold that while our *knowledge* of the world is inherently a construction from a particular perspective, there is nonetheless a real world, which can be understood in both mental and physical terms, about which our constructions can be more or less adequate.

Critical realism also supports the idea that individuals' physical contexts have a causal influence on their beliefs and perspectives. While this proposition is widely accepted in everyday life, constructivists have tended to deny the "reality" of such influences, while positivism and some forms of post-positivist empiricism tended to simply dismiss the reality or importance of individuals' perspectives, or to "operationalize" these to behavioral or attitudinal variables. From a realist perspective, not only are both individuals' perspectives and their situations real phenomena, they are *separate* phenomena that causally interact with one another.

This perspective has several benefits for qualitative research. In particular, a realist perspective can provide a framework for better understanding the relationship between actors' perspectives and their actual situations. This issue has been a prominent concern in the philosophy of social science for many years (Gellner, 1973; MacIntyre, 1967; Menzel, 1978), and is central to "critical" approaches to qualitative research. Critical realism treats both actors' perspectives and their situations as real phenomena that causally interact with one another. In this, realism supports the emphasis that critical theory places on the influence that social and economic conditions have on beliefs and ideologies. Sayer (1992, pp. 222–223) stated that the objects of "interpretive" understanding (meanings, beliefs, motives, and so on) are influenced both by the material circumstances in which they exist and by the cultural resources that provide actors with ways of making sense of their situations. However, critical realism approaches the understanding of this interaction without assuming any *particular* theory of the relationship between material and ideational phenomena, such as Marxism.

Mind and Culture

This approach to symbolic/meaningful phenomena has obvious relevance for the concept of culture, since contemporary approaches to culture typically identify this as part of the symbolic/meaningful realm of human experience. However, few realists have explicitly addressed the concept of culture; the major exception is the sociologist Margaret Archer (1996), whose work I discuss shortly. A recent review of the concept of culture across the disciplines (Baldwin, Faulkner, Hecht, & Lindsley, 2005) indicates that there is no current consensus about the definition of this term, and that traditional definitions that have largely been abandoned in anthropology are still widely used in other disciplines.

Qualitative researchers in particular have tended, on the whole, to uncritically adopt a traditional definition of culture as the shared beliefs and values (and sometimes practices) held by the members of a particular society or social group. A common additional assumption is that these shared beliefs and values are what unite the members of a social group. There seems to be little awareness that there is anything problematic about this view, or that the concept of culture deserves particular scrutiny.

For example, the 1,000-page *SAGE Encyclopedia of Qualitative Research Methods* (Given, 2008) does not even contain an entry for "culture," only one for "cultural context" (Morgan & Guevara, 2008); the authors did not attempt to define culture, but took the concept for granted. Similarly, the third edition of Schwandt's *SAGE Dictionary of Qualitative Inquiry* (2007) has only a one-paragraph overview of the concept. While Schwandt acknowledged that "what constitutes culture and how it is best described and interpreted are matters of much debate," he stated that in ethnography, culture refers "to a form or pattern abstracted from observed behavior. Presently, that pattern is most often spoken of as an ideational system—that is, a kind of knowledge and understanding that members of a group share" (p. 59).

As I argued in Chapter 1, one of the major implications of realism for qualitative research is that it relegitimates *ontological* questions about the phenomena we study, as distinct from epistemological ones. If our concepts refer to (not "reflect" or "correspond to") real phenomena, rather than to abstractions from sense data or to our own constructions, it makes sense to ask, to what phenomena or domains of phenomena do particular concepts refer, and what is the nature of these phenomena? A realist ontological perspective challenges some common assumptions about culture, and provides an alternative understanding that can reveal aspects of human sociocultural processes that the traditional view obscures or distorts.

However, my argument does not rely entirely on a critical realist analysis of the traditional view of culture as "shared and socially transmitted." Such conceptions of culture have repeatedly been challenged in the anthropological and sociological literature over the past 50 years, often by prominent scholars. Despite this, the critiques have not dislodged these assumptions from their position of widespread acceptance, particularly in fields other than anthropology.

One of the ontological problems that has recurrently occupied social scientists is the relationship among culture, society (or social structure), mind or personality, and the biological or behavioral organism. Cole (1991), for example, argued that much of what psychologists call "social" is really cultural, and that we need a more psychologically useful concept of culture. D'Andrade stated that

> such terminological quarreling might seem to be academic foolishness. However, most of the battles about the nature of culture have been enlightening, perhaps because they make explicit our assumptions about what is out there, and perhaps because as our assumptions become more explicit, we find that there are more kinds of things out there than we had thought. (1984, p. 114)

Rather than review the different approaches to these issues and their relative advantages and difficulties, I will present a position that I see as particularly compatible with the realist approach that I am taking here. This position is based on the concise but influential formulation by Kroeber and Parsons (1958) of the distinctions among culture, social system, personality, and biological organism. Although I find their distinctions particularly useful, I believe that the grounds on which they made these distinctions are philosophically and theoretically outdated, and I propose a different, realist way of conceptualizing these distinctions. I then develop the implications of their model for a number of key issues in current debates over culture.

Kroeber and Parsons interpreted the relationships among the four concepts of culture, social system, personality, and the biological organism as the historical product of two analytic distinctions. The first of these distinctions was an attempt to separate a sociocultural sphere of investigation from that of the biological sciences, basically along the lines of the heredity-environment distinction. The organism belonged to the biological sphere, but society and culture (at first more or less undifferentiated) were seen as independent of the biological characteristics of the organism, and as transmitted by learning rather than heredity.

The second distinction, a much later one, restricted culture to systems of symbolic-meaningful entities such as ideas and values, while using "society" to refer to systems of interactions among individuals and collectivities. This distinction was stated more fully by Parsons:

> The social-system focus is on the conditions involved in the interaction of actual human individuals who constitute concrete collectivities with determinate membership. The cultural-system focus, on the other hand, is on "patterns" of meaning, e.g., of values, of norms, of organized knowledge and beliefs, of expressive "form." (1961, p. 34)

Kroeber and Parsons noted that a similar distinction had taken place at the biological level, separating a specifically psychological component, usually termed "personality," from the biological organism.

These two distinctions generated a fourfold model of the relationships among these concepts, as seen in Figure 2.1.

While I want to retain this fourfold model, I think the particular grounds on which Kroeber and Parsons made these two distinctions are outdated and no longer plausible. First, basing the separation of the biological and social sciences on the heredity-environment distinction leads to serious conceptual difficulties. As is now generally recognized, it makes no sense to speak of any characteristic of an individual as being due to hereditary rather than environmental causes, or vice versa; every phenotypic trait of an organism is the result of the interaction of genetic and environmental factors, and "relative importance" is meaningless as applied to the cause of any characteristic considered by itself (Dobzhansky, 1962, pp. 42–46; Lewontin, 1974). It *is* meaningful to ask about the relative importance of genetic and environmental factors in producing the *differences* with respect to a particular trait among individuals *in a specified population*, or between specified populations, but such differences are almost never due exclusively to

Figure 2.1 Kroeber and Parsons's Model

culture	society or social system
personality	biological organism

hereditary or environmental factors. Consequently, it is futile to attempt to distinguish sociocultural from biological phenomena on the basis of whether the characteristics in question are innate or acquired.

A more satisfactory separation of sociocultural from biological phenomena employs the distinction between the individual and the system or collectivity of individuals; in fact, Kroeber and Parsons's analysis is more consistent with this distinction than with the heredity-environment distinction (see Parsons, 1961, pp. 33–34). "Organism" and "personality" refer to entities and processes at the individual level; "society" and "culture" to entities and processes at the system or collectivity level. This distinction, employing the concept of level of organization or complexity (Pattee, 1973; Simon, 1969), avoids incorporating causal assumptions into the distinctions among these concepts.

The basis for Kroeber and Parsons's second distinction, that between culture and society, and also between personality and the biological organism, was not explicitly presented in their paper, although Parsons's later statement, quoted earlier, clearly indicates that he saw this in terms of the distinction between symbolic-meaningful phenomena and physical-behavioral ones. This is consistent with Putnam's analysis of the mind/body distinction as based on that between an ideational or mental language or framework and a physical one; that is, that social and cultural concepts belong to the physical and mental frameworks, respectively. They are distinguished from those concepts referring to mind and the biological organism, respectively, by the fact that they pertain to collectivities rather than to individuals. As a society can be seen as consisting of a group of individuals and the behavioral relationships among them, so a culture can be conceived as the associated set of symbolic/meaningful properties of these individuals and the distributive and communicative relationships among these. This view is similar to the distinction made by Toulmin (1972, p. 142) between two perspectives on scientific endeavors, seen as human action: as traditions of procedures, techniques, and concepts, to be studied as the history of ideas, and as professions consisting of organizations, roles, and individuals, to be understood in terms of the activities of individual scientists and scientific groups.

My interpretation of Kroeber and Parsons's fourfold distinction among these concepts can be represented as a 2 × 2 matrix (see Figure 2.2). Having said this, I want to emphasize that I am *not* arguing that culture and society can be analyzed as separate systems. Culture and society, like mind and body (though for somewhat different reasons), are inextricably intertwined in networks of mutual influence, as the earlier quotes from Bhaskar and Putnam make clear. As a result, any attempt to understand sociocultural phenomena must take account of both social and cultural aspects of these phenomena. Sayer (1992) stated that "social phenomena are concept-dependent . . . what

Figure 2.2   Reinterpretation of Kroeber and Parsons's Model

	Symbolic/Mental	Physical
Collectivity	culture	society or social system
Individual	mind or personality	biological organism

the practices, institutions, rules, roles, or relations *are* depends on what they mean in society to its members" (p. 30, italics in original). What I *am* arguing is that culture and society can be seen as ontologically distinct, and that this distinction has some important implications for our theorizing about, and use of, the concept of culture.

This way of distinguishing society and culture is strikingly similar to Archer's (1996, 2007) realist analysis of these two concepts, although she makes no mention of Kroeber and Parsons's model. She frames the distinction as that between "structure" (i.e., social structure) and culture, but does not explicitly define what she means by culture, although she repeatedly refers to the distinction between structure and culture as between material and ideational phenomena (e.g., 2007, p. 49).

However, Archer consistently refers to the cultural and structural domains as "levels," and asserts that it is necessary for theories about the relationships between the two "to recognize the relative autonomy of structure and culture" (1996, p. xi). My grounding of the social/cultural distinction in Putnam's analysis of the mind/body distinction, in contrast, does not assume any particular relationship between the two, and is quite compatible with diverse causal connections that are not easily accommodated to the idea of these as "levels." (I discuss the problem of "levels" in more detail shortly.) In Chapter 9, I present an analysis of some causal connections between culture and social structure in one specific context.

My realist reformulation of the concept of culture conflicts with a number of influential ideas about culture. In the remainder of this chapter, I will deal with some of the most important of these alternative assumptions, explaining why I think they are untenable. Specifically, I will argue that culture is not an abstraction; that it is not a "level" in a hierarchical relationship with society or personality; and that it is not inherently or necessarily shared. I will devote most of my argument to the last of these points, because it is the one that is most widely and uncritically held across the social sciences, and it is the one where I feel a realist alternative has the most important implications; some of these implications are taken up again in Chapter 4. I will also try to show how the concept of culture that one employs has important methodological consequences for one's fieldwork and analysis.

However, to modify the predominantly negative tone of what follows, I want to emphasize what I think culture *is:* a domain of phenomena that are real, rather than abstractions; both symbolic-meaningful (i.e., part of the mental rather than physical perspective) and collective (that is, a property of groups rather than of single individuals); that cannot be reduced to individual behavior or thought or subsumed in social structure; and that is causally inter-related with both behavior and social structure. Stated baldly, some of this may seem to be little more than common sense, but I think its implications are worth investigating, because many formulations of culture have incorporated different assumptions that I think are unwarranted and unproductive.

CULTURE IS NOT AN ABSTRACTION

The view of culture as an abstraction is common both in the social sciences generally (Baldwin et al., 2005) and in qualitative research. In addition to Schwandt's statement, cited earlier, the article on applied ethnography in the second edition of the *SAGE Handbook of Qualitative Research* (Chambers, 2000) stated that "culture is an *abstraction* that has been applied, with various degrees of success, to small groups (i.e., the 'culture' of the classroom) and to large groups (i.e., nation-states)" (p. 852; italics in original).

An influential presentation of this view of culture as an abstraction from behavior was that of the anthropologist David Schneider. Schneider argued that the construction of a "cultural account" of a particular domain is a matter of correctly abstracting symbols and meanings from one's observations and interviews (1976, p. 198; 1980, pp. 126–133). He defined an abstraction as "simply an analytically defined operation that is applicable to, and can be drawn from, observations of behavior" and that "exists in the mind of the observer" (1976, p. 198) rather than in some external reality.

The view of culture as an abstraction from behavioral observations (including verbal behavior) is a vestigial remnant of positivism. As discussed in Chapter 1, positivism held that the meaning of every scientific term must ultimately be specifiable in terms of direct and public observational data, and that theoretical terms, those that could not be given a direct operational definition, were "useful fictions," abstractions from data that might be valuable in making predictions, but which had no claim to any reality. This view of theoretical concepts as simply abstractions from observational data was eventually shown to be untenable (e.g., Hempel, 1952), and this was a major factor in the demise of positivism.

The conception of culture as something real, rather than an abstraction, has important methodological implications. Since culture refers to mental and symbolic entities, rather than physical or behavioral ones, its characteristics must be inferred rather than observed or "abstracted" from observations.

These inferences must be supported by evidence and defended against various "validity threats" (Maxwell, 1992, 2005; see Chapter 8). A cultural analysis should not only meet criteria of simplicity, adequacy, and logical coherence, but should be tested against the full range of relevant data and all plausible alternative analyses (Maxwell, 1995); I present an application of this strategy in Chapter 10.

CULTURE IS NOT A "LEVEL"

Another implication of a realist interpretation of Kroeber and Parsons's model is that culture is not a "level" that stands in a hierarchical relationship to the other "levels" of social structure, personality, and biology. Such a "levels" conception of the relationship among the four concepts, ironically, was later elaborated by Parsons (1966, pp. 6–29), who saw these as comprising a hierarchy of control agencies, proceeding from the cultural system (values) downward to the social system (norms and collectivity), personality (the learned behavioral organization of the individual), and the organism (genetic constitution), which is the point of interaction of the system of action with the physical environment. Parsons apparently shifted from the first to the second view of culture, but never resolved many of the difficulties with the latter conception (Schmid, 1992).

This view of culture as a "level" is also alive and well in contemporary social science (Baldwin et al., 2005), but is in conflict with the one advanced here. The most serious point of disagreement is that, with the definition of the society-culture distinction as norms vs. values, much of what I have considered culture was assigned by Parsons to the social sphere. One consequence of this is that the development of cultural theory was directed along more limited and less productive lines (Sheldon, 1951, pp. 40–42). The "stratigraphic" conception of the four concepts was also criticized by Geertz (1965, pp. 50–55), who argued that this formulation, and the attempt to tie putative cultural universals to presumed requirements of the lower levels, have in fact hindered the theoretical integration of the four fields and the discovery of genuine functional interrelationships between them. "Culture" and "social structure" do refer to a higher level of organization than the individual, but this does not have any necessary implications for hierarchy or control; many realist scholars (e.g., Sayer, 1992) argue that culture and social structure are deeply entangled, and that causal relationships run in both directions. The problem of the relationship of norms to values is an important and difficult one, but I do not think that a separation of the two into different levels or hierarchically related systems is the best approach to it.

The view that culture, society, personality, and organism are linked in a linear sequence of control implies that a society's adaptation to its environment is initially mediated by the "lower" levels in the hierarchy, such as subsistence activities, and that the "higher" levels, especially ideational systems, have a less direct role in the adaptation process. This approach was challenged by, among others, Keesing (1974, pp. 76–77) and Rappaport (1967, 1971). In contrast, Kroeber and Parsons's model, as I employ it, does not entail any particular theory of sociocultural change, and is compatible with the work of Rappaport and others who saw culture as having a direct role in environmental adaptation. I discuss a specific example of this in Chapter 9.

One implication of the critical realist position I present here is that it legitimates and clarifies the concept of "ideological distortion"—that cultural forms may obscure or misrepresent aspects of the economic or social system or the physical environment—while affirming the causal interaction between the physical and social environment and cultural forms. In particular, realism is compatible with what have been called "ideological" or "nonreflectionist" approaches to culture, in which cultural forms that contradict aspects of social structure may serve ideological functions that act to sustain the social system (including class domination) or constitute adaptive responses to the physical or social environment (e.g., Maxwell, 1978; McKinley, 1971a, 1971b; Murphy, 1967; Sypnowich, 2010; Willis, 1977); I discuss this in more detail in Chapter 9. An emphasis on causal processes, rather than regularities or laws, in explaining sociocultural phenomena also allows explanations to be tailored to single cases and unique circumstances, so that different individuals or social groups may have different responses to similar situations, depending on differences in specific personal or cultural characteristics that are causally relevant to the outcome.

CULTURE IS NOT NECESSARILY SHARED

Finally, from the realist perspective I've presented here, the concept of culture cannot be restricted to a set of *shared* concepts, symbols, and beliefs. A culture is a *system* of individuals' conceptual/meaningful structures (minds) found in a given social system, and is not intrinsically shared, but participated in (Aberle, 1960); although sharing is one *possible* form of participation, it is not the only one. Culture cannot be represented by a model on the same scale as the individual, i.e., as a "shared" set of meanings or beliefs that could be held by a single individual, but requires a model at a higher level of complexity.

The view that culture is inherently shared, by definition or empirical fact, has been subjected to repeated challenges in anthropology. These challenges have been both theoretical (Aberle, 1960; Hannerz, 1992; Kronenfeld, 2008; Linton, 1936; Pelto & Pelto, 1975; Urban, 1991; Wallace, 1970) and empirical (Atran & Medin, 2008; D'Andrade, 1984; E. Heider, 1972; K. Heider, 1978; Sanjek, 1977; Sankoff, 1971; Shore, 1996; Swartz, 1982). Further, the idea that what is shared by individuals is most central to the functioning of a sociocultural system has also been questioned; diversity may be of equal or greater significance (Wallace, 1970), and I take up this issue in Chapter 4.

A systematic alternative to the traditional conception of culture was developed by Wallace (1970), who distinguished between what he called the "replication of uniformity" and "organization of diversity" approaches to culture; some implications of this distinction are discussed in Chapter 4. The replication of uniformity model assumes that culture and community are based on similarity—shared beliefs and values—and that the key task of any society is to maintain and transmit these core similarities. The organization-of-diversity model, in contrast, rejects this assumption that similarity is the basis of culture, and looks at culture as a system of *different* beliefs and values that are connected through interaction. Wallace pointed out the lack of evidence for the functional necessity of shared goals, motives, or beliefs, and the increasing empirical evidence for cognitive diversity, and argued that ordered, stable societies depend not on a uniformity of beliefs and motives, but on a systematic relationship between diverse cognitive systems that permits prediction of behavior. More recently, in a detailed analysis of the environmental beliefs and practices of several communities, Atran and Medin (2008) argued that "for our purposes, it is just a nonstarter to treat or define cultures or groups in terms of shared properties" (p. 265), and that "the study of culture is the study of variation within and across populations" (p. 222).

A strikingly similar critique of the traditional concept of culture was expressed by Erikson, a sociologist:

> The idea that people *do* different things in the service of some overall pattern of coordination is entirely familiar to social scientists and is usually called "division of labor." . . . The idea that people *think* or *feel* different things in the service of an overall pattern of coordination, however, seems a good deal farther fetched, but that is more or less what I am arguing. In the same sense that people contribute different skills and abilities to the organization of *work*, so people contribute different temperaments and outlook to the organization of *sensibility*. (1976, p. 83)

Pratt (1988) similarly stated that linguistics has been dominated by an assumption of homogeneity, what she called a "linguistics of community," and argued that more attention needs to be paid to a "linguistics of contact," which abandons this assumption and focuses on relations across differences.

A concept of culture that explicitly incorporates individual diversity is strikingly analogous to the domain of phenomena in psychology known as "socially situated cognition" (Resnick, Levine, & Teasley, 1991) and to what Perkins (1992) called "distributed intelligence," although culture is not limited to cognition but can include affect as well. Hutchins, using the concept of "socially distributed cognition," claimed that

the ideational definition of culture [as shared concepts] prevents us from seeing that systems of socially distributed cognition may have interesting cognitive properties of their own. In the history of anthropology, there is scarcely
a more important concept than the division of labor. . . . The emphasis on
finding and describing "knowledge structures" that are somewhere "inside"
the individual encourages us to overlook the fact that human cognition is
always situated in a complex sociocultural world and cannot be unaffected
by it. (1995, p. xiii)

However, many of those writing about situated cognition use this phrase
interchangeably with "socially shared cognition," obscuring precisely what
I see as most important about the concept. Addressing this problem, Cole
(1991) argued that the term "shared" is ambiguous, since it has two distinct
meanings: "held in common" or similar, and "divided up" or distributed. He
elaborates on the latter meaning as "the division of cognitive labor." Resnick
et al. (1991) provided extensive empirical evidence for the socially situated
and distributed nature of cognition, evidence that supports the arguments for
intracultural diversity presented earlier, and Kronenfeld (2008), drawing from
linguistics, cognitive science, and anthropology, developed a detailed theory of
culture as a decentralized system of distributed cognition, illustrating this with
carefully analyzed empirical examples.

Shore (1996) clearly stated the position I take here:

As anthropologists have come to better understand the social life of everyday
knowledge, they have increasingly adopted a "distributive" view of culture.
Culture is not accurately conceived of as a neat packaging of traditions possessed equally by all members of a community. A distributive view of culture
sees culture as a complex knowledge system unevenly appropriated in social
and political time and space. (p. 209)

Shore grounded this approach to culture in Lakoff and Johnson's "experiential realism" (1999, p. 334), one of the versions of critical realism discussed
in Chapter 1.

However, I think Shore was overly optimistic about the adoption of this
view. Certainly outside of anthropology, the "learned, shared, and socially
transmitted" definition of culture is still dominant (Varenne, 2008). In his
chapter in the SAGE Handbook of Qualitative Research, Chambers continued
the definition of culture cited earlier by stating that "an operational definition
might be that culture is apparent when distinctly shared meanings are discovered to be present in any given group" (2000, p. 852).

Methodologically, the realist view of culture proposed here implies that
uniformity or sharing (and its presumed importance and consequences)
must be demonstrated rather than assumed (Berkhofer, 1973; Maxwell, 1999;
Urban, 1991, p. 1). In particular, statements about a culture must be based on

more than a few "key" informants. Not only must systematic sampling be done in order to support such statements and to assess the actual conceptual diversity present in a society (E. Heider, 1972; Sankoff, 1971), but there is evidence that key informants themselves assume greater uniformity than actually exists (Pelto & Pelto, 1975, p. 7; Poggie, 1972).

Atran and Medin (2008) forcefully restated this perspective:

> The distributional concept of culture implies a methodology that departs in distinct ways from traditional anthropology, where the intrepid explorer becomes immersed in culture X and returns to report how Xers think and behave. . . . Rarely in ethnography does the explorer ever specify precisely which Xers think and behave this way (nor do they hint that all Xers might not think and behave this way). . . . Like modern biology, the distributional view of cultural phenomena does not take individual variation as deviation but as a core subject of study. (p. 220)

There have been two common strategies for "explaining away" evidence of intracultural diversity. The first has been to see surface variation as grounded in an "underlying" or a "higher-level" uniformity (e.g., Schneider, 1980, pp. 122–123). This explanation of diversity was criticized by Yanagisako, who stated that the premise that "higher" levels are less variable than "lower" ones "has nowhere been adequately supported by cultural data" (1978, p. 26) and argued that the assumption is not true for Japanese-American kinship.

The second way of dealing with intracultural diversity is to treat variation within the larger culture as the result of subcultures within this culture. Denzin and Lincoln's (2005a) interpretation of philosophical diversity within qualitative research, in terms of specific paradigms being shared by subgroups of qualitative researchers, is an example of this strategy. This simply takes the problem to a lower level, and is often unsupported by empirical evidence that these "subcultures" are themselves uniform.

McCawley (1982) addressed this issue by examining the debate between two positions in linguistics, generative semantics and interpretive semantics, that had generally been seen as unitary paradigms. He showed that both of these "paradigms" in fact consisted of two packages of positions on a large number of issues, each package corresponding to the views of some prominent members of two communities of linguists. However,

> neither of these communities was completely homogeneous, no member of the community retained exactly the same set of views for very long, . . . and the relationships among the views that were packaged together as "generative semantics" or as "interpretive semantics" were generally far more tenuous than representative members of either community led people (including themselves) to believe. (1982, p. 1)

A valid cultural analysis must incorporate procedures designed to counteract these two theoretical biases.

In summary, I have argued, first, that meaningful or symbolic phenomena can be productively understood using a realist approach that sees such phenomena as real, but as comprehended by means of a different conceptual framework than that used for physical and behavioral phenomena. Second, I have claimed that this understanding is compatible with, and supportive of, "interpretive" approaches to qualitative research. Finally, I have attempted to show how this realist approach challenges some traditional ideas about culture, ideas that have been influential in qualitative research. In doing so, I have asserted the validity of the concept of causality in dealing with mental/meaningful phenomena, and the importance of diversity within cultures. These two issues are taken up in detail in Chapters 3 and 4, respectively.

3

Causation Is Real

Until a few years ago [causal claims] were in disrepute in both philosophy and economics alike and sometimes in the other social sciences as well. Nowadays causality is back, and with a vengeance . . . methodologists and philosophers are suddenly in intense dispute about what these kinds of claims can mean and how to test them.

Nancy Cartwright
Hunting Causes and Using Them (2007)

While I think that Cartwright downplays the extent to which questions of causality and causal explanation have been important in the philosophy of science over the last 40 years, following the demise of logical positivism and of the "deductive-nomological model" as a credible theory of scientific explanation (Kitcher & Salmon, 1989; Salmon, 1984, 1998), her statement clearly identifies the current ferment over issues of causality. I believe that contemporary realist approaches to causality provide a valuable conceptual framework both for doing and for justifying qualitative research that is intended to draw causal conclusions. In this chapter, I focus on how a realist perspective differs from positivist/quantitative and constructivist views of causality, and on how qualitative researchers can use this perspective in their work.

The ability of qualitative research to address causality has been a contested issue for some time. Divergent views on this question are currently held within both the qualitative and quantitative traditions, and there is little sign of a movement toward consensus. However, the emergence of realism as a distinct alternative to both positivism/empiricism and constructivism, as a philosophical stance for social science, has provided a new way to address this issue (Manicas, 2006; Maxwell, 2004a). I will first outline the positivist/ empiricist and constructivist positions on causal explanation in relation to qualitative research, and then describe a realist approach that avoids many of the problems created by these positions.

While there are many differences between positivism and realism (Schwandt, 1997, pp. 133–134), one of the most important of these is their divergent views of causality. The positivist view (also called the "regularity" or "successionist" theory of causation) was derived from David Hume's analysis of causality,[1] as elaborated by J. S. Mill and others. Hume's fundamental idea was that we cannot directly perceive causal relationships, only what he called the "constant conjunction" of events. He denied that we can have any knowledge of causality beyond the observed regularities in associations of events, and repudiated any reference to unobservable entities and mechanisms. (For this reason, some positivists rejected the concept of "cause" entirely, arguing that it had no meaning beyond this observed regularity.)

This position was given its most systematic statement by Hempel and Oppenheim (1948) in what they called the "deductive-nomological" theory of causation. This approach "seeks laws and principles of the utmost generality" (Salmon, 1989, p. 182), and sees scientific explanation as the fitting of specific facts and events into this framework of laws, which may be statistical as well as deterministic. This "covering law" approach was the standard view of causality in the philosophy of science for much of the twentieth century (Salmon, 1989).

Mohr (1982) labeled this approach to causal explanation "variance theory"; it defines causality as a consistent relationship between variables. It treats the actual process of causality as unobservable, a "black box," and focuses on discovering whether there is a systematic relationship between inputs and outputs. In this view, causal inference requires both some sort of systematic comparison of situations in which the presumed causal factor is present or absent, or varies in strength, and the implementation of controls on other possible explanatory variables. Mohr argued that "the variance-theory model of explanation in social science has a close affinity to statistics. The archetypal rendering of this idea of causality is the linear or nonlinear regression model" (1982, p. 42), and that this conception of causality is "the basis of ordinary quantitative research and of the stricture that we need comparison in order to establish causality" (1996, p. 99).

A common interpretation of this position (e.g., Light, Singer, & Willett, 1990) is that only experimental research is capable of establishing causal

---

[1] Not all philosophers believe that Hume in fact held a regularity theory of causation. Strawson (1989), drawing on the work of many other philosophers, argued that Hume was actually a realist with respect to causation, and Coventry (2006) characterized Hume's position as "quasi-realist."

conclusions, with randomized experiments as the "gold standard" for causal investigation. A broader version is that nonexperimental quantitative methods, such as structural equation modeling, can also be used to make causal claims (e.g., Mulaik, 2009; Murnane & Willett, 2010). Most proponents of these views hold that qualitative methods are limited to suggesting causal hypotheses or providing supporting data for "causal" quantitative research (e.g., Shavelson & Towne, 2002; see Maxwell, 2004a).

This approach to causation had a far-reaching impact on qualitative research. Becker described the detrimental effect that Hume's theory has had on sociological writing, leading researchers to use vague or evasive circumlocutions for causal statements, "hinting at what we would like, but don't dare, to say" (1986, p. 8). Some qualitative researchers accepted the requirements that this approach to causality entails, and denied that they were making causal claims that were more than speculative (e.g., Lofland & Lofland, 1984, pp. 100–102).

However, other qualitative researchers reacted to the hegemony of the "regularity" approach by denying that causality is even a valid concept in the social sciences. A particularly influential statement of this position was by Lincoln and Guba (1985), who argued that "the concept of causality is so beleaguered and in such serious disarray that it strains credibility to continue to entertain it in any form approximating its present (poorly defined) one" (p. 141). They later grounded this view in a constructivist stance, stating that "there exist multiple, socially constructed realities ungoverned by natural laws, causal or otherwise" (Guba & Lincoln, 1989, p. 86), and that "'causes' and 'effects' do not exist except by imputation" (p. 44).

These two reactions to the regularity view have been so influential that the two-volume *SAGE Encyclopedia of Qualitative Research Methods* (Given, 2008) had no entries for cause or causation, and the only nondismissive mention of causation in the third edition of the *SAGE Handbook of Qualitative Research* (Denzin & Lincoln, 2005b) was in the chapter on qualitative evaluation and public policy (House, 2005), for which the issue of causation is almost impossible to avoid.

Both of these reactions identified causality with the "regularity" theory of causation, and ignored the existence of an alternative, realist approach to causality, one that saw causality as fundamentally referring to the actual causal mechanisms and processes that are involved in particular events and situations. For the philosophy of science in general, this approach was most systematically developed by Salmon (1984, 1989, 1998), who referred to it as the "causal/mechanical" view. In this approach, "explanatory knowledge opens up the black boxes of nature to reveal their inner workings. It exhibits the ways in which the things we want to explain come about" (Salmon, 1989, p. 182).

In the philosophy of the social sciences, very similar views were developed, by critical realists and others. Sayer (1992) argued that

> much that has been written on methods of explanation assumes that causation is a matter of regularities in relationships between events, and that without models of regularities we are left with allegedly inferior, "ad hoc" narratives. But social science has been singularly unsuccessful in discovering law-like regularities. One of the main achievements of recent realist philosophy has been to show that this is an inevitable consequence of an erroneous view of causation. Realism replaces the regularity model with one in which objects and social relations have causal powers which may or may not produce regularities, and which can be explained independently of them. In view of this, less weight is put on quantitative methods for discovering and assessing regularities and more on methods of establishing the qualitative nature of social objects and relations on which causal mechanisms depend. (pp. 2–3)

These mechanisms are seen not as general laws, or as having invariant outcomes, but as situationally contingent; their actual context is inextricably part of the causal process (Cartwright, 1999, p. 73; Little, 1995/1998, p. 197 ff.; Pawson & Tilley, 1997).

Mohr (1982) called this approach to causal explanation "process theory," in distinction from variance theory. Process theory deals with *events* and the processes that connect them; it is based on an analysis of the causal *processes* by which some events influence others. Process explanation, since it deals with specific events and processes, is less amenable to statistical approaches. It lends itself to the in-depth study of one or a few cases or a relatively small sample of individuals, and to textual forms of data that retain the chronological and contextual connections between events. Similar distinctions to that between variance theory and process theory include Blumer's distinction between "variable analysis" and the "process of interpretation" (1956), Ragin's between variable- and case-oriented approaches (1987), and Yin's between factor theories and explanatory theories (1993, pp. 15 ff.).

The development of a process approach to causality in the social sciences has not been limited to self-identified critical realists. Dissatisfaction with the Humean, regularity understanding of causality has been widespread in philosophy, and a process or realist approach has been taken up by a diverse group of social scientists in psychology, sociology, political science, economics, and history (e.g., Falleti & Lynch, 2009; George & Bennett, 2005; Groff, 2007; Lawson, 2003; Little, 2010; Morrison, 2009; Tilly, 2008). Little (2010), writing mainly to historians, provided a particularly trenchant statement:

> it is very important for historians to arrive at deeper understandings of the metaphysics [ontology] of social causation. This means, first, understanding the complete inadequacy of the traditional positivist interpretations of

causation: "causation is no more than regularity." This Humean view does not serve the natural sciences well, and it certainly does not help us when it comes to social causation. So it is necessary to explore a different model of causation that fits better with what we know about the actual workings of social processes. The model developed above is "causal realism." (Little, 2010, p. 218)

Both regularity/variance theory and process theory are forms of causal explanation. Process theory is not merely "descriptive," as opposed to "explanatory" variance theory; it is a different *approach* to explanation. Variance theory typically involves a "black box" approach to the problem of causality in the social sciences. Lacking direct access to social and cognitive processes, researchers must attempt to correlate differences in output with differences in input, and control for other plausible factors that might affect the output. In contrast, process theory, which is much more suitable for qualitative methods, can often directly investigate these causal processes though observation of social settings and interviews with participants.[2]

Such a "process" approach to causation has been advocated by a significant number of qualitative researchers (e.g., Britan, 1978, p. 231; Erickson, 1986, p. 82; Fielding & Fielding, 1986, p. 22). Weiss argued that

> in qualitative interview studies the demonstration of causation rests heavily on the description of a visualizable sequence of events, each event flowing into the next. . . . Quantitative studies support an assertion of causation by showing a correlation between an earlier event and a subsequent event. An analysis of data collected in a large-scale sample survey might, for example, show that there is a correlation between the level of the wife's education and the presence of a companionable marriage. In qualitative studies we would look for a process through which the wife's education or factors associated with her education express themselves in marital interaction. (1994, p. 179)

Similarly, Miles and Huberman stated that "field research is far *better* than solely quantified approaches at developing explanations of what we call *local causality*—the actual events and processes that led to specific outcomes" (1984, p. 132, italics in original), and Sayer argued that "[causal] explanation requires mainly interpretive and qualitative research to discover actors' reasoning and circumstances in specific contexts—not in abstraction from them" (2000, p. 23). McAdam, Tarrow, and Tilly, writing for qualitative sociologists, argued that "compared to other techniques, scholars have made relatively little use of ethnographic methods to systematically interrogate the dynamics of contention,

---

[2] To anticipate a distinction explained in Chapter 4, variance theories are based on the identification of similarities and differences in the values of variables (virtual relationships), while process theories focus on the *actual* relationships of entities and events.

despite the fact that the strength of the method is its attentiveness to process" (2008, pp. 307–331).

An example of the value of such a process approach is provided by a mixed-method study of patient falls in a hospital (Morse & Tylko, 1985; Morse, Tylko, & Dixon, 1987) that included qualitative observations of, and interviews with, elderly patients who had fallen, focusing on *how* they moved around in the hospital environment and the reasons they fell. The researchers used these data to identify causes of falls, such as the use of furniture or IV poles for support, that had not been reported in previous quantitative studies; this identification was made possible by the study's focus on the process of patient ambulation and the specific events and circumstances that led to the fall, rather than on attempting to correlate falls with other, previously defined variables.

A realist understanding of causality thus provides a philosophical justification for the ways in which qualitative researchers typically approach explanation, whether they explicitly use the term "cause" or not. There are three specific aspects of qualitative research that are supported by this understanding: the use of qualitative methods to identify causality in single cases, the essential role of context in causal explanation, and the legitimacy of seeing individuals' beliefs, values, motives, and meanings as causes.

IDENTIFYING CAUSALITY IN SINGLE CASES

A realist approach justifies qualitative researchers' claims to be able to identify causality in single case studies, without necessarily employing control groups or formal pre/post comparisons. Salmon (1998) stated that

> Hume concludes that it is only by repeatedly observing associated events that we can establish the existence of causal relations. If, in addition to the separate events, a causal connection were observable, it would suffice to observe one case in which the cause, the effect, and the causal relation were present. (p. 15)

Salmon then argued that "causal processes are precisely the connections Hume sought, that is, that the relation between a cause and an effect is a physical connection" (p. 16).[3] Scriven (2008) similarly argued that "causation can be directly observed, in lab or home or field, usually as one of many contextually embedded observations, such as lead being melted by heating a crucible, eggs being fried in a pan, or a hawk taking a pigeon" (p. 18).

---

[3] Note that Salmon is talking about physical science (cf. 1989, p. 180). As discussed shortly, realists dealing with the social sciences typically consider mental as well as physical processes to be causal, although mental processes are not amenable to direct observation.

A long line of experimental research on perception supports the view that we can in fact observe causal relationships. Sperber (1995), in his introduction to a book on causal cognition, states that the "anti-Humean idea, that causal relations may be perceived and not just inferred, has been espoused, developed, and experimentally tested by the Belgian psychologist Andre Michotte (1946), and is elaborated on in several contributions to this book" (p. xvi). In fact, experimental research supports a distinction (in non-human animals as well as humans) between what has been called "natural" causal perception in a single event, and "arbitrary" causal judgment based on the identification of regularities (Dickinson & Shanks, 1995; Kummer, 1995). These two types of causal knowledge, which closely correspond to the distinction presented earlier between realist and regularity conceptions of causation, appear to involve quite different cognitive processes (Premack & Premack, 1995).

Miles and Huberman (1994), drawing on their experience with multisite educational policy research, gave a detailed explanation of how qualitative methods can provide credible accounts of such causal relationships and processes (pp. 144–165), and showed how to develop and test "causal maps" for single-case studies. They argued that "qualitative analysis, with its close-up look, can identify *mechanisms*, going beyond sheer association. It is unrelentingly *local*, and deals well with the *complex* network of events and processes in a situation" (p. 147, italics in original). They concluded that "if you've done it right, you will have respected the complexity of local causality as it has played out over time, and successfully combined 'process' and 'variable' analysis" (p. 160).

Similarly, Becker (2008) argued that many classic qualitative studies in the social sciences "analyze directly observed processes, chains of events that produce the outcomes we want to understand. . . . Process analysis presents substantial difficulties for quantitative studies, which generally have to substitute such makeshifts as panel studies, population measurements at several selected times, etc. for realistic, more or less continuous empirical observation." Thus, Jankowski (1991), reporting on his 10-year participant observation study of urban gangs in three cities, stated that

> unable to observe gang violence directly, researchers have treated it as a dependent variable, something to be explained using structural and individual-oriented independent variables. This study . . . seeks to understand the anatomy of violence as well as to explain it. (p. 138)

As Becker (1996) noted elsewhere, "It is invariably epistemologically dangerous to guess at what could be observed directly." The ability of qualitative methods to directly investigate causal processes in single cases is a major contribution that this approach can make to social research and evaluation.

CAUSATION AND CONTEXT

Realist social researchers place considerable emphasis on the context-dependence of causal explanation (e.g., Huberman & Miles, 1985, p. 354; Sayer, 1992, pp. 60–61). Pawson and Tilley (1997) summed up this position in their formula "mechanism + context = outcome" (p. xv). They maintained that "the relationship between causal mechanisms and their effects is not fixed, but contingent" (p. 69); it depends on the context within which the mechanism operates (see also Cartwright, 1999, p. 73). This is not simply a claim that causal relationships vary across contexts; it is a more fundamental claim, that the context within which a causal process occurs is, to a greater or lesser extent, intrinsically involved in that process, and often cannot be "controlled for" in a variance-theory sense without misrepresenting the causal mechanism (Sayer, 2000, pp. 114–118). For the social sciences, the social and cultural contexts of the phenomenon studied are crucial for understanding the operation of causal mechanisms.

Thus, Goldenberg (1992), in a case study of the reading progress of two students and the effects of their teacher's behavior on this progress, stated that "if we see these dimensions as variables divorced from this context, we risk distorting the role they actually play" (p. 540). And Miles and Huberman (1994, pp. 151–165) argued that "the components of a causal map are of a different nature than a disembodied beta coefficient or partial correlation; they are not probabilistic, but specific and determinate, grounded in understanding of events over time in the concrete local context" (p. 159). In this view, causality is fundamentally *local* rather than general, and general causal claims must be grounded in valid site-specific causal explanations.

MEANING AND CAUSALITY

Finally, as argued in Chapter 2, critical realist social scientists see the meanings, beliefs, values, and intentions held by participants in a study as just as real as physical phenomena, and as playing a causal role in individual and social phenomena. For example, Manicas (2009) stated that "at the heart of social science explanation is the idea of a social mechanism with persons as causal agents . . . since persons are the dominant causes of what occurs in society, the first problem for the social scientist is to understand action as it is understood by the actors" (p. 33). Similarly, Sayer (1992), in a critical realist approach to research methods, argued that "social phenomena are concept-dependent. . . . What the practices, institutions, rules, roles, or relationships *are* depends on what they mean in society to its members" (p. 30).

Seeing meanings, beliefs, values, and so on as part of reality thus provides a consistent grounding for accepting a causal role for meanings, and supports an interpretivist approach to understanding social phenomena without entailing a radical constructivism that denies the existence or causal relevance of a physical world. This point is often misunderstood or missed, because there is a widespread view that realism is the doctrine that "the world is independent of the mental" (Callinicos, 1995, p. 82). The versions of realism discussed here treat mental phenomena as *part of* reality, not as a realm separate from it, although it is a part that is understood by means of a different conceptual framework from that used for the physical world.

Combining this view with a process-oriented approach to causality can resolve the long-standing perceived contradiction between "reason" explanations and "cause" explanations, and integrate both in explanatory theories. Unfortunately, Weber's sharp distinction between causal explanation and interpretive understanding (1905; Layton, 1997, pp. 184–185) had a profound influence on qualitative research, obscuring the importance of reasons as causal influences on actions, and thus their role as essential components of any full explanation of human action. Realism can deal with the apparent dissimilarity of reason explanations and cause explanations by showing that reasons can plausibly be seen as real phenomena in a causal nexus leading to the action.

In combination, these components of a realist approach to causality provide a powerful strategy for addressing causal explanation in qualitative research, one that allows qualitative researchers, in many circumstances, to develop causal explanations independently of quantitative, variance-theory strategies. In addition, this strategy complements the strengths of quantitative research and emphasizes the potential contribution of qualitative methods to mixed-method research.

These three uses of a realist concept of causality are also valuable in defending qualitative research from the dismissive and marginalizing attacks of so-called "science-based research," which seeks to impose a quantitative, variance-theory standard on all social research (e.g., King, Keohane, & Verba, 1994). I have elsewhere (Maxwell, 2004a, 2004c) presented specific ways in which qualitative researchers can use a critical realist concept of causality to challenge the assumptions on which these attacks are based, and to argue that that it is possible for qualitative researchers to be fully "scientific" in the sense of being able to systematically develop and validate causal explanations for the phenomena they study. (Of course, not all qualitative researchers aspire to do this; much qualitative research is explicitly grounded in the arts and humanities rather than the sciences.)

I think that much of what qualitative researchers already do in developing and assessing evidence for their conclusions can be applied to the task of causal explanation, for two reasons. First, evidence for causality is not in principle different from evidence for any other sort of conclusion; the function of evidence in general is to enable the researcher to develop, modify, and test conclusions, and many of the qualitative procedures for doing this are applicable to causal investigation. While some qualitative researchers hold, following Weber, that assessing the validity of interpretive claims is different in principle from assessing causal explanations, Sayer argued that "in so far as reasons and beliefs can be causes of social events, the evaluation of interpretive understanding is not so different from that of causal explanations as is often supposed" (1992, p. 223). Second, many qualitative researchers are already making and assessing causal claims, but without framing these in explicitly "causal" language. Any argument that something "influences," "impacts," "shapes," "produces," or "transforms" something else is a causal claim, and requires appropriate sorts of evidence to support that claim. Making the causal implication explicit allows a more rigorous evaluation of such claims.

However, developing causal explanations in a qualitative study is not an easy or straightforward task. Furthermore, there are many potential validity threats to *any* causal explanation, threats that will need to be addressed in the design and conduct of a study. In this, the situation of qualitative research is no different from that of quantitative research; both approaches need to identify and deal with the plausible validity threats to any proposed causal explanation. This ability to rule out plausible alternative explanations or "rival hypotheses," rather than the use of any specific methods or designs, is widely seen as the fundamental characteristic of scientific inquiry in general (Campbell, 1986, p. 125; Platt, 1964; Popper, 1934/1959; Scriven, 2008). Thus, I turn now to how qualitative research can accomplish these tasks.

Becker, in discussing George Herbert Mead's theory of society, stated that in Mead's view,

> the reality of social life is a conversation of significant symbols, in the course of which people make tentative moves and then adjust and reorient their activity in the light of the responses (real and imagined) others make to those moves. . . . Social process, then, is not an imagined interplay of invisible forces or a vector made up of the interaction of multiple social factors, but an observable process of symbolically mediated interaction. (1966, p. 69)

However, Becker then made a fundamental point about the observation of social processes: "Observable, yes; but not easily observable, at least not for scientific purposes" (1966, p. 69). Dunn argued similarly that "there are still no cheap ways to deep knowledge of other persons and the causes of their actions" (1978, p. 171).

Shortly, I discuss some specific strategies that qualitative researchers can use in developing causal explanations. Some of these are standard qualitative data collection and analysis methods: intensive, long-term involvement, the collection of rich data, and narrative analysis. Others are less commonly used in qualitative research: intervention, comparison, the "modus operandi" strategy (Scriven, 1976), and the development of causal narratives and maps.

I am not claiming that these methods are either thoroughly developed or foolproof. Becker argued more than 40 years ago that

> these methods have all kinds of problems, some because their logic has never been worked out in the detail characteristic of quantitative methodologies; others because you gather your data in the middle of the collective life you are studying. (1970, p. vi)

Observing (and analyzing) social processes is hard work, requiring both substantial time and methodological skill. Most books on qualitative methods discuss the skills involved in such observation, though usually without directly relating these to causal inference. I see three strategies as particularly useful for causal explanation in qualitative research: intensive, relatively long-term involvement; collecting "rich" data; and using narrative or "connecting" approaches to analysis.

INTENSIVE, LONG-TERM INVOLVEMENT AND "RICH" DATA

Becker and Geer (1957) claimed that long-term participant observation provides more complete data about specific situations and events than any other method. Not only does it provide more, and more varied, data, but the data are more direct and less dependent on inference. Repeated observations and interviews, and the sustained presence of the researcher in the setting studied, can give a clearer picture of causal processes, as well as helping to rule out spurious associations and premature theories. They also allow a much greater opportunity to develop and test interpretations of the meanings for participants of situations and events.

For example, Becker (1970, pp. 49–51) argued that his lengthy participant observation research with medical students not only allowed him to get beyond their public expressions of cynicism about a medical career and uncover an idealistic perspective, but also enabled him to better understand how these different views were shaped by, and expressed in, different social situations, and how students dealt with the conflicts between these perspectives.

"Rich" data (often, and erroneously, called "thick description"; see Maxwell & Mittapalli, 2008) are data that are detailed and varied enough that they provide a fuller and more revealing picture of what is going on, and of the processes involved (Becker, 1970, p. 51 ff.). In the same way that a detailed, chronological description of a physical process (for example, of waves washing away a sand castle, or the observations of patient falls described earlier) often reveals many of the causal mechanisms at work, a similar description of a social setting or event can reveal many of the causal processes taking place. In a social setting, some of these processes are mental rather than physical, and are not directly observable, but can often be inferred from behavior (including speech).

In addition, Becker (1970) claimed that rich data

> counter the twin dangers of respondent duplicity and observer bias by making
> it difficult for respondents to produce data that uniformly support a mistaken
> conclusion, just as they make it difficult for the observer to restrict his observa-
> tions so that he sees only what supports his prejudices and expectations. (p. 53)

NARRATIVE AND CONNECTING ANALYSIS

Causal explanation is contingent on the analysis strategy used, as well
as the data collected. The distinction between categorizing and connecting
analysis, described in Chapter 8, is particularly important for deriving causal
conclusions from your data. Categorizing strategies such as coding, which
depend on splitting up and reorganizing data into categories and analyzing
the relationships within and between categories, fragment the actual causal
processes embedded in these data, and allow only generic statements of causal
relationships among categories. The analysis of local causality is dependent on
preserving these links and using an analytic strategy that identifies and elucidates the actual connections between events and the complex interaction of
causal processes in a specific context.

Such strategies have received much less explicit development than categorizing ones, as discussed in Chapter 8. Narrative analysis is the most widely
recognized strategy that preserves connections within the data from a single
observation or interview, but "narrative analysis" covers a wide range of techniques (Lieblich, Tuval-Mashiach, & Zilber, 1998), some of which have more
in common with categorizing than connecting strategies. While categorization
in qualitative research is quite different from categorization in quantitative
research, for causal explanation its value is primarily comparative, identifying
differences and similarities and relating these to other differences and similarities. A different type of analysis is needed for processual explanation.

Although narrative analyses are usually not explicitly concerned with
causality, the tools they employ can be applied to the purpose of elucidating
causal connections. Abbott (1992) gave a detailed account of how a reliance on
variance theory distorts sociologists' causal analyses of cases, and argued for a
more systematic and rigorous use of narrative and process analysis for causal
explanation. Similarly, the strategy that Erickson (1992) called "ethnographic
microanalysis of interaction" can be used to identify and explicate causal
processes in observational data. This strategy "begins by considering whole
events, continues by analytically decomposing them into smaller fragments,
and then concludes by *recomposing* them into wholes. . . . [This technique]
returns them to a level of sequentially connected social action (1992, p. 217,
italics in original).

A variety of other narrative or processual approaches to causation have been developed in different fields, including analytic narratives (Bates, Greif, Levi, Rosenthal, & Weingast, 1998) and process tracing (Little, 1995/1998, p. 211 ff.). What these have in common is a focus on understanding the specific causal chains and interactions that led to a particular outcome in a single case.

However, Sayer (1992, pp. 259–262) noted that narratives have specific dangers. They tend to underspecify causality in the processes they describe, and often miss the distinction between chronology and causality; their linear, chronological structure tends to obscure the complex interaction of causal influences; and their persuasive "storytelling" can avoid problematizing their interpretations and deflect criticism. Researchers need to be aware of these issues, and address them in drawing conclusions.

In addition to these widely used qualitative methods, there are other tools available to qualitative researchers that are not commonly associated with qualitative research, but which can be usefully applied in particular circumstances to develop and test causal explanations. I will briefly present three of these: intervention, comparison, and the "modus operandi" method.

INTERVENTION

Although some qualitative researchers have seen deliberate manipulation as inconsistent with qualitative approaches (e.g., Lincoln & Guba, 1985), this view is by no means universal. The integration of qualitative methods with experimental interventions has a long history in the social sciences (e.g., Lundsgaarde, Fischer, & Steele, 1981; Milgram, 1974; Trend, 1978; Weisner, 2002). The issues of quantification and of experimental manipulation are independent dimensions of research design (Maxwell, Sandlow, & Bashook, 1986) and are not inherently incompatible (Maxwell & Loomis, 2003).

However, interventions can also be used less formally within more traditional qualitative studies that lack a "control group." For example, Goldenberg, in a study of two students' reading progress and the effect that their teacher's expectations and behavior had on this progress (1992), shared his interpretation of one student's failure to meet these expectations with the teacher. This resulted in a change in the teacher's behavior toward the student, and a subsequent improvement in the student's reading. The intervention with the teacher, and the resulting changes in her behavior and the student's progress, supported Goldenberg's claim that the teacher's behavior, rather than her expectations of the student, was the primary cause of the student's progress or lack thereof. The logic of this inference, although it resembles that of time-series quasi-experiments, was not simply a matter of "variance theory" correlation of the intervention with a change in outcome; Goldenberg provided a detailed account of the *process* by which the change occurred, which corroborated the identification of the teacher's behavior as the cause of the improvement in a way that a simple correlation could never do.

Furthermore, in field research the researcher's presence is *always* an intervention in some ways (Hammersley & Atkinson, 2007; Maxwell, 2002; see Chapter 5), and the effects of this intervention can be used to develop or test causal theories about the group or topic studied. For example, Briggs, in her study of an Eskimo family (1970), used a detailed analysis of how the family reacted to her often inappropriate behavior as an "adopted daughter" to develop her theories about the culture and dynamics of Eskimo social relations.

COMPARISON

While explicit comparisons (such as between intervention and control groups) for the purpose of causal inference are most common in quantitative, variance-theory research, there are numerous uses of comparison in qualitative studies, particularly in multicase or multisite studies; Miles and Huberman (1994, p. 254) provide a list of strategies for comparison, and advice on their use. "Controlled comparison" (Eggan, 1954) of different societies is a long-standing practice in anthropology, and research that combines group comparisons with qualitative methods is widespread in other fields as well. Such comparisons (including longitudinal comparisons and comparisons within a single setting) can address one of the main objections raised against using qualitative case studies for causal inference—their inability to explicitly address the "counterfactual" of what would have happened *without* the presence of the presumed cause (Shadish et al., 2002, p. 501).

In addition, single-setting qualitative studies, or interview studies of a relatively homogeneous group of interviewees, often incorporate less formal comparisons that contribute to the interpretability of the case. There may be a literature on "typical" settings or individuals of the type studied that make it easier to identify the relevant causal processes in an exceptional case, or the researcher may be able to draw on his or her own experience with other cases that provide an illuminating comparison. In other instances, the participants in the setting studied may themselves have experience with other settings or with the same setting at an earlier time, and the researcher may be able to draw on this experience to identify the crucial mechanisms and the effect that these have.

For example, Regan-Smith's study of exemplary medical school teaching and its effect on student learning (1992) included only faculty who had won the "Best Teacher" award; from the point of view of quantitative design, this was an "uncontrolled," preexperimental study. However, all of the previously mentioned forms of informal comparison were used in the research. First, there is a great deal of published information about medical school teaching, and Regan-Smith was able to use both this background and her own extensive knowledge of medical teaching to identify what it was that the teachers she studied did in their classes that was distinctive, and the differences in student responses to these strategies. Second, the students Regan-Smith interviewed explicitly contrasted these teachers with others whose classes they felt were not as helpful to them, explaining *why* the former's teaching was effective.

THE "MODUS OPERANDI" STRATEGY

This strategy, originally proposed by Scriven (1976), resembles the approach of a detective trying to solve a crime, an inspector trying to determine the cause of an airplane crash, or a physician attempting to diagnose a patient's illness. Basically, in situations in which the causal process is not directly observable, the modus operandi strategy involves searching for "clues" (what Scriven called the "signatures" of particular causes) as to whether particular processes were operating and if they had the causal influence hypothesized. This is also an important strategy for assessing the validity of a proposed explanation, and will be discussed in this context in Chapter 8.

My point in presenting these strategies is that qualitative researchers already have available to them many tools for generating and testing causal explanations and the evidence to support these. I believe that a realist understanding of causality can help qualitative researchers to use these tools more effectively, and to develop new ways of assessing their conclusions.

I reiterate that I am not claiming that a realist approach is the single "correct" understanding of causality. I accept the possibility of multiple useful approaches to causality, and see value in a dialogue between these. Cartwright (2007) provided a detailed argument for what she called "causal pluralism," the view that what causes are and what they do varies from case to case.[4] She stated that current approaches "are not alternative, incompatible views about causation; they are rather views that fit different kinds of causal systems" and that "there is no single interesting characterizing feature of causation; hence no off-the-shelf or one-size-fits-all method for finding out about it, no 'gold standard' for judging causal relations" (p. 2). I believe, however, that the realist approach I describe here is particularly compatible with qualitative methods and premises, and can be of significant value to qualitative researchers.

---

[4] Although this work deals mainly with variance/regularity approaches to causation, due in part to Cartwright's focus on causal explanation in economics, her earlier work makes it clear that she is an advocate of what she calls "local realism" (1999, p. 23), and an opponent of causal reductionism and universal causal laws: "It is capacities that are basic, and laws of nature obtain—to the extent that they do obtain—on account of the capacities; or, more explicitly, on account of the repeated operation of a system of components with stable capacities in particularly fortunate circumstances" (1999, p. 49).

4

Diversity Is Real

I argued in Chapter 2 that intracultural diversity is a real and important phenomenon, one often ignored, minimized, or suppressed by "uniformist" views of culture. In this chapter, I extend this argument for the reality of diversity to social as well as cultural phenomena, and attempt to show that diversity is not only ubiquitous, but is of central importance in understanding these phenomena. In particular, it raises serious questions about the nature of social solidarity and community, and the roles that similarity and difference play in these.

The recognition of diversity as a real phenomenon, rather than as peripheral and secondary to the inherent, shared nature of some category of entities or processes, is particularly prominent in biology. A central feature of the Darwinian revolution was that it replaced a Platonic view of variation among organisms (that variations within a species were simply imperfect approximations to the "ideal" or "type" of the species) with a realist view that saw actual variation as the fundamental fact of biology and the cornerstone of evolutionary theory (Gould, 1985; 1996, pp. 41–42; Lewontin, 1973; Pelto & Pelto, 1975, pp. 14–15). The evolutionary biologist Mayr (1982, pp. 45–47) saw the former position as an example of what he called "essentialism": the view that the norm or the "typical" individual is the important characteristic of a species, and that individual variation is largely random "noise" around this mean. In opposition to this, he argued for what he called "population thinking," which focuses on variation rather than mean values. Mayr stated that "the most interesting parameter in the statistics of natural populations is the actual variation, its amount, and its nature" (1982, p. 47). Example 4.1 provides a practical application of this understanding.

In making this argument for the reality and importance of diversity, I link critical realism to postmodernism—specifically, to what has been called

49

Example 4.1

Steven Jay Gould's essay "The Median Isn't the Message" conveys both the reality of diversity and its practical importance. Gould wrote this essay after being diagnosed with mesothelioma, a particularly lethal form of cancer, and discovering that the median survival time after discovery was only eight months. However, as an evolutionary biologist, he realized that the median was not the fundamental reality, but only an abstraction calculated from the actual variation in survival times. He stated,

> We still carry the historical baggage of a Platonic heritage that seeks sharp essences and definite boundaries. (Thus we hope to find an unambiguous "beginning of life" or "definition of death," although nature often comes to us as irreducible continua.) This Platonic heritage, with its emphasis in clear distinctions and separated immutable entities, leads us to view statistical measures of central tendency wrongly, indeed opposite to the appropriate interpretation in our actual world of variation, shadings, and continua. In short, we view means and medians as the hard "realities," and the variation that permits their calculation as a set of transient and imperfect measurements of this hidden essence. If the median is the reality and variation around the median just a device for its calculation, the "I will probably be dead in eight months" may pass as a reasonable interpretation.
>
> But all evolutionary biologists know that variation itself is nature's only irreducible essence. Variation is the hard reality, not a set of imperfect measures for a central tendency. Means and medians are the abstractions. Therefore, I looked at the mesothelioma statistics quite differently—and not only because I am an optimist who tends to see the doughnut instead of the hole, but primarily because I know that variation itself is the reality. I had to place myself amidst the variation. (Gould, 1985)

Gould in fact lived for another 20 years, and died from an unrelated form of cancer.

"affirmative" (Rosenau, 1992) or "moderate" (Kvale, 1995) postmodernism. A central component of all of the various approaches that have been labeled "postmodern" is the idea that difference is fundamental rather than superficial, and that the goal of dissolving and reconciling all differences in some ultimate unity is illusory (Bernstein, 1992; Leach, 1992; Rosenau, 1992). Affirmative or moderate postmodernism accepts this premise, and the repudiation of "totalizing metanarratives" that attempt to provide a single, unified, definitive account of some phenomenon (Rosenau, 1992, p. 6), without abandoning the quest for valid understandings of the world. Thus, Ezzy (2002, pp. 15–18) argued that while some postmodernists deny that reality exists, others simply want to problematize our assumptions about reality in light of the complexity of our process of understanding it, citing Kvale's claim (1995, p. 21) that while moderate postmodernism rejects the idea of universal truth, it "accepts the possibility of specific, local, personal, and community forms of truth with a focus on daily life and local narrative" (Ezzy, 2002, p. 18).

I see this affirmative understanding of postmodernism as compatible with science and empirical research, rather than fundamentally opposed to these. I also see it as compatible with a critical realist position that denies that there is any privileged perspective on or understanding of the world, and thus accepts that there can be multiple valid perspectives and accounts of the world. However, in attempting to join these two perspectives, my goal is not to *reconcile* realism and postmodernism. Instead, I want to put the two perspectives in dialogue with one another, and to show that, jointly, they have some important implications for our understanding of diversity (cf. Maxwell, 1999).

If postmodernists are right that difference is fundamental rather than superficial, and if diversity is a real and important phenomenon, rather than simply irrelevant "noise" or secondary to what individuals have in common, I see two main implications for research. First, we need to better understand the diversity that actually exists within social institutions and societies, and to investigate the ways in which social solidarity and community are created and sustained that may not depend on the similarities between us. Second, we need to use methods for social research that do not presume commonality or similarity or impose an illusory uniformity on the phenomena we study, as described in Chapter 2 with respect to culture. I will discuss these two issues in turn.

A Realist/Postmodern Understanding of Diversity and Community

Social and political theorists have generally assumed that diversity, despite its moral and practical benefits, is inherently in conflict with solidarity and community. They have typically taken for granted that individual or group differences are intrinsically a source of tension, and need to be overcome or transcended through the recognition or creation of commonalities. Conversely, they have usually defined community in terms of shared values and practices, and assumed that social solidarity is the result of what we have in common with others, the ways in which we are similar.

Even theorists who challenged the assumption that solidarity is based on what we have in common, such as Richard Rorty, did not provide an explicit account of how community or solidarity can be generated without similarity. As a result, they tended to fall back on similarity as the ultimate basis for solidarity.

> Feelings of solidarity are necessarily a matter of which similarities and differences strike us as salient. . . . [Solidarity] is thought of as the ability to see more and more traditional differences (of tribe, religion, race, customs, and the like) as unimportant when compared to similarities. (Rorty, 1989, p. 192)

Likewise, Burbules and Rice (1991), despite their avowed goal of "celebrating difference" and promoting dialogue across differences, repeatedly referred to differences as "conflicts," "problems," and "challenges," and as being "difficult to overcome." Although they listed three benefits of dialogue across differences, none of these involves seeing difference as beneficial to community or solidarity *per se*, only as an "opportunity" for improving our identities, our understanding of others, and our communicative practices.

These authors have not been able to conceive of community or solidarity in a way that does not fundamentally depend on similarity, or to envision a morally acceptable social order that does not involve consensus or commonality at some level. Giroux (1991) framed the dilemma this creates as including "how a politics of difference can be constructed that will not simply reproduce forms of liberal individualism, [and] how a theory of difference can be developed that is not at odds with a politics of solidarity" (pp. 40–41).

Confronting the two unacceptable alternatives of a purely procedural, utilitarian, exchange-based model of social order that has no place for solidarity or community, and of a communitarian ideal that privileges homogeneity, most theorists have chosen to try to reconcile the assumed necessity of shared beliefs and values with a respect for difference; they see unity and diversity as end points on a continuum, and seek a balance between the two (e.g., Strike, 1994. p. 25).

Others, facing this dilemma, abandoned the goal of community entirely:

> The ideal of community . . . privileges unity over difference, immediacy over mediation, sympathy over the limits of one's understanding of others from their point of view. . . . Those motivated by it will tend to suppress differences among themselves or implicitly to exclude from their political groups persons with whom they do not identify. (Young, 1990, p. 300)

To oppose similarity-based models of community and solidarity by arguing for difference and diversity *per se* lacks credibility because, despite the demonstrable value of diversity for both individuals and societies, difference cannot by itself constitute a basis for solidarity; any assertion that it *should* be such a basis is not just utopian, but incoherent. Consequently, advocates of diversity have been forced to smuggle similarity back into their theories as the ultimate source of solidarity, attempting to broaden and universalize its scope and to embed diversity within it. Thus, while Burbules and Rice denied that dialogue across differences involves eliminating these differences or imposing a single view, they still seemed to see its goal as "consensus or common understanding," and to seek a dialogue that "can sustain differences within a broader compact of toleration and respect" (1991, p. 402).

The only way out of this dilemma is to find another dimension to bring into the discussion, one that escapes the totalizing opposition between similarity and difference. In this chapter, I argue that in all human societies, there are two fundamentally different kinds of relationships that are involved in the creation and maintenance of solidarity: relations of similarity, and relations of contiguity. (I discuss this distinction further in Chapter 7.) I will first clarify the distinction between these two dimensions, and then present and analyze several examples that illustrate the significance of contiguity-based solidarity. Finally, I will discuss some of the problems and limitations of contiguity as a source of solidarity.

Similarity and Contiguity as Sources of Solidarity

The distinction between similarity and contiguity, as two aspects of thought and modes of relationship, was first explicitly stated by David Hume in his *A Treatise of Human Nature* (1739/1978). Hume defined three ways in which ideas may be associated: by resemblance (similarity), by contiguity in time or place, and by cause and effect. He then argued that causation is a complex relation based on the other two, leaving resemblance and contiguity as the two primary modes of association. Hume used this distinction widely, but not systematically, in the *Treatise*, discussing, for example, how sympathy was the result of the operation of both resemblance and contiguity: "Nor is resemblance the only relation, which has this effect. . . . The sentiments of others have little influence, when far remov'd from us, and require the relation of contiguity, to make them communicate themselves entirely" (1739/1978, p. 318).

This distinction was developed (apparently independently of Hume) by Saussure (1916/1986) and Jakobson (1956) as a key principle of structuralist linguistics—the distinction between paradigmatic (similarity-based) and syntagmatic (contiguity-based) relations in language (Lyons, 1968, pp. 70–81). The distinction was widely applied during the 1960s and 1970s, by Levi-Strauss (e.g., 1963, 1966) and others to the analysis of myth, and by Barthes (1968) to semiology, and later by Bruner (1986) to distinguishing two modes of thought: the paradigmatic, or logico-scientific, mode and the narrative mode. With the exception of Hume, however, its explicit use has largely been confined to the analysis of cultural and linguistic rather than social phenomena, and its application to social solidarity has been implicit and unrecognized.

My use of this distinction is grounded in a realist approach that emphasizes ontological questions about the nature of these relationships. Saussure (as described by Jakobson, 1956, p. 61) held that relationships of similarity and difference are *virtual* relationships, while relationships of contiguity are *actual* relationships. Similarity is a virtual relationship because there is no necessity that there be a real process or connection involved in the relationship; similarity and difference are established simply by comparison, independent of time and space. In contrast, relationships of contiguity posit, explicitly or implicitly, a real connection between two things. This can be physical (as in a physical description of a sequence of events, each one impacting subsequent ones), mental (as with a chain of thought, in which one idea or statement leads to another), or a combination of these. Sayer (1992, p. 88 ff.) developed the same distinction, as part of his realist approach to social science, as that between formal and substantive relationships.

I argue that similarity and contiguity are different and, to a significant extent, independent sources of social solidarity. Similarity-based solidarity derives from the ways in which people recognize or construct *resemblances* between one another, ways in which they see themselves as *alike*. Contiguity-based solidarity, on the other hand, derives from the ways in which people *interact*, and thereby come to know and care about one another. Contiguity is not inherently a matter of either similarity or difference; it is a separate dimension of relationship, often associated with difference and complementarity rather than similarity. Contiguity is not limited to face-to-face contact, though this is the typical case; it can involve relationships of interaction at a distance.

The similarity-contiguity distinction is not simply a way of reframing the similarity-difference opposition. Similarity and contiguity are fundamentally different *dimensions* of relationship, rather than being opposites on a single continuum. Both similarity and its opposite, difference, are matters of likeness or resemblance. Contiguity, on the other hand, is a matter of actual connection, influence, or interaction, or their absence—an issue of concrete relationship in time and space, not a virtual relationship of comparison.

One possible response to the argument I am making is that the sorts of connection that are generated by contiguity do not satisfy the criteria for the term "solidarity." Contiguity-based interdependence has been seen by most theorists as based on self-interest and rational choice, and as the antithesis of solidarity and community, despite Durkheim's admonition that it is wrong to oppose a society that derives from a community of beliefs to one whose foundation is co-operation, by granting only the first a moral character and seeing in the latter only an economic grouping. In reality, co-operation has also its intrinsic morality. (1984 [1893], pp. 173–174)

Unfortunately, Weber's distinction between "communal" and "associative" relationships, the latter being based on rational calculation rather than emotional identification (Nisbet, 1966, p. 80), has been far more influential than Durkheim's attempt to see both similarity and interdependence as forms of solidarity. I believe that the examples I discuss shortly demonstrate that Durkheim's concept of "organic solidarity" captures an important component of how solidarity is actually created in communities, and that the examples of contiguity-based bonds I describe clearly *do* fall within the accepted meaning of solidarity.

Contiguity and Solidarity in Traditional Communities

The importance of contiguity as a basis for solidarity is difficult to demonstrate empirically, because both similarity and contiguity are present in all communities; in methodological terms, the two factors are "confounded." It is therefore easy, as Hannerz (1992) and others have pointed out, to assume that similarity is the operative factor in creating solidarity and social order, and to ignore data that point to substantial intracultural diversity, as argued in Chapter 2.

Thus, to support my claim that contiguity makes a crucial contribution to solidarity, I will present two sorts of evidence. The first, presented in this chapter, is based on several examples of the *loss* of solidarity and community in traditional, face-to-face contexts, showing that what was lost in these cases was not similarity, but contiguity. The second sort of evidence, presented in Chapter 10, derives from the theories held by members of one traditional society, demonstrating that the members of this society themselves think of solidarity as based to a substantial extent on contiguity rather than similarity.

The first example is taken from a study by Erikson (1976) of how a flood, caused by the collapse of a mining-company dam, shattered the Appalachian community of Buffalo Creek, demolishing neighborhoods and killing many of the residents. Erikson argued that the trauma of the flood was social as well as psychological, "a blow to the basic tissues of social life that damages the bonds attaching people together and impairs the prevailing sense of communality" (p. 154).

The striking fact about the Buffalo Creek flood was that, unlike in many other disasters, the community did not recover quickly from its effects. The survivors' feelings of solidarity with their fellows were seriously damaged, and the damage persisted for years after the flood:

> The community, what remains of it, seems to have lost its most significant quality—the power it generated in people to care for one another in times of need, to console one another in times of distress, to protect one another in times of danger. (Erikson, 1976, p. 226)

This loss was not due to a decline in similarity with one another, or to the erosion of shared values or norms. Erikson noted that even the shared experience of loss "does not appear to have become a new basis for community, as has so often been the case in other disasters" (p. 203). And in analyzing the perceived "collapse of morality" among the survivors, he states that "the [moral] consensus has held; local standards as to what qualifies as deviation remain largely intact, even though a number of people see themselves as drifting away from that norm" (p. 207).

The loss, instead, was a loss of contiguity, of long-standing connection with one's neighbors. As one community member analyzed the situation,

> Perhaps the communities people were placed in after the disaster had a lot to do with the problem. If there had been time enough to place people [near] the same families and neighbors they were accustomed to, it might have been different. Instead, they were haphazardly placed among people that were strangers with different personalities. I have conflicts with people I don't even know. . . . Things like that just didn't happen in Lundale. Everybody knew you and your personality. (Erikson, 1976, p. 149)

Similarly, Erikson invoked contiguity rather than similarity in explaining the "collapse of morality" in Buffalo Creek:

> The unfamiliar people who move next door and bring their old styles of life with them may be acting improperly by some objective measure or they may not, but they are always acting in an unfamiliar way, and the fact of the matter may very well be that relative strangers, even if they come from the same general community, are almost by definition less "moral" than immediate neighbors. They do not fall within the pale of local clemency, as it were, and so do not qualify for the allowances neighbors make for one another on the grounds that they know the motives involved. ("We don't worry none about that, it's just the way Billy is.") (p. 207)

Erikson suggested that one of the main factors in Buffalo Creek's failure to recover a sense of community is that the traditional solidarity was based on ties of contiguity that the inhabitants were involved in from birth.

In places like Buffalo Creek, where attachments between people are seen as part of the natural order of things—inherited by birth or acquired by proximity—the very idea of "forming" friendships or "building" relationships seems a little odd. . . . So people are not sure just what to do. (p. 226)

Many of the survivors whose relationships were destroyed by the flood and the subsequent relocation were unable to forge new solidary ties; they had no experience in recreating these ties with strangers, or with using similarity as an alternative basis for generating solidarity.

My second illustration of contiguity-based solidarity is taken from the work of Clifford Geertz (1959), who argued that in traditional Javanese villages, "the primary tie between families [is] that of residential propinquity" (p. 168). This is very similar to Toennies's characterization (1887/1957, p. 161) of *gemeinschaft*: "Neighborhood . . . is the basis of their union." Elsewhere, Geertz characterized "communal" or "primordial" bonds generally as based on "immediate contiguity and kin connection mainly" (1963, p. 109). The core ritual of these villages, a communal sharing of food called a *slametan*, involved only the households immediately surrounding that of the sponsor, and "symbolizes the mystic and social unity of those participating in it" (1960, p. 11).

These villages exhibited a diverse range of belief systems, including Hindu-based, Islamic, and pancretistic elements, but individual differences in religious views "were softened by the easy tolerance of the Javanese for a wide range of religious concepts, so long as basic ritual patterns—that is, slametans—were supported" (1959, p. 149). Erikson (1976, p. 59) also noted the traditional tolerance for individual differences in Buffalo Creek, and Williams (1988), discussing the "street work" of men in the urban neighborhood she studied, argued that "in the intricate world of the street, men do all they can to understand the details of one another's biographies. Because they memorize others' reputations, they tolerate a great deal of deviance and diversity" (p. 81).

These traditional ties were disrupted when Javanese villagers moved to larger towns and became increasingly involved in relationships that lacked the sustained face-to-face contact that existed in the villages. This led to the rise of similarity-based, ideological ties, centered on religious and political beliefs. These ideologies, in which different groups began to see themselves as in essential conflict, further eroded the contiguity-based solidarity that had previously existed.

Geertz provided a detailed case study of how, in a period of increasing religious and political tension, a death in one urban neighborhood precipitated a local breakdown of the slametan, the successful performance of which required the cooperation of different religious groups. He attributed the ritual's collapse to the discontinuity between its traditional cultural basis and the participants' current lives. In the urban setting, social groupings were to a significant extent based on similarities of class, occupation, religion, politics, age, and sex, in addition to residential contiguity, and these groupings created cross-cutting ties of similarity as well as contiguity. He argued that

> in the midst of all this pluralistic checking and balancing, the slametan remains unchanged, blind to the major lines of social and cultural demarcation in urban life. . . . In the [urban neighborhood], the holding of a slametan increasingly serves to remind people that the neighborhood bonds that they are strengthening through a dramatic enactment are no longer the bonds which most emphatically hold them together. (1959, pp. 168–169)

Similarities and differences that were largely irrelevant to solidarity in the villages, where contiguity was primary, became the main criteria for solidarity in the urban neighborhoods.

Michael Ignatieff, in a review of several books about the Bosnian conflict (1994), made many of the same points. Acknowledging that what doomed Bosnia was the lack of trust between Muslims, Croats, and Serbs, he asserted that

> it was not that such trust was lacking "on the ground": all three communities were deeply interwoven by intermarriage and a shared common life. . . . Far from being a fatal frontier between two antithetical civilizations—Christendom and Islam—Bosnia was the place where the two had learned, over five centuries, to understand each other and to coexist. (1994, p. 3)

What eventually divided the Bosnian groups from one another was not presumably "primordial" ties of similarity reasserting themselves, but external influences—the imperialist or nationalist ambitions of neighboring states, most recently Serbia. "Nationalist ideology went to work on these cultural differences, defining them as essential, pure, and indissoluble signs of national identity" (Ignatieff, 1994, p. 4).

This view of the shift in the nature of solidarity, as expressed in Geertz's and Ignatieff's analyses, is the reverse of Durkheim's original evolutionary scheme, in which organic solidarity succeeds and substantially replaces mechanical solidarity. Geertz and Ignatieff have implicitly done with Durkheim what Marx did with Hegel: they found Durkheim standing on his head, and stood him on his feet. In this revised view, traditional societies are united by contiguity as much as by similarity; the development of what I call the "ideology of similarity," in the hegemonic form that can override and destroy bonds of contiguity, is predominantly a modern phenomenon. A recent popular book, Bill Bishop's *The Big Sort: How the Clustering of Like-Minded America Is Tearing Us Apart* (2008), argued that local communities in the United States are becoming more and more homogeneous, threatening the communication, interaction, and solidarity that links these communities with one another.

I argue that social and cultural diversity, and the contiguity-based solidarity that is compatible with such diversity, are fundamental properties of human societies throughout history. Such diversity can be traced back to the earliest stages of biological life; as Mayr and others have insisted, diversity is the essential requirement for evolution. This argument does not ignore the fact that diversity in modern societies has some very different properties and consequences from its presence in earlier ones, only that diversity within community is not a recent development, and needs to be incorporated in our theories of, and research on, community and solidarity.

However, the idea that solidarity in traditional societies is based to a significant extent on contiguity as well as similarity is not simply a theoretical abstraction; it is often the perspective of the members of these societies themselves. I present a detailed account of one such society in Chapter 10.

These examples, which could be multiplied indefinitely, demonstrate the importance of contiguity-based relationships in creating solidarity in traditional communities. It is clear that similarity is not the sole or fundamental basis for solidarity, and that there exists an alternative source of solidarity that is compatible with difference, a source that could in principle help to resolve the problems associated with difference.

Commonsense Recognition of Contiguity in Contemporary Societies

Despite the lack of recognition in Western social theory of contiguity as an alternative basis for solidarity, there is a widespread, commonsense awareness of the importance of complementarity and interaction in creating solidarity and supporting diversity. Out of numerous possible examples (I have reluctantly omitted, for example, a discussion of Rudolph the Red-Nosed Reindeer), I have tried to select diverse instances in which the distinction between contiguity and similarity is particularly clear.

Shaffer and Anundsen (1993), in a book on creating community, devoted very little attention to similarities such as shared values; instead, they focused on building connections, interdependence, caring, and commitment. They gave an example of "an urban professional, tired of associating with others like himself, who joined an amateur league hardball team and discovered the kind of heterogeneous community he had enjoyed in his hometown" (p. xiv). They ended by calling for an expansion of community to include the entire planet, an expansion based not on similarity, but on our connectedness and interdependence with the rest of the earth, what they call "developing an ecological self" (p. 321).

Similarly, Bensimon and Neumann (1993), discussing leadership in higher education, argued that administrative teams should be both *complex*—incorporating and expressing diverse views and cognitive styles—and *connected*—fostering interaction, relationship building, and caring. They stated that they "view connectedness as providing the foundation that makes complex and creative thinking (i.e., real teamwork) possible and tolerable" (p. 110). Simple teams, on the other hand, tend to seek cognitive consistency and are less tolerant of differences; these teams usually lack lateral or cross-cutting relationships that draw members into an interconnected whole that can support diversity (pp. 88–90).

Finally, Willett (1993), in a qualitative study of two first-grade classrooms in an international community characterized by substantial diversity, found striking differences between the classrooms. In one, the teacher focused on common tasks and characteristics, and differences were deemphasized. Informal subgroupings occurred mostly on the basis of similarities in language proficiency, culture, and gender, and there was little dialogue across these subgroups. In the second classroom, the teacher encouraged discussion of differences and collective decision making. Children were grouped at different times by propinquity, shared interests, or individual similarities, and subgroup membership changed frequently; as a result, the children in the classroom knew a great deal about each other.

In the first classroom, Willett found that solidarity was largely limited to the subgroups; despite the teacher's emphasis on similarities among the children, there was little sense of community in the class as a whole, and subgroups sometimes disrupted class activities. In the second classroom, where diversity was openly accepted and discussed, and interaction across differences was encouraged, solidarity existed both within the subgroups and in the class as a whole; both children and parents described this classroom as "close-knit." This emphasis on heterogeneous grouping, and its advantages for creating cooperation and solidarity, has since become more common (e.g., Boaler & Staples, 2008).

Contiguity, in conjunction with difference, can create complementarity and thereby generate solidarity that is compatible with heterogeneity. In addition, as some of the earlier examples illustrate, contiguity can produce understanding of others' behavior that reduces the felt need for similarity in order to allow predictability. For these reasons, the recognition of contiguity as a distinct source of solidarity supports the valuing of difference. It also suggests that the common conception of contemporary society as characterized by the loss of a presumed earlier homogeneity and consensus is fundamentally misconstrued. While the theoretical recognition and practical use of contiguity as a source of solidarity is not a panacea for the problems that difference can create, it can reframe these problems and suggest solutions that make the two ideals of diversity and community more compatible.

Similarity and Contiguity as Ideologies of Solidarity

I have mainly discussed similarity and contiguity as two types of relationship that can serve as sources of solidarity. However, both can also function as *ideologies* of and for solidarity. The Buffalo Creek example depicts a contiguity-based ideology for solidarity, while the Javanese and Bosnian examples illustrate the rise of a similarity-based ideology. Such ideologies tend to imply that solidarity is or should be based on only one or the other of these two types of relationship.

Similarity as an ideology for solidarity, which is widespread in Western societies, contributes to the widely held belief that some degree of homogeneity is essential for solidarity, and that solidarity is difficult or impossible to achieve with those who are substantially different from oneself except by creating or emphasizing similarities. (This "ideology of similarity" is similar to what Adorno called the "logic of identity"; see Young, 1990.) This ideology fosters a lack of mutual understanding, respect, and empathy between groups and individuals who differ from one another, and makes it difficult to see or accept ways in which difference and complementarity can be a source of solidary relationships.

This ideology is deeply embedded in our language for talking about relationships. M. C. Bateson (1989), in discussing her relationships with her colleagues, provided numerous examples of solidarity deriving from complementary differences rather than similarities. Yet she struggled with our culture's ideological separation of complementarity and solidarity:

> When I search for a word for my relationships with the women described in this book, I feel a need for a term that would assert both collegiality and the fact that the process is made possible by our differences. The thesaurus betrays me, denying me a term that affirms both symmetry and complementarity. . . . We are rich in words that describe symmetrical relationships, from buddy to rival to colleague. We are also rich in words that describe strongly asymmetrical relationships, many of which imply hierarchy and have curious undertones of exploitation or dominance. But none of these words meets my needs. (pp. 156–157)

I'm not arguing that solidarity *should* be based on contiguity, or that contiguity is morally superior to similarity. My goal is to demonstrate that solidarity often *is* based on contiguity, and to suggest that attempts to understand and develop solidarity need to recognize and use this fact. This is particularly important because, in addition to the problems that critics of "community" as a similarity-based ideal have identified, similarity-based strategies are not always effective in generating solidarity. Ignatieff, in analyzing the failure of Western nations to come to Bosnia's aid, noted the very real weakness of the narratives of moral empathy that tie us all together in the so-called "global village." One such narrative, which was repeated like a mantra—Sarajevo is a European city, Sarajevo is us—had stunningly little effect. . . . Intellectuals who called for solidarity with Sarajevo in the name of Europe did not understand that the concept of Europe divides as much as it unites. (1994, pp. 4–6)

He suggested that more attention to actual strategic interests, "some deeper understanding of what is at stake in a place like Bosnia" (p. 4), could have added pragmatic weight to moral empathy. I would add that a clearer sense of our *connectedness* to the Bosnians, of how what happens there affects us and how what we do affects them, could increase our *moral* as well as our pragmatic concern.

However, having so far mainly criticized the Western emphasis on similarity, I want to point out some of the drawbacks of contiguity as an ideology for solidarity. First, and most obviously, contiguity as an ideology for solidarity fails to acknowledge and support solidarity with people with whom we aren't in contact; this may be the major reason why most theorists have rejected contiguity as a moral basis for solidarity.

Second, the contiguity-based concept of "organic solidarity," involving difference and complementarity, can be used to justify inequality and oppression; historical examples of such use include rationalizations for slavery, the Indian caste system, and patriarchal male-female relations. For example, Bateson (1989) described how caretaking, with its inherent asymmetry, can easily be transformed into domination or exploitation, the solidary bond distorted into an ideological justification for oppression.

Young (1990), in denying that community as an ideal is compatible with a politics of difference, criticized both the similarity-based and contiguity-based aspects of this ideal. However, she did not explicitly distinguish the two aspects of community, arguing, for example, that "[community] devalues and denies difference in the form of temporal and spatial distancing" (p. 302).

I argue, in contrast, that contiguity and similarity are co-occurring sources of solidarity in all human groups, and that neither of these is reducible to the other. The widespread characterization of community as involving both "common ties" and "social interaction" (e.g., Bernard, 1973, pp. 3–4) implicitly acknowledges this duality. However, the Western identification of "community" with "common" has largely prevented the explicit recognition of sources of solidarity and community other than similarity, and has led to the rejection of community as a legitimate goal by many writers who value diversity over similarity. I think that explicitly distinguishing similarity and contiguity shows how the ideal of community that Young criticizes is not simply utopian, but is inconsistent with the nature of actual communities, and reveals ways in which communitarian goals are compatible with a politics of difference.

As noted earlier, these arguments for the importance of diversity are strikingly similar to Durkheim's analysis (1893/1984) of mechanical and organic solidarity. For Durkheim, "mechanical solidarity, or solidarity by similarities" derives from those beliefs and sentiments that the members of a society hold in common—what he called the "*conscience collective*," generally translated "collective consciousness." Organic solidarity, in contrast, is based on individual difference, complementarity, and the division of labor.

Unfortunately, Durkheim was unable to conceive of a mechanism by which diversity and complementarity could generate genuine solidarity, and eventually abandoned the concept of organic solidarity entirely, arguing that solidarity had to be based on a continuation of the *conscience collective* (Hawthorn, 1987, pp. 123–124; Nisbet, 1966, pp. 84–86). Durkheim's view has been perpetuated in virtually all subsequent work on social solidarity, which has assumed that solidarity must necessarily involve some fundamental similarity. Parsons, for example, incorporated in his influential theories of society Durkheim's later assumption that shared values (Parsons's definition of culture) were the source of social order.

Challenges to this position came almost exclusively from theorists holding a conflict model of society that denied the very existence of the sort of integration that Parsons's theory was intended to explain, so that the possibility of solidarity based on complementarity was never systematically developed in sociology. Schmid argued that "Parsons seems unable to imagine the empirical possibility of conflict-free social relations where actors are orienting themselves, not to a common culture, but to quite different, and possibly contradictory, parts of it" (1992, p. 99).

One scholar who developed a view of solidarity that did not depend on similarity or consensus, a view grounded in her own experience in religious and political groups, was the feminist theologian Sharon Welch (1990). Noting the "American proclivity to see pluralism and complexity as problems to be solved rather than constitutive elements of social organization" (p. 35), she argued that "the intention of solidarity is potentially more inclusive and more transformative than is the goal of consensus," and that "the search for consensus is a continuation of the dream of domination" (pp. 132–133). While her focus was mainly on issues of ethics and justice rather than social theory, her concept of a feminist "epistemology of solidarity" that is based on concrete relations and material interaction, rather than universal values (p. 137 ff.), is compatible with, and supports, the analysis I develop here.

In summary, I have argued that a major reason that diversity and solidarity have been seen as antithetical has been the absence of an empirically and conceptually adequate theory of how solidarity is created and maintained in communities, a theory that does not assume at the outset that similarity is the ultimate basis for solidarity. I believe that this dilemma is a false one, based on a misunderstanding of the nature of solidarity and community. Like Corlett (1989), I have tried

> to show how overcoming the urge to say that human beings, or subsets of them, are all the same leads arguments neither back to the atomistic prejudices of nineteenth century individualism nor ahead to the solitary ecstasy of avant-garde eruptions. (p. 7)

A more explicit recognition of contiguity as a source of solidarity can reframe our understanding of the nature of solidarity and community, and lead to practical solutions to the problems that difference and the ideology of similarity have created.

Diversity and Methodology

I now turn to the methodological implications of a realist view of diversity. I believe that both quantitative and qualitative methods contain biases that tend to conceal the existence of diversity and make it more difficult to understand its nature and influence. These methodological biases can undercut the value of an approach that has the theoretical potential to illuminate the extent and consequences of diversity. Thus, Strauss (1992) argued that Bourdieu's analysis of socialization in terms of "habitus," the mental structures unconsciously created by individuals from the practices of everyday life, has exactly this problem:

> In *Outline* [*of a Theory of Practice*] he never analyzes the habitus of any particular individuals, but instead, like all too many social researchers, makes assumptions about the contents of the habitus of his Kabyle informants on the basis of social facts such as the organization of their households or the rhythms of their agricultural calendar. This leads him to ignore the potential for intracultural variation and change that is built into his theory of habitus formation and to stress instead the reproduction of hegemonic relations, at least for "traditional" societies. In other words, although Bourdieu's theory takes us away from what I call "fax" models of socialization, his own practice falls back into them. (p. 9)

Qualitative research, which accepts the particularity of its subject and is aimed at developing in-depth understandings of single cases or small samples, would seem to be particularly suited to understanding diversity. However, qualitative research also has methodological biases towards uniformity. The sample size and sampling strategies used in qualitative studies are often inadequate to identify and characterize the actual diversity that exists in the setting or population studied, and lead to simplistic generalizations. Shulman (1986/1990) claimed that

> too frequently we find educational [ethnographers] making sweeping general statements based on woefully limited data. Inferences that demand careful cross-site analyses, for example, are based on examination of a single case, or on several cases whose variations do not reflect principles of theoretical sampling. (p. 50)

In addition, qualitative researchers tend to use data collection and analysis methods that emphasize uniformity, such as relying on key informants and focusing on shared themes and concepts, as described in Chapter 2.

Critical ethnography has been proposed (e.g., by Kincheloe & McLaren, 2000) as an approach to research that incorporates postmodernism's concern with difference, and that avoids the problems of other research strategies that impose uniformity. Critical approaches to social theory are often based on "conflict" rather than "consensus" theories of social order, and incorporate explicitly postmodern views of society. While I agree with much of this argument, I am not convinced that critical ethnography by itself can solve the problem of uniformism. I see two main limitations on critical ethnography's ability to address these issues.

First, critical ethnography has some of the same biases with respect to sample size, data collection strategies, and analytic methods as other qualitative approaches. These methodological biases tend to suppress or overlook diversity, and lead to accounts that claim greater uniformity than is actually the case.

Second, critical ethnography often assumes that there is a single correct emancipatory understanding that, when realized, will lead all groups to unified action toward liberation (Hammersley, 1992b; cf. Leach, 1992). Hammersley argued that

> once the teleological model has been abandoned, there is no longer any guaranteed potential for change of the kind to which critical theorists are committed, and therefore it is no longer clear why one set of ideals should be regarded as "true human consciousness," rather than another. . . . It becomes possible that there will be multiple, contradictory critical theories advanced by researchers who are linked with different oppressed groups. And the linchpin of critical theory, that it is concerned with the emancipation of all, even of the oppressors, has been lost. (1992b, p. 108)

Ultimately, challenging uniformism in social and educational research will require a new theory of social and cultural coherence and integration, as suggested earlier. However, advances in theory will not remove the method-ological biases in our research methods. I think that an important step toward these changes is to recognize both the reality of diversity and the potential for bias, to be aware of the danger of assuming uniformity in the phenomena stud-ied. Kincheloe and McLaren (2000, p. 280) called on postmodern researchers to adopt what they call a "critical humility" that respects the complexity of the social world and accepts its own fallibility.

A second step toward overcoming uniformist bias is to engage in a deliber-ate search for variability. Not only must systematic sampling be done in order to identify the actual variability in a group or setting (Heider, 1972; Sankoff, 1971), but these data must be analyzed in ways that retain these differences and attempt to understand their significance (Maxwell, 1986).

A final methodological strategy is to *combine* quantitative and qualita-tive methods. The joint use of the two approaches can serve both as a form of methodological triangulation, each method compensating for the weaknesses of the other, and also as a way of generating *divergent* perspectives, deepening rather than simply confirming our understanding (Greene, 2007). Qualitative methods and approaches, which focus on particular phenomena and processes and their unique contexts, can help to overcome the biases inherent in uni-versalizing, variable-oriented quantitative methods. Conversely, quantitative methods can provide systematic evidence for diversity, and can help to correct the tendency for the qualitative researcher to ignore complexity and to focus on typical characteristics and shared concepts and themes. A collaboration between irreducibly different approaches can enable social and educational research to better understand and deal with the diversity that is a fundamental part of our world.

Postmodernism

This emphasis on the diversity that is inherent in societies and cultures is where the realist perspective I present here connects most directly with postmodern-ism. Rosenau identified as key characteristics of postmodernism its search for "diversity rather than unity, difference rather than synthesis, complexity rather than simplification" (1992, p. 8) and the possibility of a plurality of interpre-tations of any text, rather than a single message (1992, p. 35). Wolf likewise saw diversity as central: "The postmodernist goal is, I take it, to encourage the author to present a less tidy picture with more contradictory voices" (1992, p. 53). The additional contribution of a realist conception of diversity is that it applies the concept of irreducible diversity, and the rejection of "totalizing metanarratives," not just to the *accounts* that researchers create, but to actual social and cultural *phenomena.*

Hannerz similarly stated that "postmodernism comes close enough to the view of culture as an organization of diversity which I take here" (1992, p. 35). However, he also warned that

> it is a problem of postmodernist thought that as it has emphasized diversity and been assertively doubtful toward master narratives, it has frequently been on the verge of becoming another all-encompassing formula for a macroan-thropology of the replication of uniformity. (1992, p. 35)

I am well aware that, as Rosenau (1992, p. 14) warned, the absence of unity in postmodernism itself allows anyone to find points of agreement with it. However, I think that the mutual emphasis on diversity in critical realist and postmodern views is not a superficial or chance similarity, but is indicative of a wider and more important parallel between the two (Maxwell, 1996a). For example, other parallels between critical realism and postmodernism are their rejection of a unitary, objectivist concept of truth, and their affirmation of the grounding of accounts in perspectives that are inevitably local rather than universal. (Clearly, the major affinity here is with what Rosenau called "affir-mative" rather than "skeptical" postmodernism.)

Contiguity as a source of coherence does not fit well with some postmod-ern views, which reject both contiguity-based and similarity-based integration (e.g., Young, 1990). However, contiguity-based integration is compatible with postmodernism's emphasis on local rather than general narratives, since conti-guity is inherently a *local* connection. What I take as most valid from postmod-ernism is not the rejection of coherence *per se*, but the rejection of *similarity* as the sole or fundamental source of coherence. I am arguing for a recognition of contiguity as a real phenomenon that provides an alternative to similarity, an alternative that avoids many of the "totalizing" features that postmodernism has attacked. A realist approach can reveal diversity that traditional approaches have ignored, and can suggest mechanisms for integration that are compatible with diversity. This perspective can provide one way out of the "hegemony of mimesis" that postmodernism has identified.

Part II

Realism and Qualitative Methods

Introduction

Part I of this book presented an introduction to critical realism and discussed several theoretical issues for which critical realism can provide a useful perspective for qualitative research. Part II addresses the methodological and practical issues involved in conducting a qualitative study, and the value of a realist perspective on these issues.

Chapter 5 deals with research design in a broad sense (Maxwell, 2005) and the conceptual issues that are central to planning a qualitative study: the goals, theories, and research questions of the researcher. I argue that each of these can be usefully seen as involving real phenomena: the actual values, concepts, beliefs, and intentions held by a researcher, and the consequences of these for the other design components and for how the research is planned and conducted.

Chapter 6 focuses on the actual conduct of a research project: the selection of settings and participants, the relations that the researcher establishes with participants and other stakeholders, and the activities involved in data collection. Here, a realist approach emphasizes the consequences of a researcher's actions (and the beliefs and intentions that motivate these) for the success of the study.

Chapter 7 (written with Barbara Miller) deals with data analysis, presenting a distinction between two types of strategies for analysis—categorizing strategies (e.g., coding), and the less clearly conceptualized set of strategies that involve seeing connections among data and among concepts. This distinction has been extensively discussed in the qualitative research literature, but has not been clearly theorized. Miller and I propose a realist conceptualization of these strategies, based on the philosophical and linguistic distinction between similarity relations and contiguity relations, discussed in Chapter 4.

Finally, Chapter 8 deals with the issue of validity (alternative terms are *quality, trustworthiness,* and *authenticity*) in qualitative research. I present an alternative to what has been the dominant approach for addressing validity in both quantitative and qualitative research: using criteria that are based on the strategies and methods employed in a study. The alternative I describe locates validity in the conclusions and interpretations of a study and their relationship to reality, rather than the study's design or methods, and assesses the validity of a study in terms of how adequately the researcher deals with plausible alternatives to these conclusions or interpretations.

5

The Realities of Research Design

In this chapter I address the implications of realism for qualitative research design, in the broad sense of the components of a study and the relationships among these (Maxwell, 2005), and more specifically for the key conceptual components of a design: the goals and purposes of the study, the conceptual framework for the study, and the specific research questions that the study is intended to answer.

Research Design

The most important implication of realism for qualitative research design is to view research designs as real entities, not simply as abstract, formal plans or models. Research designs, from this perspective, are real in at least two senses. First, as the actual conceptions of and plans for research held by the researcher, they are real parts of people's meanings, motives, and understandings, as discussed in Chapter 2, and have consequences for the conduct of the research. Second, the conduct of the research "on the ground"—the actions taken by the researcher, and the ways that these influence and are influenced by the specific context and relationships in which the study is conducted—is itself a real phenomenon that may differ substantially from what was planned, and even from what the researcher *thinks* is happening. In this second sense, designs are models *of*, and not simply *for*, research; they are intended to represent what is actually taking place, not simply what the researcher plans or intends.

Kaplan's distinction (1964, p. 8) between the "reconstructed logic" and the "logic-in-use" of a study captures some of this difference, but the first aspect of the reality of design includes not just after-the-fact reconstructions, but the researcher's prior planning for, and ongoing conceptualization of, the design. These conceptualizations, and the beliefs and motives that inform them, are not necessarily things that you are fully conscious of, and you may need to engage in systematic reflection, and to get feedback from others, to become aware of these and how they are shaping your research. (This is one implication of the critical realist view of knowledge as always partial, incomplete, and fallible, as discussed in Chapters 1 and 2.) This applies not only to our knowledge of the "external world," including knowledge of others' minds, but also to our knowledge of our *own* minds. We never have a complete, objective understanding even of our own thinking, and often discover that we were unaware of, or mistaken about, some of our own beliefs, values, and intentions.

Howard Becker's claim, in *Writing for Social Scientists*, that "you have already made many choices when you sit down to write, but probably don't know what they were" (1986, p. 17), is equally true of research design. This is one reason why designing a study, like writing, is an iterative process in which much of what you are doing is figuring out what your actual design viewpoints, commitments, and purposes are. Students in my qualitative research methods course often find that their design decisions were shaped by their prior experiences, and the beliefs and goals that these led to, in ways that they were unaware of when they began their research projects (see, for example, Maxwell, 2005, pp. 17–21, 28–31).

Becker argued that you can't assume that you have completely free choice in these matters; this assumption leads to the belief that what theory you will use for your study is a matter of free choice, when in fact your prior beliefs about the phenomena you're studying have already constrained (and substantially constitute) the theory that you are *actually* using. As Becker said, "you cannot 'use' Marx if Durkheim's ideas shaped your thinking" (1986, p. 17).

This doesn't mean that you are a helpless prisoner of your unconscious concepts and beliefs. You can change these, but a necessary step in doing this is becoming aware of what these prior concepts and beliefs are. This allows you to use these productively in designing and conducting your research, and helps you to keep them from being an obstacle to carrying out the study and a threat to the validity of your conclusions. I have developed an exercise called a "researcher identity memo" (Maxwell, 2005, pp. 27–28) that I think provides valuable scaffolding for doing this. I discuss this issue of "researcher identity" in more detail later, under "Goals," but it is also relevant to your conceptual framework.

The second sense in which research designs are real phenomena refers to the actual nature and interaction of the components of the research in practice, independent of what the researcher believes or intends about these. The actual setting, and social roles and relationships within that setting, may substantially alter the conduct of the research, making the *real* design as implemented significantly different from the intended design. Your presence in a setting may have unintended consequences for what the participants do, so that a planned "naturalistic" study of this setting is anything but that. Similarly, the sort of interviews you planned may turn out to be very unlike what you intended, if the participants have a different understanding of, or goals for, this interaction (see Example 5.1). I discuss this issue in more detail shortly.

Such a realist approach to design enables you to consider not only your intended design and how well you are employing this, but also the actual design embodied in your actions, and the interaction of this with the physical and social environment, interactions that are influenced by many things external to the design itself, ones that you may not be fully aware of.

Example 5.1

Interviewing Joshua

Nancy Knapp, as part of her dissertation research on how second-grade students thought about learning to read, interviewed several students in one classroom, using a carefully planned interview guide. However, one student, Joshua, resisted answering her questions until she agreed to spend equal time drawing and looking at "Waldo" books with him. To her surprise, it was through "doing Waldos" with Joshua (which involved very little actual "reading" in the usual sense) that she learned the most about Joshua's developing sense of narrative and his struggles with phonetic decoding, and the value of minimal-text books such as the Waldo series as a gateway to literacy for struggling students. The actual design of her interviews with Joshua ended up being very different from what she had intended, resulting in changes not only in her data collection and analysis, but also in her goals, conceptual framework, and research questions. It was only in analyzing and reflecting on her data and her research process that Knapp became aware of some aspects of these changes. These reflections revealed the importance of serendipity and an openness to renegotiating her relationships with participants (an issue that I discuss in more detail in Chapter 6). As Knapp said, "I want to relinquish the position, and the more insidious inner belief, that I know at least all the important questions, if not all the important answers, in my research."

Source: Adapted from Knapp (1997).

This approach also helps you, in reading research reports, to understand the *real* design of a published study, its "logic-in-use," which may differ substantially from the "reconstructed logic" presented in the report. To do this, it is necessary to examine the actual conduct of the study (insofar as this can be determined from the published account) rather than simply depending on the author's assertions about the design (Maxwell & Loomis, 2003; see Example 5.2).

Example 5.2

Blumstein and Schwartz's book *American Couples* (1983) presented the results of their study, drawn from both survey questionnaires and open-ended interviews. The authors described the results of their study as based entirely on the survey data, while the qualitative data simply provided illustrative instances:

> We use the phrase "we find. . . ." in presenting a conclusion based on statistical analysis of data from the questionnaires. . . . The interview data help us interpret our questionnaire findings, but unless we are using one of the parts of the interview that is readily quantifiable, we do not afford them the same degree of trust we grant to information derived from the questionnaires.
>
> The interviews serve another purpose. We use the interview materials to illustrate both majority patterns and important exceptions. (p. 23)

And they characterized the chapters in their book that deal with relationship histories, which are based mainly on the interviews, by stating that "In these chapters, which have nothing to do with our analysis of the data but are included only for their illustrative value" (p. 22).

However, this doesn't explain why they conducted in-depth interviews, lasting 2½ to 4 hours, with both partners, separately and together, for 300 couples; transcribed and coded these interviews; and followed up with questionnaires to fill in any gaps. It also seems inconsistent with the fact that, in addition to their extensive use of quotes in the thematically organized sections of the book, they devote 213 pages, almost half of the results section of their book, to detailed case studies of 20 couples' relationships.

A closer analysis of their account reveals that triangulation of the two methods was an important feature of the study, in order to "see couples from several vantage points" (p. 15), and that the case studies "helped to illuminate some of the ways in which money, sex, and work

(Continued)

(Continued)

shape the nature of [the partners'] relationships" (p. 332). It appears that the "reconstructed logic" of the design was heavily influenced by a quantitative ideology of what counts as "results," distorting the study's "logic-in-use" and the actual contribution of the qualitative component.

Source: Adapted from Maxwell and Loomis (2003).

For these reasons, you need to not only carefully plan what you intend to do, but also to be attentive to what is *actually* happening in the research, and to adjust your actions to make the design more relevant and productive. Simply attempting to implement a previously designed plan for your research may lead to disaster if you are not aware of, and responsive to, the ways in which the research context is altering the actual design of the study.

Unfortunately, most works dealing with research design focus on the first of these aspects of design (the researcher's plans and intentions, and the possible choices among such plans), and largely ignore the second, except as a practical consideration in adhering to the intended design. This matches the standard definition of the term "design" as applied to research: "a plan or protocol for carrying out or accomplishing something (esp. a scientific experiment)" (*Webster's Ninth New Collegiate Dictionary*).

Most works dealing with research design from this perspective use one of two different conceptions of design. The first of these is typological: it treats designs as distinct, standard arrangements of research methods that each have their own coherence and logic. This view sees a research design as a possible answer to the question "What design are you using?" These types of designs, which Robson (2011) called "fixed" designs, are prevalent in quantitative research, in which it is critical to adhere to the original plan in order to ensure comparability of the data and to maintain design features intended to address particular validity threats. Using a specific design that has been previously developed and systematically analyzed to address possible validity concerns often makes the most sense for such studies.[1]

The second traditional approach to design is to see a design as a series of stages or tasks in planning or conducting a study. While some versions of

---

[1] However, Shadish et al. (2002), in what is one of the most detailed and sophisticated expositions of experimental design, make the same criticism of typological approaches to design that I have. They state that "we claim a general utility for thinking in terms of structural design elements rather than in terms of a finite set of designs" (pp. xvii–xviii). They argue that focusing on design elements allows the creation of new designs, and the borrowing of specific elements from other types of designs, providing researchers with a flexible set of tools for improving their research and generating valid conclusions.

this view of design are circular and recursive (e.g., Marshall & Rossman, 1999, pp. 26–27), all are essentially linear in the sense of being a one-directional *sequence* of steps from problem formulation to conclusions or theory, though this sequence may be repeated. Such models usually resemble a flowchart, with a clear starting point and goal and a specified order for doing the intermediate tasks.

Both typological and sequential concepts of design provide a model *for* conducting the research—a prescriptive guide that tells you the key features of your research plan or what tasks you need to accomplish and the order in which you do these. In contrast, the model of research design described shortly, which I call an interactive or systemic model, is a model *of* as well as *for* research. It is intended to help you understand the *actual* structure of your study, as well as to plan this study and carry it out. This is consistent with the more general meaning of "design": "the arrangement of elements or details in a product or work of art" (*Webster's Ninth New Collegiate Dictionary*).

Such a view of design as an ongoing, interactive process is a much better fit for qualitative research than are models that rely on fixed categories of "designs" or a linear sequence of activities. Qualitative research is necessarily inductive in its approach to design, and this inductive strategy means that the research plan itself is constantly changing in response to new information or changing circumstances. This sort of research needs a model of design that captures the actual design as it plays out during the research, rather than an exclusively prescriptive model for how the research *should* be done.

This conception of design as a model of, as well as for, research is exemplified in a classic qualitative study of medical students (Becker, Geer, Hughes, & Strauss, 1961). The authors begin their chapter on the "Design of the Study" by stating that

> In one sense, our study had no design. That is, we had no well-worked-out set of hypotheses to be tested, no data-gathering instruments purposely designed to secure information relevant to these hypotheses, no set of analytic procedures specified in advance. Insofar as the term "design" implies these features of elaborate prior planning, our study had none.
>
> If we take the idea of design in a larger and looser sense, using it to identify those elements of order, system, and consistency our procedures did exhibit, our study had a design. We can say what this was by describing our original view of the problem, our theoretical and methodological commitments, and the way these affected our research and were affected by it as we proceeded. (1961, p. 17)

Thus, qualitative research design, to a much greater extent than quantitative design, is a "do-it-yourself" rather than an "off-the-shelf" process. There are many qualitative design *traditions*, but not a menu of specific designs that you choose from or a fixed set of steps that you progress through. In qualitative research you need, to a substantial extent, to *construct* your design, rather than to follow a prescribed pattern or sequence. Design in qualitative research is an ongoing process that involves "tacking" back and forth between the different components of the design, assessing the implications of goals, theories, research questions, methods, and validity threats for one another.

One of my students, Don Tyson, once asked me how you could make progress using a nonlinear model of design. The answer I should have given at the time (but didn't) is that it's much like a soccer team moving the ball down the field, passing it back and forth and sometimes backward, but progressing as a whole in terms of improvising opportunities and setting up a shot at the goal. Qualitative research design is much more like soccer than it is like American football, which relies heavily on a "playbook" of designed plays, each with a planned sequence of actions, to advance the ball.

A fairly extreme, but appropriately cautionary, statement of the view of design that I present here is attributed to General Dwight Eisenhower, who was in charge of the Allied invasion of Normandy in World War II: "In preparing for battle, I have found that planning is essential, but plans are useless" (Shubin, 2008, p. 4). Shubin, a paleontologist, argues that this quote "captures field paleontology in a nutshell. We make all kinds of plans to get us to promising fossil sites. Once we're there, the entire field plan may be thrown out the window. Facts on the ground can change our best-laid plans" (p. 4). As Eisenhower said, planning your design is essential, but you will need to continually assess how this design is actually working during the research, how it influences and is influenced by its environment, and to make adjustments or more substantial changes so that your study can accomplish what you want.

The model of research design I present here (Figure 5.1), which I call an "interactive" model (I could just as well have called it "systemic"), has a definite structure. However, it is an interconnected and flexible structure. Elsewhere (Maxwell, 2005; Maxwell & Loomis, 2003), I describe in detail the key components of this model, and present a strategy for understanding and creating coherent and workable relationships among these components. Here, I will briefly describe this model and its realist premises.

This model of research design has five components. The first three of the components (goals, conceptual framework, and research questions) are real phenomena, but they exist in the researchers' minds, although they have observable behavioral manifestations and consequences for the research. They represent the researcher's actual thoughts about the phenomena studied, and intentions for the research. The fourth component, methods, exists as actual behaviors as well as ideas: the processes of selecting settings and participants, the relationships that are established with participants and other stakeholders,

Figure 5.1   An Interactive Model of Research Design

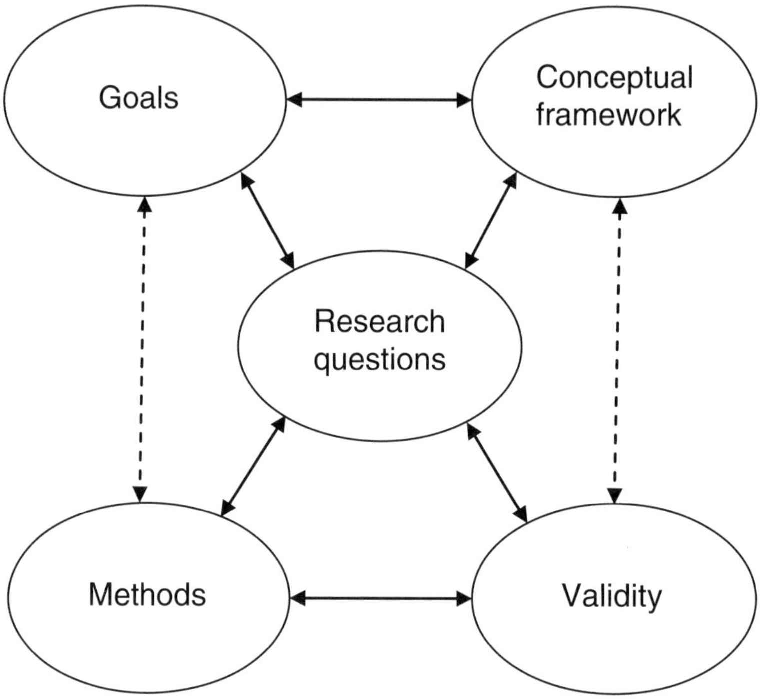

Source: Maxwell (2005).

and the procedures used for data collection and analysis. These are discussed in Chapters 6 and 7. The fifth component, validity, concerns the relationship of the conclusions and inferences drawn from the study to the actual phenomena studied; I discuss this in Chapter 8. Example 5.3 provides a more detailed description of each of these components.

These components are not substantially different from the ones presented in many other discussions of research design (e.g., LeCompte & Preissle, 1993; Miles & Huberman, 1994; Robson, 2011; Rudestam & Newton, 1992, p. 5). However, contrary to what is implied in some research methods textbooks, none of these components is fixed in advance or a necessary starting point for the research. Students in my courses often discover important aspects of their goals and conceptual frameworks, and make additions or changes to their research questions, after they begin collecting or analyzing their data. These components are generally developed (or made more explicit) as *part of* the design process, which continues after the study is begun.

Example 5.3

The five components of my design model are as follows:

1. *Goals*: Why is your study worth doing? What issues or problem(s) do you want it to clarify, and what practices and policies do you want it to influence? Why do you want to conduct this study, and why should we care about the results?

2. *Conceptual Framework*: What do you think is going on with the issues, settings, or people you plan to study? What theories, beliefs, and prior research findings will guide or inform your research, and what literature, preliminary studies, and personal experiences will you draw on for understanding the people or issues you are studying?

3. *Research Questions*: What, specifically, do you want to understand by doing this study? What do you *not* know about the phenomena you are studying that you want to learn? What questions will your research attempt to answer, and how are these questions related to one another?

4. *Methods*: What will you actually do in conducting this study? What approaches and techniques will you use to collect and analyze your data? There are four parts of this component of your design: a) the relationships that you establish with the participants in your study; b) your selection of settings, participants, times and places of data collection, and other data sources such as documents (what is often called "sampling"); c) your data collection methods; and d) your data analysis strategies and techniques.

5. *Validity*: How might your results and conclusions be wrong? What are the plausible alternative interpretations and validity threats to these, and how will you deal with these? How can the data that you have, or that you could potentially collect, support or challenge your ideas about what's going on? Why should we believe your results?

Source: Maxwell (2005).

Thus, what is innovative about this model is that the components are related to one another as an interacting system. Each component is closely tied to several others in relationships of mutual and ongoing influence, rather than being linked in a fixed linear or cyclic sequence. These relationships are displayed in Figure 5.1.

A key feature of this model is that the connections among the components are not rigid rules or fixed implications. Instead, they represent actual influences, rather than simply logical relationships. These influences are two-way; each of the five components can influence any of the others.

In particular, the upper triangle of this model (the focus of this chapter) should be a closely integrated unit. Your research questions should have a clear relationship to the goals of your study, and should be informed by what is already known about the phenomena you are studying and the theoretical concepts and models that can be applied to these phenomena. In addition, the goals of your study should be informed by current theory and knowledge, while your decisions about what theories and knowledge are relevant depend on your goals and questions.

Similarly, the bottom triangle of the model should also be closely integrated. The methods you use must enable you to answer your research questions, and also to deal with plausible validity threats to these answers. The questions, in turn, need to be framed so as to take the feasibility of the methods and the seriousness of particular validity threats into account, while the plausibility and relevance of particular validity threats, and the ways these can be dealt with, depend on the questions and methods chosen. The research questions are the heart, or hub, of the model; they connect all of the other components of the design, and should inform, and be sensitive to, these components.

The main implication of this interactive model is that you can't just work separately on each piece and then put them together. Design requires thinking about the connections between the pieces—the implications that each piece has for others—throughout the process.

There are many other factors besides these five components that will influence the design of your study; these include your resources, research skills, perceived problems, ethical standards, the research setting, and the data you collect and results you draw from these data. In my view, these are not part of the *design* of a study, but either belong to the *environment* within which the research and its design exist, or are *products* of the research. You will need to take these factors into account in designing your study, just as the design of a ship needs to take into account the kinds of wind and waves it will encounter and the sorts of cargo it will carry. Figure 5.2 presents some of the factors in the environment that can influence the design and conduct of a study, and displays some of the key linkages of these factors with components of the research design.

One way in which the design model presented here can be useful is as a tool or template for conceptually mapping the design of a specific study, either as part of the design process or in analyzing the design of an already-completed study. This involves filling in the circles for the five components

Figure 5.2   Contextual Factors Influencing a Research Design

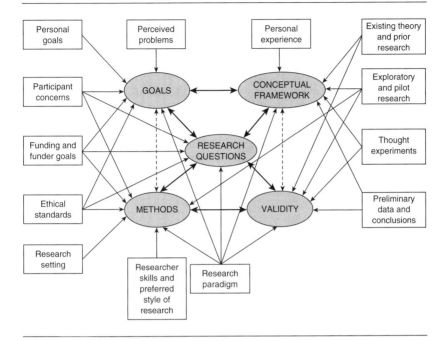

Source: Maxwell (2005).

of the model with the *actual* components of a particular study's design, a strategy that I call a "design map" (Maxwell, 2005; Maxwell & Loomis, 2003).

The main point that I want to make is that these components are real phenomena, with complex aspects and consequences for the research. This also has a deeper implication: that it is critical to understand how the researcher's goals, beliefs, and questions influence his or her actions, and how the latter affect the research setting and participants.

Goals

Your goals—using this term in a broad sense that includes your motives, desires, and purposes in doing the research—are an essential part of your study's design. They are the actual ends that you want to achieve through conducting the research, and their key function is to guide the design and conduct of the study so that it actually accomplishes these goals. Goals are real properties of the researcher, as discussed earlier, and have a profound influence on the design of a study. This influence may be conscious and intentional, or unrecognized and implicit.

Researchers frequently make a sharp separation between their research and the rest of their lives. This practice has usually been based, implicitly or explicitly, on the positivist ideal of the "objective" and "disinterested" scientist, in which any personal involvement has been treated as "bias." However, it is clear from autobiographies of scientists (e.g., Watson, 1968) that research decisions are often far more personal than this, and the importance of subjective motives and goals in science is supported by a great deal of historical, sociological, and philosophical work. The attempt to exclude subjective and personal concerns is not only impossible in practice, but is actually harmful to good research, in two main ways. First, it creates the illusion that research is typically guided only by rational and impersonal motives and decisions. This obscures the actual motives, assumptions, and agendas that researchers have, and leads them to ignore the influence of these on their research process and conclusions. It also leads researchers to hide their actual motives and practices when they don't conform to this ideal, and contributes to a kind of "impostor syndrome" in which each researcher feels that only he or she is failing to live up to the goal of scientific neutrality and disinterest.

Second, and in some ways even more damaging, this separation cuts the researcher off from a major source of insights, questions, and practical guidance in conducting the research and analyzing the data. I discuss this issue later in this chapter, in dealing with the researcher's conceptual framework.

The particular aspects of a design that are most directly and intentionally affected by your goals are your topic selection, research questions, and methods. However, these goals may also shape your assumptions about the phenomena studied and your selection of relevant theory, and can themselves create a validity threat to the study's conclusions (insofar as these goals affect your relationships, data collection, or analysis in ways that problematize these conclusions).

Also, as noted earlier, "real" does not mean "fixed"; your goals for a study can change radically, as a result of external circumstances or through reflection and critique (or both). Writing a "researcher identity memo" (Maxwell, 2005) is one way to become more aware of your goals and their implications and consequences. Example 5.4 describes how one researcher, Alan Peshkin, used such a process to understand his own goals and their effects on his research.

A realist stance toward goals implies that you should identify your beliefs and values *as* yours, rather than projecting them into the external environment. Phrases such as "we must," "there is a need to," and "it is imperative that" are

Example 5.4

Alan Peshkin's personal goals, rooted in his own values and identity, profoundly influenced several ethnographic studies he did of schools and their communities (1991, pp. 285–295; Glesne & Peshkin, 1992, pp. 93–107). In his first study, in a rural town he called Mansfield, he liked the community and felt protective toward it. This shaped the kind of story that he told, a story about the importance of community and its preservation. In contrast, in his second study, an ethnography of a fundamentalist Christian school (which he called Bethany Baptist Academy, BBA) and its community, he felt alienated, as a Jew, from a community that attempted to proselytize him:

> When I began to write. . . . I knew I was annoyed by my personal (as opposed to research) experience at BBA. I soon became sharply aware that my annoyance was pervasively present, that I was writing out of pique and vexation. Accordingly, I was not celebrating community at Bethany, and community prevailed there no less robustly than it had at Mansfield. Why not? I was more than annoyed in Bethany; my ox had been gored. The consequence was that the story I was feeling drawn to tell had its origins in my personal sense of threat. I was not at Bethany as a cool, dispassionate observer (are there any?); I was there as a Jew whose otherness was dramatized directly and indirectly during eighteen months of fieldwork. (Glesne & Peshkin, 1992, p. 103)

In hindsight, Peshkin realized that if he had been less sympathetic toward Mansfield, he could have told a different, equally valid story about this community, whereas if he had identified with Bethany and wanted to support and perpetuate it, he could legitimately have shown how it was much like Mansfield.

In a third study, this one of an urban, multiethnic, and multiracial school and community that he called Riverview, Peshkin resolved at the outset to try to identify the aspects of his identity that he saw emerging in his reactions. He "looked for the warm and the cool spots, the emergence of positive and negative feelings, the experiences I wanted to have more of or to avoid" (1991, p. 287), and recorded these on 5 x 8 cards.

Peshkin identified six different subjective "I"s that influenced this study, each embodying its own goals. These included the Ethnic-Maintenance I and the Community-Maintenance I that he had discovered in his earlier studies; an E-Pluribus-Unum I that supported the ethnic and racial "mingling" that

(Continued)

(Continued)

he saw going on; a Justice-Seeking I that wanted to correct the negative and biased images of Riverview held by its wealthier neighbors; a Pedagogical-Meliorist I that was disturbed by the poor teaching that many minority students received in Riverview and sought to find ways to improve this; and a Nonresearch-Human I that was grateful for the warm reception he and his wife received in Riverview, generated a concern for the people and community, and moderated otherwise sharp judgments he might have made.

Peshkin strongly recommended that all researchers systematically monitor their subjectivity:

> I see this monitoring as a necessary exercise, a workout, a tuning up of my subjectivity to get it in shape. It is a rehearsal for keeping the lines of my subjectivity open—and straight. And it is a warning to myself so that I may avoid the trap of perceiving just what my own untamed sentiments have sought out and served up as data. (1991, pp. 293–294)

In addition to influencing his questions and conclusions, Peshkin's personal goals were intimately involved in his choice of methods. As he stated, "I like fieldwork, it suits me, and I concluded that rather than pursuing research with questions in search of the 'right' methods of data collection, I had a preferred method of data collection in search of the 'right' question" (Glesne & Peshkin, 1992, p. 102).

red flags that you're not owning your beliefs, but instead are transforming them into purportedly "objective" and impersonal statements about the things you study. This is often done in order to make your goals seem less subjective and give your claims greater impact. However, doing so not only misrepresents their actual nature, but also makes it harder for you to recognize when your goals are distorting your conclusions.

There are two types of goals that I want to distinguish, because they have very different implications for the design of your study. I call these practical goals and intellectual goals. Practical goals are focused on *accomplishing* something—meeting some need, changing some situation, or achieving some practical objective. Intellectual goals, in contrast, are focused on *understanding* something—gaining insight into what is going on and why this is happening, or answering some question that previous research has not adequately understood. Both of these kinds of goals are real parts of your design, but they address different aspects of the world external to that design. Your intellectual goals deal with what *is*—the nature of the phenomena you are studying.

Practical goals, in contrast, deal with what *could be*—how you want to *change* these phenomena, to make them *different* from the way they currently are (or are currently changing).

For this reason, your intellectual goals are more directly relevant to your conceptual framework and research questions than your practical goals. Intellectual goals can often be easily converted into viable research questions— ones that your study could actually answer. Practical goals, on the other hand, because they don't directly deal with what actually exists, are more problematic for developing research questions. Questions based directly on practical goals, such as "How can this program be improved?," aren't good research questions because they don't target a real phenomenon, but a *hypothetical* one—what *might* happen, rather than what *is* happening or *did* happen. The goal *itself* is real in sense of being part of your own thinking, but any answer to the question isn't a real aspect of the situation you're studying: it is potential, rather than actual. Such questions, however, can often be transformed into workable questions by focusing on the actual phenomena studied, e.g., "How did this policy influence the outcomes of the program?"

Using practical goals to develop research questions thus requires an intermediate step: asking what you need to better *understand* about the phenomena you're studying *in order to* accomplish these goals. (One example of the latter is understanding what *participants* believe needs to be done to achieve these goals, and how they think that this could be accomplished.) Framing your actual research questions in terms of the latter understandings that you want to gain gives you better guidance for selecting sites or participants, collecting and analyzing data, and deciding what validity threats you need to deal with and how you can do this.

Developing useful research questions requires attention to both your goals and your conceptual framework for your study, and I next turn to the latter component of your research design.

Conceptual Frameworks

Your conceptual framework is the component of your design that incorporates your understanding of the events, settings, individuals, and processes being investigated, their interrelationships, and the relevant contextual influences on these. It consists of the actual concepts, beliefs, and assumptions that you hold about these phenomena and contexts, including the relationships among these phenomena and contexts. In a broad sense, it is your model, or theory, of the things you are studying and the events and processes that influence these. While your intellectual goals deal with what you *don't* know and want to learn, your conceptual framework deals with what you *do* know, think you know, or hypothesize about the things you plan to study. A critical realist perspective implies that such knowledge, like all knowledge, is never absolute or certain, and is always subject to revision in the light of new evidence or theories.

As with goals, it is useful to distinguish your conscious, explicit beliefs from your actual beliefs; you may not be fully aware of the latter. Your conceptual framework will change during the course of your study, both because the information you gather will lead to new ideas and understandings, and because the process of doing this may lead you to become aware of, or to question, parts of your previous conceptual framework. Thus, the kind of exercises that I recommended for developing a better understanding of your goals are also useful for examining your conceptual framework.

From a realist perspective, there are no fixed rules or constraints on how you construct your conceptual framework or what sources you use for this. The criterion for evaluating a conceptual framework is how effectively it represents what really exists and is actually occurring. No conceptual framework, model, or theory can capture everything about the phenomena you study; every theory is a lens for making sense of the world, and every theory both reveals some aspects of that reality, and distorts or conceals other aspects. The issue is how useful any particular theory or model is in understanding and dealing with the phenomena in question.

The term "framework" can be misleading in suggesting that your conceptual framework must be a single, coherent, integrated system of concepts. While this may be an ideal, it is rarely achieved, and isn't necessary for your conceptual framework to be useful. Since, as noted earlier, no theory or model can be a complete picture of what exists, it may be desirable to have multiple theories, each helping you to understand some aspect of the phenomena you're studying (Anyon, 2009; Dressman, 2008; Maxwell, 2008, 2009). Awareness of alternative theories can help you to avoid the "ideological hegemony" (Becker, 1986, pp. 147–149) of a single dominant theory, which can distort your conceptions of the things you study, as well as lead you to overlook things that don't fit this theory or alternative ways of making sense of your data.

In addition, you don't have to adopt theories as wholes; you can borrow particular ideas from different theories and use these to construct a conceptual framework that best fits your particular topic or problem. As Abbott and others have argued, these theoretical modules or heuristics can function as specific conceptual tools in a larger "toolkit," rather than only as a single "framework" or "paradigm." It will be helpful for you to think about how these diverse pieces might fit together, or what their implications are for one another.

I therefore recommend thinking broadly about the range of available sources from which your conceptual framework can be drawn or modified (Example 5.5). This is not an exhaustive list, but covers the most commonly used sources.

Example 5.5

Possible Sources for Your Conceptual Framework

1. *Prior theory and research.* This is often treated as the main or only source of your conceptual framework, so much so that this section of a dissertation is often called the "literature review." Here, I mainly want to emphasize that this source, although important and usually essential, isn't the only way to gain valuable ideas for your conceptual framework, and, as described earlier, may have a negative influence on your understanding of the phenomena you're studying. (For more extensive discussions of this source, see Maxwell, 2005, pp. 41–46; 2006.) Qualitative researchers typically use insights or concepts taken from existing theories, and relate their findings to these theories, but their research often draws on these theories selectively and eclectically, rather than deliberately seeking to apply or contribute to a particular theory.

2. *Experiential knowledge.* The ideas and understandings that you have gained from your own experience with the types of people, settings, or problems you want to study are a key source of concepts and theories for your conceptual framework. Unfortunately, many students, and other researchers as well, systematically ignore what they know from direct experience, because it isn't seen as being as credible or prestigious as "the literature," as well as because, by positivist standards, it is "subjective" and therefore suspect. Anselm Strauss argued that "[positivist] canons lead to the squashing of valuable experiential data. We say, rather, 'mine your experience, there is potential gold there!'" (Strauss, 1987, p. 11). Such experiential knowledge is often more credible than that drawn from prior research, because it is grounded in direct acquaintance with the settings, people, or phenomena you propose to study. However, like all knowledge, it is subject to significant validity threats, which must be addressed to establish the credibility of your conclusions (see Chapter 8).

3. *Pilot studies.* Pilot studies serve some of the same functions as prior research, but they can be focused more precisely on your own concerns and theories, and on the specific setting or kinds of people you plan to study. You can design pilot studies specifically to test your ideas or methods and explore their implications, or to inductively develop theory. In particular, pilot studies can provide insights into the meanings, beliefs, and values held by the sorts of people you plan to study—a key part of the reality you want to understand, as argued in Chapter 2. In a qualitative study, your ideas about these meanings and perspectives should constitute a key component of your conceptual framework.

(Continued)

(Continued)

4. *Thought experiments.* Thought experiments—speculation about how something might function, or what could cause a particular outcome— have a long and respected history in the physical sciences (much of Einstein's work was based on thought experiments), and are regularly used in social sciences such as economics. However, they have received little attention as an explicit source of insights in qualitative research. Many of the kinds of memos that I have recommended earlier can be seen as thought experiments—opportunities to think about the phenomena you're studying and develop ideas that can be used or tested in your research. For a more detailed presentation of how to use thought experiments in social research, see Lave and March (1975) and Maxwell (2005, pp. 58–63).

Source: Adapted from Maxwell (2005).

A valuable strategy in developing your conceptual framework is concept mapping (Miles & Huberman, 1994, pp. 18–22; Novak & Gowin, 1984). The goal of a concept map is to capture visually your actual "mental model" of what you're studying, and to help you improve that model. Many students create concept maps, but such maps are often little more than a spatial arrangement of the key topics and ideas that inform their study. As described earlier, your conceptual framework consists not only of your concepts and beliefs that are relevant to the phenomena you are studying, *but also the relationships you see among these*; the latter are rarely explicitly incorporated in the map, except by lines that remain unexplained. A useful concept map, one that really helps you to understand and develop your conceptual framework, needs to *describe* the relationships that you believe exist among your concepts, and generally needs an accompanying narrative that accomplishes this (see Example 9.1).

Research Questions

As with all of the other components of your design, the development of your research questions should be an iterative, ongoing process, not a one-shot "step" in designing your study. Jointly, your goals and your conceptual framework provide the most important material for developing the research questions for your study. These research questions state the things that your research is intended to discover, or gain a better understanding of. For this reason, I have placed research questions at the center or hub of my model of research design. Your research questions connect directly to all of the other four components of your design, and need to influence, and be responsive to, these components.

In addition, your research questions should be responsive to the actual phenomena you are studying and the situations in which you do this, as Figure 5.2 illustrates. As your understanding of these phenomena and situations (your conceptual framework) develops, this should inform your research questions, and may lead to significant refocusing and revision of these. This focusing (and I use this metaphor in the sense of bringing *into* focus the things you are studying, sharpening your understanding of these phenomena, as well as more precisely selecting *what* you focus on) enables your questions to more accurately guide your data collection and analysis, as well as to anticipate and deal with potential validity threats.

However, it is possible for your questions to be *too* focused; they may create tunnel vision, leaving out things that are important to the goals (both intellectual and practical) of your study. Research questions that are precisely framed too early in the study may lead you to overlook areas of theory or prior experience that are relevant to your understanding of what is going on, or cause you to not pay enough attention to a wide range of data, data that can reveal important and unanticipated phenomena and relationships. This is often a result of smuggling unexamined assumptions about the things you're studying into the research questions themselves, imposing a conceptual framework that doesn't fit the reality you're trying to understand. A research question such as "How do teachers deal with the experience of isolation from their colleagues in their classrooms?" assumes that teachers *do* experience such isolation. Such an assumption needs to be carefully examined and justified, and may work better as a subquestion to broader questions about the nature of classroom teachers' experience of their work and their relations with colleagues.

There are three distinctions among types of research questions that I want to emphasize, all of which are connected to a realist ontology. The first is between questions stated in terms of a *category* of individuals, settings, or activities, and those stated in terms of *specific* instances of these. Thus, a research question could be framed either as "How do elementary math teachers understand mathematical ability," or as "How do the math teachers *in this elementary school* understand mathematical ability?" In the latter statement, the teachers studied are treated not as a *sample* from some larger population of teachers to whom the study is intended to generalize, but as a *case* of a group of teachers who are studied in a particular context (the specific school and community).

The former wording is standard in quantitative research, and is common even in qualitative research. However, it often conflicts with the actual purpose of a qualitative study, which may not be to generalize, but to understand a specific, local phenomenon or situation. As argued in Chapter 3, even causal explanation is, from a realist perspective, primarily a *local* phenomenon, and valid general explanations must be based on an understanding of local processes in context. More broadly, I argued in Chapter 4 that diversity is a real phenomenon, and that generalizations are abstractions from that diverse, local reality. Framing research questions in general terms can interfere with your investigation of the specific features of, and influences on, the actual individuals or settings you're studying.

The second distinction I want to make is between questions framed in terms of observable data, and those framed in terms of unobservable, but presumably real, phenomena. Thus, the previous question could be stated as "How do these elementary math teachers *describe* mathematical ability," rather than "How do they *understand* mathematical ability?" The former approach, generally known as "instrumentalism" (Norris, 1983), avoids the risk of making inferences from the data to unobservable entities; this was a major goal of positivism, which sought to define all scientific concepts in terms of observable data and procedures, and to eliminate unobservable entities from scientific theories. However, this goal eventually was shown to be irreparably flawed, as discussed in Chapter 1, and a realist approach to scientific concepts, seeing these as legitimately referring to unobservable entities and processes, is now prevalent. It is completely legitimate, and often more productive, to frame your research questions in terms of the actual phenomena and processes that you think may be involved in the things you study, even if you can't directly observe these. (However, this then requires you to present *evidence* to support your conclusions about these, as discussed in Chapter 8.)

The third distinction is between questions that are framed, explicitly or implicitly, in terms of variance theory, and those framed in terms of process theory. Variance questions tend to focus on *differences* and their explanation; for example, "Do second-career teachers remain in teaching longer than teachers for whom teaching is their first career, and if so, what factors account for this?" In contrast, an example of a process question would be "How do second-career teachers decide whether to remain in teaching or to leave?"

As described in Chapter 3, variance theory is particularly well suited to quantitative approaches, which emphasize accurately measuring differences and correlating these with other differences. Qualitative research, in contrast, is much more effective for understanding the actual processes that are involved in particular situations or outcomes, what Miles and Huberman (1994) called "local causality." Variance questions can implicitly lead you to think in variance terms, overlooking the real strengths of a qualitative approach, which are understanding *how* and *why* something happens, rather than simply *whether* it does so and to what extent.

One student, Bruce Wahl, wrote to me about having changed his research questions while he was analyzing the data for his dissertation, an evaluation of math projects for community college students that engaged different learning styles:

> I don't know if you remember, but two years ago when I was writing my proposal, you stressed that I should be writing my research questions beginning with words like "how" and "what" and "why" instead of the yes/no questions I was asking. For example, my first question was, "Do the projects help students to grasp mathematical concepts?" As I am writing up the interview results, I finally understand what you were saying. What I really wanted to know was "How do the projects help (or not help!) the students to grasp mathematical concepts?" It seems so clear now, it is a wonder that I didn't understand it back then. I have rewritten the five research questions for myself with that in mind and will include those new, and I hope, improved questions with the [dissertation] draft I deliver next week.

The Interconnections Among the Design Components

The main point of thinking about research design systemically or interactively is that there really are interactions among the components of your design, seen as both the actual conceptions that you have of your study and the actual implementation of this "on the ground." In particular, your goals, conceptual framework, and research questions need to be responsive to one another, so that changes in one component don't create a disconnection or incompatibility with the other components. The goal of my design model is to represent the actual, functioning parts of a study and how they relate to one another.

For a much more detailed discussion of the practical issues involved in designing a research study, with more suggestions, examples, and exercises, see my book *Qualitative Research Design: An Interactive Approach* (Maxwell, 2005).

6

Research Relationships and Data Collection

This chapter deals with the implications of realism for your engagement with the actual situations and people that you study. This engagement involves three aspects of qualitative methods: selecting settings and participants; negotiating relationships with participants, gatekeepers, and other stakeholders; and collecting data. I see these as three of the four basic components of qualitative methods (Maxwell, 2005); the fourth, data analysis, is discussed in Chapter 7.

Selecting Settings and Participants

The selection of settings and participants for a research project is often called "sampling," but this term is more appropriate for quantitative than qualitative research (Morgan, 2008), and some qualitative researchers prefer the term "selection," believing that "sampling" is too closely associated with survey sampling (e.g., Stake, 1995). In most quantitative studies, the goal is to generalize from the settings or participants selected to some defined population, or to compare groups or individuals that differ on particular independent variables in terms of their values for other, dependent variables. These goals require systematic attention to the representativeness of the sample selected, or to the comparability of the groups or individuals compared; for these purposes, some form of probability sampling (or random assignment of individuals or settings to particular conditions) is optimal.

In qualitative research, this sort of generalization, which Yin (1993) called "statistical generalization," is uncommon, for two reasons. First, the number of participants or settings included in a qualitative study is typically too small to confidently make such generalizations, even with a probability sample. (Even random sampling is very vulnerable to sampling error if the sample size is small, and using small random samples is a common mistake in selecting qualitative sites or participants.)

Second, the goal of most qualitative studies is not to generalize a claim *that* a difference exists between different settings, groups, or categories of individuals, or that a relationship exists between specific variables for some population. Instead, it is to understand the processes, meanings, and local contextual influences involved in the phenomena of interest, for the specific settings or individuals studied. (This is the distinction between variance and process approaches, described in Chapter 3.) This does not mean that qualitative research is incapable of generalization. Qualitative research involves a different strategy for generalizing its findings, which Yin (1993) called "analytic generalization." This strategy is discussed in Chapter 8.

As a result, the guiding principle in selecting settings and participants for a qualitative study is usually not to ensure representativeness or comparability, but, first, to identify groups, settings, or individuals that best exhibit the characteristics or phenomena of interest, and second, to select those that are most accessible and conducive to gaining the understandings you seek.[1] The first of these principles is often called "purposive sampling"—the strategic selection of where, when, and from whom data will be collected, based on the objectives of the study (Palys, 2008). Palys argued that "purposive sampling is virtually synonymous with qualitative research," and that decisions about whom and what to include should be based on "what [you] want to accomplish and what you want to know" (p. 697). In terms of my design model (Chapter 5), these represent, respectively, your goals and your research questions.

I would add to these two additional considerations. First, your current understanding of the phenomena you want to study (your conceptual framework) is critical; this is the primary issue for what Strauss (1987; Strauss & Corbin, 1990, p. 176 ff.) called "theoretical sampling," which involves selecting participants, activities, or incidents on the basis of their relevance to the theory you are developing. Second, you need to consider the relationships that you have, or expect to be able to establish, with participants or other stakeholders

---

[1] There are some situations in which random sampling is a useful strategy for a qualitative study. If you want your participants to be representative of some larger population, and you are able to include a large enough number of participants, then some form of probability sampling may be appropriate (e.g., Huberman, 1989), although you need to be aware of the pitfalls in making inferences from even a random sample to a population (Huck, 2009, p. 121 ff.). In addition, random sampling may be useful for other purposes besides representativeness, such as ensuring that the selection process is perceived as fair (e.g., Starnes, 1990, p. 33).

in the research settings or populations you study, and how these will facilitate of hinder your goals; I discuss this in more detail shortly. All of these are real considerations in making selection decisions, because they will influence the data you can gather and the understandings you will gain from these.

The second principle listed earlier, selecting those settings and individuals that are most accessible and conducive to gaining the understandings you seek, is often labeled "convenience sampling," and negatively contrasted with both probability and purposeful sampling (e.g., Glesne, 2011, p. 45; Patton, 2001). However, the realities of access, cost, time, and difficulty necessarily influence *every* decision about what settings and participants to include in a study, and to dismiss these considerations as "unrigorous" is to ignore the real conditions that will influence how data can be collected and the ability of these data to answer your research questions. Palys stated that "there is no one best sampling strategy because which is best depends on the context in which researchers are working and the nature of their research objective(s)" (2008, p. 697).

To make convenience the primary or sole criterion for these decisions is dangerous, both because it diminishes or ignores the first criterion—where you can best obtain the information and understandings you seek—and because it exposes your conclusions to serious validity threats. However, your research design needs to take into account the practical realities of your possible choices of settings and participants, and how these may affect the success of your study. In some cases (common in ethnographic fieldwork; Chapter 10 presents one example), you may have little choice; the participants in my dissertation research largely chose me, rather than vice versa.

In addition, Weiss (1994, pp. 24–29) argued that there are situations in which convenience sampling is necessarily the main criterion—for example, in attempting to learn about a group that is difficult to gain access to, or a category of people who are relatively rare in the population and for whom no data on membership exist, such as "house husbands." He listed several strategies for maximizing the value of such convenience samples in qualitative research.

However, I also want to emphasize a realist point developed in more detail in Chapter 8—that *no* selection strategy guarantees that you will *actually* select the settings and participants that best allow you to answer your questions or achieve your goals. Purposive selection is not a fixed "procedure" that you can mechanically follow; its productive application requires using *all* of the information you have available to you to help you decide which setting and participants will best meet your purposes. (It also requires a clear understanding of your goals and what you want to understand, as argued in Chapter 5.) Maxwell (2005), Miles and Huberman (1994, pp. 27–29), Palys (2008), and many other qualitative sources list specific strategies and purposes that can be employed in purposively selecting settings and participants for a qualitative study.

In many situations, optimal selection decisions will require considerable knowledge of the context of the study. In Jane Margolis's study of classroom discourse norms in a college department (1990), she could only interview a small percentage of the students, and needed to develop some criteria for selecting participants. Her dissertation committee (of which I was a member) recommended that she interview sophomores and seniors, believing that this would provide the optimal diversity of views. When she consulted with members of the department, however, they told her that sophomores were too new to the department to fully understand the norms of discourse, while seniors were too deeply involved in their theses and in planning for graduation to be good informants. Juniors turned out to be the choice that would best meet the criteria of having the desired information and being most likely to provide this in interviews.

Researcher Subjectivity and Research Relationships

In order to actually obtain data about the settings, or from the participants, that you've selected, you need to establish *relationships* with gatekeepers for these settings and with the participants themselves. As Bosk (1979, p. ix) said, qualitative fieldwork is a body contact sport; with few exceptions, you need to actually interact with your participants and other people in the settings you study. Hammersley and Atkinson (2007, pp. 16–22) referred to this interaction as "reflexivity": "the fact that we are part of the social world we study" (p. 21) and must therefore understand how we influence and are influenced by this world. This mutual influence is both a necessary aspect and facilitator of data collection, and a potential validity threat to your conclusions.

A major factor in this reflexivity is the personal characteristics that you bring to the research—the prior experiences, beliefs, purposes, values, and subjective qualities that shape how you conceptualize the study and engage in it. There is a saying that in quantitative research, the researcher *has* instruments, but in qualitative research, the researcher *is* the instrument. While I think the latter claim is also true of quantitative research, it seems indisputable that the personal characteristics of the researcher play a major role in the conduct of a qualitative study.

These two aspects of the researcher's role—personal subjectivity and research relationships—are emphasized in an edited volume on qualitative psychology (Tolman & Brydon-Miller, 2001). The editors identified two key characteristics of the sorts of qualitative research they present, which they describe as "interpretive" and "participatory." They stated that [interpretive and participatory] methods are relational in that they acknowledge and actively involve the relationships between researchers and participants, as well as their respective subjectivities. . . . Researchers using these methods reject the possibility of a neutral stance; thus, rather than attempting to eliminate bias, we explore and embrace the role of subjectivity. (p. 5)

These two components are also integral parts of my realist model of research design. The first, the researcher's identity and perspective, includes the purposes and conceptual framework of a study, implicit as well as explicit (discussed in Chapter 5), as well as other properties that the researcher brings to the study that are not formally incorporated in this model.

The second component, research relationships, is one part of the actual methods used in the research. Here, I use "methods" in a broad sense that includes all of the things that the researcher actually does to acquire and make sense of the data collected. By calling this a "realist" model, I mean that I see these components (as well as others not discussed here) not simply as theoretical abstractions or methodological principles, but as real phenomena, things that have an influence on the research, the data collected, and the conclusions.

RESEARCHER SUBJECTIVITY

The traditional view of "subjectivity" treats this as "bias," something to be eliminated, or at least controlled, in the interest of "objectivity." This is consistent with the positivist view (discussed in Chapter 1) of research conclusions as based on rigorously collected "sense data" that were objectively verifiable. The collapse of this view implies that no such "immaculate perception" exists, and that the standpoint of the researcher is inevitably involved in, and interacts with, the data that are collected. A critical realist perspective, therefore, requires researchers to take account of the actual beliefs, values, and dispositions that they bring to the study, which can serve as valuable resources, as well as possible sources of distortion or lack of comprehension.

Thus, Alan Peshkin, discussing the role of subjectivity in the research he had done, concluded that

the subjectivity that originally I had taken as an affliction, something to bear because it could not be foregone, could, to the contrary, be taken as "virtuous." My subjectivity is *the* basis for the story that I am able to tell. It is a strength on which I build. It makes me who I am as a person *and* as a researcher, equipping me with the perspectives and insights that shape all that I do as a researcher, from the selection of topic clear through to the emphases I make in my writing. Seen as virtuous, subjectivity is something to capitalize on rather than to exorcise. (Glesne & Peshkin, 1992, p. 104)

The grain of truth in the traditional view of subjectivity as bias (with which critical realists would agree) is that researchers' personal (and often unexamined) motives, beliefs, and theories have important consequences for the validity of their conclusions. If your research decisions and data analyses are based on personal desires or theoretical commitments *without* a careful assessment of the implications of these for your methods and conclusions, you are in danger of creating a flawed study or reaching incorrect conclusions. However, this does not require the *exclusion* of your subjectivity. Tolman, in discussing her research on adolescent girls' sexuality, argued that

> like a therapist, as a listener I bring myself knowingly into the process of listening, learning from my own thoughts and feelings in response to what a girl is saying in her story. . . . This attention to myself increases my ability to stay clear about what my own ideas and feelings are and how they do or do not line up with a girl's words, thus avoiding "bias" or imposing my own story over the girl's. (Tolman, 2001, p. 132)

Tolman's perspective, and the similar views of many other qualitative researchers, is consistent with, and supported by, a realist analysis of the phenomenon of subjectivity. Rather than treating subjectivity as a variable to be controlled and ideally reduced to zero, realists see it as a component of the actual process of understanding, one that can have a variety of consequences, both good and bad. Only through a clear comprehension of this process, in the particular context in which it occurs, is it possible to identify the actual mechanisms leading to these consequences, and to adjust the research to take best advantage of the positive consequences and minimize the negative ones. Even researchers who take an interpretive or constructivist stance toward qualitative research often approach this process in ways that are quite consistent with a critical realist understanding. For example, Tappan states that "the interpreter's perspective and understanding initially shapes his interpretation of a given phenomenon, but that interpretation is open to revision and elaboration as it interacts with the phenomenon in question, and as the perspective and understanding of the interpreter, including his biases and blind spots, are revealed and evaluated" (2001, p. 50).

A great deal has been written about subjectivity as an essential constituent of understanding in qualitative research (e.g., Berg & Smith, 1988; Jansen & Peshkin, 1992). What has been less well explored is *how*, specifically, one becomes aware of this subjectivity and its consequences, and how one uses this subjectivity productively in the research. The sort of in-process monitoring described by Tolman is one way to do this, but one that is fluid, idiosyncratic, and rarely described in the sort of detail that would allow someone else to learn the technique.

One strategy for understanding the influence of your beliefs and prior experiences on your research is reflective analysis and writing, or what qualitative researchers often call "memos" (Maxwell, 2005, pp. 11–13). Peshkin, in order to better understand his own subjectivity during his study of a multiethnic school and community (1991), "looked for the warm and the cool spots, the emergence of positive and negative feelings, the experiences I wanted to have more of or to avoid" (p. 287), and recorded these on 5 × 8 cards. (A diary or field journal, or a computer file of memos, would also work, but index cards allow more immediacy of recording.) In analyzing these cards, he identified six "I's," aspects of his identity that influenced his research, and was able to better understand both the benefits and the risks of these identities.

I use a much shorter and simpler version of this technique in my qualitative methods courses, an exercise that I call a "researcher identity memo." The purpose of this memo is to help students examine their background, purposes, assumptions, feelings, and values as they relate to their research, and to discover what resources and potential concerns their identity and experience may create. They are asked to write about their prior connections (social and intellectual) to the topics, people, or settings they plan to study; how they think and feel about these topics, people, or settings; and the assumptions they are making, consciously or unconsciously, about these, as well as how they see these as influencing their research. Preissle (2008) referred to such memos, which may be published as well as used for personal reflection, as "subjectivity statements."

Like other memos, these offer an exercise in reflection, "thinking on paper" about these issues to explore their complexities and implications. The goal is partly to "bracket" one's experiences and perspectives, seeing them more clearly and thus being better able to see past them, and partly to recognize the insights and conceptual resources that these experiences and perspectives provide. It should not be a one-time activity that is completed and then put aside, but an ongoing exploration of one's identity and perspective in relation to the research, which may change during the study. The exercise is often a powerful experience for students, enabling them to discover things about themselves that they were unaware of, and a valuable tool for understanding their own connection to their topic and setting, as well as the consequences of this for their research. For more discussion, and an example of such a memo, see Maxwell (2005).

RESEARCH RELATIONSHIPS

The second component of the researcher's role is the researcher's relationships with those studied. This relationship is usually addressed in qualitative-methods books and research reports, but it has often been reduced to narrow and oversimplified concepts such as "entry," "access," or "rapport," obscuring the complexity, fluid nature, and ongoing development of the research relationship. The relationships that the researcher creates with the participants in the research are real phenomena; they shape the context within which the research is conducted, and have a profound influence on the research and its results (see Example 5.1). Thus, their actual nature and operation need to be understood in order to use them productively. As I stated earlier, these relationships are also an essential part of the design of a study; they form one component of the methods that the researcher uses to collect and analyze data (Maxwell 2005, pp. 82–87).

This is true for *all* research that involves actual interaction with either participants or gatekeepers, not just qualitative research—see, for example, Mishler's discussion (1986) of the futility of attempting to eliminate the effect of the relationship between the interviewer and respondent in survey research. However, the relationships created during a qualitative study are typically much more complex and more directly implicated in the research process than in quantitative research, and the researcher's relationships are profoundly entangled with—indeed, they often substantially constitute—the data collection process. Hammersley and Atkinson argued that

> once we abandon the idea that the social character of research can be standardized out or avoided by becoming a "fly on the wall" or a "full participant," the role of the researcher as active participant in the research process becomes clear. (2007, p. 17)

Lawrence-Lightfoot and Hoffman Davis, in their presentation of portraiture as a qualitative method, criticized the tendency, even in qualitative research, to treat relationship as a tool or strategy for gaining access to data, rather than as a connection (1997, p. 135). They took what they call a "revisionist" view, that "relationships that are complex, fluid, symmetric, and reciprocal—that are shaped by both researchers and actors—reflect a more responsible ethical stance *and* are likely to yield deeper data and better social science" (pp. 137–138). They emphasized the continual creation and renegotiation of trust, intimacy, and reciprocity. From a realist perspective, this involves seeing research relationships neither as variables to be controlled or manipulated, nor simply as "constructions" created by the researcher and/or participants, but as real, complex processes that have profound, and often unanticipated, consequences for the research. As Lawrence-Lightfoot and Hoffman Davis argued, "the relationship . . . will be shaped by both temporal and temperamental dimensions—that is, by the duration of time spent and the frequency of encounters between the researcher and the actor, as well as by their personalities and the chemistry of their interactions" (1997, p. 138).

Conceptualizing the research relationship in terms of "rapport" (e.g., Seidman, 1998, pp. 80–82) is also problematic, because it frames the relationship in terms of a single continuous variable, rather than emphasizing the *nature* of the relationship. Seidman's point that it is possible to have too much rapport, as well as too little, is valuable, but the *kind* of relationship, as well as the amount of rapport, is critical. In addition, "rapport" may be an exploitative or oppressive imposition on the participant; Burman (2001, p. 263) criticized the concept of "rapport" as a commodification of relationship into manipulative strategies to promote disclosure.

Particularly insightful accounts of the process of creating relationships with participants, and the influence these had on the research, are Rabinow's analysis of his changing relationships with his informants and the influence of these on his understanding of the Moroccan community in which he conducted his research (1977); Bosk's discussion of how his relationships with the surgeons he studied both facilitated and constrained his research (1979); Eckert's description of the relationships she established in her study of social class and identity in high schools (1989); and Briggs's (1986) sociolinguistic analysis of how his relationship with his Mexicano hosts in a New Mexico village both precluded the kinds of interviews he had planned to conduct and taught him a great deal about the culturally appropriate ways to gain information in this village. Glesne (2011, pp. 141–150) provided a detailed discussion of the different aspects of field relations that need to be considered in planning and conducting a qualitative study.

As implied earlier, there are ethical and political issues that should inform the kinds of relationships that researchers and the participants in a study create. Many of these are addressed by the contributors to Tolman and Brydon-Miller's volume, all of whom believe that qualitative research should be "participatory" in the sense of working collaboratively with research participants to generate knowledge that is useful to the participants as well as the researcher, contributing to personal and social transformation (Tolman & Brydon-Miller, 2001, pp. 3–4). In particular, a major issue in relationships is that of difference between researcher and participant. Brown and Gilligan stated that "when a conversation has different meanings for the people engaged in it and especially when one of the two has the power to structure the meeting, it is important to ask whether there can be genuine dialogue" (1992, p. 25). Many of the contributors to the Tolman and Brydon-Miller volume address issues of differential power, and describe participatory strategies that help to overcome or address such differences.

However, there is often an unstated assumption, implicit in the Brown and Gilligan quote, that difference *per se* is an inherent problem for relationship and dialogue, one that must be overcome by recognizing or creating commonalities. This view, that relationship depends on similarities—shared attributes or "common ground"—is one that I have addressed at length in

Chapters 2 and 4. I believe that difference is a real phenomenon that is often disregarded or misrepresented by both quantitative and qualitative research methods (Maxwell, 1996a), and that there is a constant danger of mystifying one's understanding of relationship by ignoring differences, particularly relative differences in power or privilege. Researchers need to guard against romantic and illusory assumptions of equality and intimacy that distort the actual relationships they engage in, as well as to develop strategies that enable them to understand the actual nature, amount, and consequences of diversity in their relationships. However, they also need to avoid assuming that solidarity is necessarily a matter of similarity, and to be prepared to recognize the actual processes through which difference can contribute to relationship and solidarity, as argued in Chapter 4.

There is more discussion in the qualitative literature of the importance of relationship than there is specific guidance in how to establish mutually productive and ethically acceptable research relationships. Welch's work, described in Chapter 4, is an important exception, as are the papers by Lykes, Chataway, and Maguire in Tolman and Brydon-Miller (2001), and the classic work on field research by Wax (1971). Somewhat broader, more philosophical advice was given by the moral philosopher Alasdair MacIntyre, who argued that "the understanding of others is indeed an understanding of difference" (1993, p. 5), and drew important lessons from this for research relationships.

Example 6.1

One technique for addressing this issue of establishing mutually productive and equitable relationships is the reflective memo. In my course on qualitative research methods, I ask students to write a memo that addresses the following questions:

1. What kind of relationships have you established, or do you plan to establish, with the people whom you are studying? What consequences do you think these will have for your study? What alternative kinds of relationships could you create, and what advantages and disadvantages would these have?

2. How do you think you will be perceived by the people you interact with in your research? How will this affect your relations with these people? What could you do to better understand this perception, and to correct possible misperceptions?

3. What explicit agreements do you plan to negotiate about how the research will be conducted and how you will report the results, both to the people you are working with and to others? What *implicit* understandings about these issues do you think these people (and you) will

(Continued)

(Continued)

have? How will both the implicit and explicit terms of the study affect your research? Do any of these need to be discussed or changed?

4. What ethical issues or problems do these considerations raise? How do you plan to deal with these?

Data Collection

The main implication of realism for qualitative data collection is that data are usefully seen, not simply as "texts" to be interpreted, or as the "constructions" of participants (although they are this), but as *evidence* for real phenomena and processes (including mental phenomena and processes) that are not available for direct observation. These data are used to make *inferences* about these phenomena, which can then be tested against additional data. This follows directly from the basic premises of critical realism: that there is a real world that we seek to understand, but that our understandings of this world are inevitably incomplete and fallible, and unavoidably shaped by the particular assumptions and perspective that we bring to the research—the "lens" through which we view the world.

I deal with some of the consequences of this view of data as evidence, and the validity issues that this raises, in Chapter 8. The most important implication of this view for data collection is that you should always be considering, in planning and conducting your data collection, how the data that you collect can enable you to develop and test your emerging understandings of the phenomena you are studying. Both the use of data to develop theory and the "verification of statements against data" (Strauss & Corbin, 1990, p. 108) are key aspects of the "grounded theory" approach to qualitative research, but the latter use of data, to explicitly test your ideas, is less commonly addressed in the qualitative literature. This is sometimes equated with the "hypothesis testing" of quantitative research, and seen as inappropriate for qualitative research.

However, thinking about the data that you could collect in terms of how these could expand, support, or test your current understandings is not the same as the deliberate testing of prior, theoretically derived hypotheses, let alone the statistical testing of hypotheses that is characteristic of quantitative research, an issue that is controversial even in statistics (Harlow, Mulaik, & Steiger, 1997). It simply requires constantly being aware of how your views might be wrong or inadequately developed, and planning your data collection explicitly to address these issues, rather than simply proceeding along a predesigned path and accumulating data with no clear sense of how to use your data to support *and* test your preliminary conclusions. This issue is addressed in more depth in Chapter 8 (see also Maxwell, 2010a).

Most qualitative-methods texts devote considerable space to the strengths and limitations of different qualitative data collection methods (see particularly Bogdan & Biklen, 2003; Glesne, 2011; and Patton, 2001), and I don't want to repeat these discussions here. Instead, I want to address two key conceptual issues in selecting and using data collection methods: the relationship between your research questions and data collection methods, and the triangulation of different methods.

THE RELATIONSHIP BETWEEN RESEARCH QUESTIONS AND DATA COLLECTION METHODS

The main point that I want to emphasize here is that the methods you use to collect your data (including your interview questions) don't necessarily resemble, or follow by logical deduction from, your research questions; the two are both real parts of your design, but distinct and separate parts. This can be a source of confusion, because researchers often talk about "operationalizing" their research questions, or of "translating" the research questions into interview questions. Such language is a vestige of logical positivist views of the relationship between theory and methods, as described in Chapter 1. From a realist perspective, there is no way to mechanically "convert" research questions into methods; your methods are the *means* to answering your research questions, not a logical transformation of the latter. Their selection depends not only on your research questions, but on the actual research situation and on what will work most effectively in that situation to give you the data you need (see Example 6.2).

Example 6.2 presents an extreme case, but the basic principle holds for any study. Your research questions formulate what you want to understand; your *interview* questions are what you ask people in order to gain that understanding. The development of good interview questions (and observational strategies) requires creativity and insight, rather than a mechanical conversion of the research questions into an interview guide or observation

Example 6.2

A striking example of the lack of a logical relationship between research questions and methods (in this case, interview questions) is Kirk and Miller's research in Peru on people's knowledge and use of coca leaves (the organic source of cocaine), which was widespread and legal, though frowned on by the government. Their open-ended interview questions about coca, drawn fairly directly from their research questions, elicited

(Continued)

(Continued)

a uniform, limited set of beliefs and practices that simply confirmed the things they had already read about coca. Becoming frustrated with the excessive reliability of their answers, they began asking less sensible questions like "When do you give coca to animals?" or "How did you find out you don't like coca?" They found that "surprisingly, these 'silly' questions worked. Our bemused informants began to open up and elaborate on their personal, if modest, commitments to coca," which was far more extensive than the previous data would have indicated.

They concluded that their original questions had failed to take account of the social context of the interaction: "The informants had smoothly slipped the punch of the feeble first question. Only with an outrageous second strategy did the researchers manage to initiate a productive exchange."

Source: Kirk and Miller (1986), pp. 25–26.

schedule, and depends fundamentally on how the interview questions and observational strategies will actually work in practice.

This doesn't mean that you should conceal your research questions from participants, or treat them simply as subjects to be manipulated to produce the data you need, as criticized earlier under "Research Relationships." Carol Gilligan (personal communication) emphasized the value of asking your interviewees "real questions," ones to which you are genuinely interested in the answer, rather than contrived questions designed to elicit particular sorts of data. Doing this helps to create a more symmetrical and collaborative relationship in which participants are able to bring their own knowledge to bear on the questions in ways that you might not have anticipated.

There are two important implications that the lack of a direct logical connection between research questions and interview questions has for your research. First, you need to anticipate, as best you can, how particular questions will actually work in practice—how people will understand them, and how they are likely to respond in the actual context of the interview. Try to put yourself in your interviewee's place and imagine how you would react to these questions (this is another use of "thought experiments"), and get feedback from others on how they think the questions (and the interview guide as a whole) will work. Second, if at all possible, you should *pilot-test* your interview guide with people as much like your planned interviewees as possible, to determine if the questions work as intended, and what revisions you may need to make.

This lack of a deductive relationship between questions and methods also holds, more obviously, for observation and other data collection methods. As with interviews, you need to anticipate what information you will actually be able to collect, in the setting studied, using particular observational or other methods, and how this information will contribute to your understanding of the issues you are studying, as discussed earlier. If possible, you should pretest these methods to determine if they will actually provide this information. Your data collection strategies will probably go through a period of focusing and revision, even in a carefully designed study, to enable them to better provide the data that you need to answer your research questions and to address any plausible validity threats to these answers (see Example 5.1).

THE USES OF MULTIPLE QUALITATIVE METHODS

Collecting information using a variety of sources and methods is one aspect of what is called triangulation (Fielding & Fielding, 1986). This strategy reduces the risk that your conclusions will reflect only the systematic biases or limitations of a specific source or method, and allows you to gain a broader and more secure understanding of the issues you are investigating. I discuss the use of triangulation generally, as a way to deal with validity threats, in Chapter 8; here, I want to focus specifically on combining different data collection methods.

One belief that inhibits triangulation is the widespread (though often implicit) assumption that observation is mainly useful for describing behavior and events, while interviewing is mainly useful for obtaining the perspectives of actors. It is true that the *immediate* result of observation is description, but this is equally true of interviewing: the latter gives you a description of what the informant *said*, not a direct understanding of their perspective. Generating an interpretation of someone's perspective is inherently a matter of inference from descriptions of their behavior (including verbal behavior), whether the data are derived from observations, interviews, or some other source such as written documents (Maxwell, 1992).

While interviewing is often an efficient and valid way of understanding someone's perspective, observation can enable you to draw inferences about this perspective that you couldn't obtain by relying exclusively on interview data. This is particularly important for getting at tacit understandings and "theory-in-use," as well as aspects of the participants' perspective that they are reluctant to directly state in interviews. For example, watching how a teacher responds to boys' and girls' questions in a science class may provide a much better understanding of the teacher's actual views about gender and science than what the teacher says in an interview.

Conversely, although observation often provides a direct and powerful way of learning about people's behavior and the context in which this occurs, interviewing can also be a valuable way of gaining a description of actions and events—often the *only* way, for events that took place in the past or to which you can't gain observational access. Interviews can provide additional information that was missed in observation, and can be used to check the accuracy of the observations. However, in order for interviewing to be useful for this purpose, you need to ask about *specific* events and actions, rather than posing questions that elicit only generalizations or abstract opinions (Weiss, 1994, pp. 72–76). In both of these situations, triangulation of observations and interviews can provide a more complete and accurate account than either could alone.

However, a number of authors, primarily dealing with the integration of qualitative and quantitative methods, have been critical of the use of triangulation (Fielding, 2008; Greene, 2007; Hammersley, 2008). Greene argued that the classic rationale for triangulation is corroboration or convergence on a single conclusion (validity), but that using different methods is often far more valuable for complementarity (revealing *different* aspects of a single complex phenomenon), expansion (investigating different *phenomena* that interact and need to be understood jointly), or initiation (to create divergent or contradictory interpretations, generate fresh insights, or force the researcher to seek a deeper and more complex understanding) (2007, pp. 98–104). These insights from the mixed-methods literature can be valuable for qualitative researchers who use a variety of methods in their work.

In summary, I have tried to indicate the ways in which a realist perspective can usefully inform qualitative selection, relationships, and data collection. The commonsense, though usually implicit, ontological realism of many qualitative researchers is already well incorporated into much qualitative research practice—for example, in the attention given to the actual perceptions of participants, the context within which the research takes place, and the ways in which these influence, and are influenced by, the methods used and the results of these. However, explicitly seeing the goal of qualitative research as gaining a better understanding of real phenomena, and the practice of qualitative research as conducted in a real context, which the researcher must interact with and adequately understand, can help researchers to better address all of these aspects of qualitative research.

7

Real and Virtual Relationships in Qualitative Data Analysis

with Barbara Miller

In this chapter, we apply a realist perspective to qualitative data analysis. We do this by distinguishing two types of analytic strategies, which we label *categorizing* and *connecting* strategies. This distinction is based on the distinction between similarity and contiguity, described in Chapter 4. To recapitulate, similarity and contiguity refer to two fundamentally different kinds of relationships between things, neither of which can be assimilated to the other. Similarity relationships are based on resemblances or commonalities independent of proximity in time or space. Ontologically, similarity relationships are *virtual* relationships, based on comparison rather than actual connection or influence. Relationships of contiguity, on the other hand, presume, explicitly or implicitly, a real connection or association that is *not* a matter of similarity.

To our knowledge, the extensively developed theoretical analysis of these two types of relationships, primarily in linguistics, has never been explicitly applied to qualitative data analysis. Although the role of similarity in categorizing is often acknowledged,[1] the importance of contiguity relations in other types of analysis is rarely stated, and the similarity/contiguity distinction itself, though sometimes implicitly recognized and described, is not linked to existing theoretical work on this distinction.

---

[1] Categorization in qualitative analysis is almost always based on similarity, despite the existence of theories of categorization (e.g., Lakoff, 1987) that include contiguity-based relationships (e.g., metonymy) as well as similarity-based ones.

In terms of the concrete processes of data analysis, the difference between these two strategies was well described by Smith (1979):

> I usually start . . . at the beginning of the notes. I read along and seem to engage in two kinds of processes—comparing and contrasting, and looking for antecedents and consequences. . .
>
> The essence of concept formation [the first process] is . . . "How are they alike, and how are they different?" The similar things are grouped and given a label that highlights their similarity. . . . In time, these similarities and differences come to represent clusters of concepts, which then organize themselves into more abstract categories and eventually into hierarchical taxonomies.
>
> Concurrently, a related but different process is occurring. . . . The conscious search for the consequences of social items . . . seemed to flesh out a complex systemic view and a concern for process, the flow of events over time. In addition it seemed to argue for a more holistic, systemic, interdependent network of events at the concrete level and concepts and propositions at an abstract level. . . . At a practical level, while in the field, the thinking, searching, and note recording reflected not only a consciousness of similarities and differences but also an attempt to look for unexpected relationships, antecedents, and consequences within the flow of items. (p. 338)

A similar distinction is found in many accounts of qualitative data analysis. For example, Seidman (1998, p. 101 ff.) described two main strategies in the analysis of interviews: the categorization of interview material through coding and thematic analysis, and the creation of several different types of narratives, which he called "profiles" and "vignettes." Other versions of this distinction are Weiss's (1994) contrast between "issue-focused" and "case-focused" analysis, and Coffey and Atkinson's (1996) between "concepts and coding" and "narratives and stories."

However, none of these authors examined the principles on which these distinctions are based, and the similarity/contiguity distinction is frequently confounded with others. For example, Ezzy (2002, p. 95) distinguished narrative analysis from coding primarily in terms of its being more holistic, interpretive, and "in process," and as employing a constructivist approach and "situated relativity."

Jakobson's application of the similarity/contiguity distinction to aphasia (1956), discussed later in this chapter, suggests that there may be a neurological basis for this distinction. Research on memory by the psychologist Tulving (1983; Tulving & Craik, 2000) and others provides some support for this view. Tulving identified two distinct, though interacting, systems of memory, which he called semantic memory and episodic memory. Semantic memory is memory of facts, concepts, principles, and other sorts of information, organized conceptually rather than in terms of the context in which they were learned. Episodic memory, in contrast, is memory of events and episodes, organized temporally in terms of the context of their occurrence. Extensive experimental research, in both humans and other animals (Dere,

Easton, Nadel, & Huston, 2008; Shettleworth, 2010, pp. 249–256; Tulving & Craik, 2000), has supported this distinction, particularly the idea of episodic memory as a distinct system, as have studies demonstrating that memory loss may selectively affect one or the other of these systems (Mayes, 2000), and brain imaging has shown that encoding or retrieving information from the two memory systems engages different areas of the brain (Nyberg & Cabeza, 2000; Wheeler, 2000).

We begin by separately describing categorizing and connecting strategies, presenting the strengths and limitations of each approach, and applying this distinction to data displays (Miles & Huberman, 1994). We then discuss ways of integrating these two approaches. We conclude with some observations on the use of computers in qualitative data analysis.

Categorizing Strategies

The most widely used categorizing strategy in qualitative data analysis is coding. In coding, the data are segmented into discrete units (Strauss, 1987, p. 29, referred to this as "fracturing" the data), and the segments are labeled and grouped by category; they are then examined and compared, both within and between categories. Coding categories "are a means of sorting the descriptive data you have collected . . . so that the material bearing on a given topic can be physically separated from other data" (Bogdan & Biklen, 2003, p. 161). Coding and then sorting by code creates a similarity-based ordering of data that replaces the original contiguity-based ordering.

Example 7.1

Types of Categories

An important distinction among types of categories, one that also draws on a realist approach to qualitative data analysis (although not employing the similarity/contiguity distinction), is that between organizational, substantive, and theoretical categories (Maxwell, 2005, pp. 97–98). I'm not presenting these as absolute distinctions; many actual coding categories can be seen as involving aspects of more than one type, or as being intermediate between two types. However, I believe that the conceptual typology is valuable.

Organizational categories are broad areas or issues that are often established prior to data collection. McMillan and Schumacher (2001)

(Continued)

(Continued)

refer to these as *topics* rather than categories, stating that "a topic is the descriptive name for the subject matter of the segment. You are not, at this time, asking 'What is said?' which identifies the meaning of the segment" (p. 469). In a study of elementary school principals' practices of retaining children in a grade, examples of such categories are "retention," "policy," "goals," "alternatives," "and "consequences" (p. 470). Organizational categories function primarily as abstract "bins" for sorting the data for further analysis; they do not specifically address what is actually happening or what meaning these topics have for participants. They are often useful as organizational tools in your analysis, as chapter or section headings in presenting your results, but they don't by themselves provide much insight into what is actually going on (cf. Coffey & Atkinson, 1996, pp. 34–35).

This latter task requires substantive and/or theoretical categories, ones that incorporate what's actually taking place, or the actual understandings of this that participants have. These latter categories can often be seen as subcategories of the organizational ones, but they are generally *not* subcategories that, in advance, you could have known would be significant, unless you are already fairly familiar with the kind of participants or setting you're studying or are using a well-developed theory. They implicitly make some sort of claim about the phenomena being studied—that is, they could be *wrong*, rather than simply being conceptual boxes for holding data.

Substantive categories are primarily *descriptive*, in a broad sense that includes description of participants' concepts and beliefs; they stay close to the data categorized, and don't inherently imply a more abstract theory. In the study of grade retention mentioned earlier, examples of substantive categories derived from interviews with principals would be "retention as failure," "retention as a last resort," "self-confidence as a goal," "parent's willingness to try alternatives," and "not being in control (of the decision)" (McMillan & Schumacher, 2001, p. 472). Categories taken from participants' own words and concepts (what are generally called "emic" categories) are usually substantive, but many substantive categories are not emic, being based on the *researcher's* description of what's going on. Substantive categories are often inductively generated through a close "open coding" of the data (Strauss & Corbin, 1990). They can be used in *developing* a more general theory of what's going on, but they don't *depend on* this theory.

(Continued)

(Continued)

Theoretical categories, in contrast, place the coded data into a more general or abstract framework. These categories may be derived either from prior theory, or from an inductively developed theory (in which case the concepts and the theory are usually developed concurrently). They often represent the *researcher's* concepts (what are called "etic" categories), rather than denoting participants' own concepts. For example, the categories "nativist," "remediationist," and "interactionist," used to classify teachers' beliefs about grade retention in terms of prior analytic distinctions (Smith & Shepard, 1988), are theoretical.

Most accounts of qualitative data analysis treat categorization as the fundamental activity in analysis, and the only one that involves manipulation of actual data, giving the impression that coding *is* qualitative data analysis. For example, LeCompte and Preissle stated that "the next step [after writing an initial summary] is to begin the time-consuming and laborious process of pulling apart field notes, matching, comparing, and contrasting, which constitutes the heart of analysis" (1993, p. 237). Numerous similar statements could be quoted (e.g., Hesse-Biber & Leavy, 2011, p. 309 ff.; Pfaffenberger, 1988, pp. 26–27; Tesch, 1990, p. 96; Webb & Glesne, 1992, pp. 796–801).

Tesch (1990, pp. 115–123) referred to this replacement of an original connected structure by a different, categorical structure as "decontextualizing and recontextualizing." She described recontextualizing as follows: "The [data] segment is settled in the context of its topic, in the neighborhood of all other segments of the data corpus that deal with the same topic" (p. 122). However, this new set of relationships is based on similarity rather than contiguity, and is thus not a "recontextualization" in the usual sense of "context," that is, a set of phenomena that are connected in time and space. These similarity-based relationships are quite different from a contiguity-based context, and confusing the two can lead to the neglect of actual contextual relationships. In addition, reordering the data in terms of particular categories can create analytic blinders, preventing the analyst from seeing alternative relationships in the data.

Both of these problems are illustrated by Atkinson's description (1992) of how his initial categorizing analysis of the teaching of general medicine affected his subsequent analysis of his surgery notes:

[O]n rereading the surgery notes, I initially found it difficult to *escape* those categories I had initially established [for medicine]. Understandably, they furnished a powerful conceptual grid. Moreover, they exercised a more powerful physical constraint. The notes as I confronted them had been fragmented into the constituent themes. (pp. 458–459)

On returning to his original notebooks, Atkinson found that

> I am now much less inclined to fragment the notes into relatively small segments. Instead, I am just as interested in reading episodes and passages at greater length, with a correspondingly different attitude toward the act of reading and hence of analysis. Rather than constructing my account like a patchwork quilt, I feel more like working with the whole cloth. . . . To be more precise, what now concerns me is the nature of these products as *texts*. (p. 460)

Other researchers (e.g., Mishler, 1984, 1986) have also seen the neglect of context as a major defect of coding and other categorizing strategies. (This critique is similar to the realist critique of the "regularity" approach to causality, in terms of the latter's neglect of context as an essential component of causal explanation, discussed in Chapter 3.) Mishler argued that "the meanings of questions and answers are not fixed by nor adequately represented by the interview schedule or by code-category systems" (1986, p. 138), and claimed that systematic methods of narrative analysis are required to understand research interviews.

The categories thus generated are then usually linked into larger patterns (e.g., Tesch, 1993, p. 303 ff.); this subsequent step can be seen as contiguity-based, but the connections are made between the categories themselves, rather than between segments of actual data. However, using connecting techniques only on the categories, rather than the data, results in an *aggregate* account of contiguity relationships, and can never reconstitute the actual, diverse contextual connections that were lost during the original categorizing analysis (see the discussion of diversity in Chapter 4). Miles and Huberman warned that

> just adding up separate variables as in a quantitative survey approach will destroy the local web of causality, and result only in a sort of "smoothed-down" set of generalizations that may not apply anywhere in the real world of the sites. (1984, p. 151)

A common alternative to coding and thematic classification in qualitative research is the "case study" (Hesse-Biber & Leavy, 2011, pp. 255–276; Stake, 1995). In this approach, the unique context of each case is retained, and the data are interpreted within that context, to provide an account of a particular instance, setting, person, or event. However, case studies often employ primarily categorizing analysis strategies (e.g., Hesse-Biber & Leavy, 2011, p. 266; Merriam, 1988; Yin, 2003); their main advantage is that the categorizing (coding, thematic analysis, etc.) occurs within a particular case rather than between cases, so that the contextual relationships are harder to lose sight of. Qualitative case studies *can* be highly contextual or connected in their analysis (e.g., clinical case description), but are not inherently so.

Most qualitative researchers are aware of the dangers of decontextualization in using categorizing techniques. Works on qualitative methods are filled with warnings about context-stripping and admonitions to retain the connection of coded data with their original context. However, attention to context is often seen only as a *check* or *control* on the use of categorizing analytic strategies; most works say nothing about how one might *analyze* contextual relationships. For example, Lofland and Lofland argued that

> splitting the materials into mundane, analytic, and fieldwork files will facilitate staying "on top" of what is happening and evolving an analysis. But it also tends to obscure that nebulous quality called "context." . . . You should therefore keep a full set of your materials in the order in which you originally collected them. . . . [I]t is useful simply for reading and reviewing from beginning to end, as a stimulus to thinking about larger patterns and larger units of analysis. (1984, pp. 134–135)

Many other qualitative researchers also seem to view context as "nebulous" and resistant to systematic analysis. The development of explicit procedures for the analysis of contextual relations has, to a substantial extent, occurred in isolation from mainstream qualitative research, and it is to this approach that we now turn.

Connecting Strategies

Narratives, portraits, and case studies are often included in qualitative research reports as an accompaniment to categorizing analysis, and Barone (1990) argued that most qualitative texts are a mixture of narrative and paradigmatic (categorizing) design features. However, such uses of narrative are largely presentational rather than analytic; even Patton, who clearly used case studies as an analytic strategy (2001, p. 447), confounded this distinction by describing the case study as "a readable, descriptive picture of or story about a person, program, [or] organization" (2001, p. 450). Such presentational techniques partially compensate for the loss of contextual ties that results from a primarily categorizing approach, but they rarely are integrated with what is seen as the "real" analysis, or go beyond what is apparent in the raw data. Here, we are concerned with narrative or contextual approaches to data *analysis*, rather than simply presentation.

Connecting analytic strategies do not simply preserve data in their original form. Instead, they are ways to analyze and reduce data; this is generally done by identifying key relationships that tie the data together into a narrative or sequence, and eliminating information that is not germane to these relationships. Patton (2001, p. 447 ff.) and Seidman (1998) discuss the steps involved in selecting data to create case studies and "profiles," respectively.

The process of doing connecting analysis has received less attention than categorizing analysis. Narrative analysis is the most prevalent approach that has emphasized alternatives to categorizing analysis, but much of narrative research, broadly defined, involves categorizing as well as connecting analysis, and the distinction has not been clearly defined.

Many connecting strategies focus on the structure or significance of the narrative conveyed by the data (the latter usually being an interview transcript). These narrative strategies are informed by different disciplines. Discourse analysis, drawing from linguistics (e.g., Gee, 2005; Mishler, 1986), usually operates on a close, textual level where the semantic connections between different parts of the text are examined. One such strategy is the functional analysis carried out by Labov and his colleagues (1972, 1982; Labov & Fanshel, 1977; Labov & Waletzky, 1967). In their early work they focused on the temporal sequence of action within a narrative; in subsequent work, they attended to the larger, social meanings conveyed by the narrative structure.

A second kind of narrative strategy is informed more by sociology, anthropology, and clinical psychology. This approach is less concerned with the structure of the text and more with the meaning of that text for the participant. Seidman's "profiles" (1998) are one example of such an approach. In creating a profile from an interview transcript, Seidman first identifies and synthesizes the basic story line by reducing the text to those elements that are seen as important parts of the person's story. These segments are then crafted into a first-person account, normally (but not invariably) keeping the same order as these appeared in the transcript.

However, contiguity-based analytic strategies are not limited to narrative approaches. What Erickson (1992) called "ethnographic microanalysis of interaction" involves the detailed description of local interactional processes, and analysis of how these processes are organized (p. 204). The analytic process "begins by considering whole events, continues by analytically decomposing them into smaller fragments, and then concludes by *recomposing* them into wholes. . . . [This process] returns them to a level of sequentially connected social action" (1992, p. 217). Thus, instead of segmenting events and then *categorizing* these segments to create a structure of similarities and differences among these, this approach segments the data and then *connects* these segments into a relational order within an actual context.

Narrative strategies, as well as other connecting strategies, do not rely exclusively on contiguity. They utilize categorization, to a greater or lesser extent, to discern the narrative structure of the data (Linde, 1993, pp. 65–66). For example, identifying elements of plot, scene, conflict, or resolution in a narrative inherently involves classification. However, such classification is used to identify the elements of a narrative in terms of how they relate to other elements, rather than to create a similarity-based reordering of the data. Thus,

Mishler (1986) described some forms of narrative analysis that employ coding and categorization, but the categories he presented are *functional* rather than substantive categories. Such categories "provide a set of codes for classifying the 'narrative functions' of different parts of the account" (Mishler, 1986, p. 82), rather than constituting the basis for a reorganization of the data. Such categorization is a tool in contextual analysis, rather than a separate analytic process.

Narrative and contextual analyses, as strategies based primarily on contiguity rather than similarity, have disadvantages of their own. In particular, they can lead to an inability to make comparisons and to gain insights from the similarity or difference of two things in separate contexts. Some of our students have avoided coding their interviews or fieldnotes, because they felt that coding would destroy the contextual relations that they considered most important. However, when we persuaded them to try this, they said that it vastly increased their understanding of the data, because it broke them out of the fixed contextual frameworks within which they were working, and allowed them to see other relationships that they had been blind to. As one student wrote,

> At first, I resisted coding. The process seemed mechanical and reductive to me. I didn't want to violate the organic unity of my interviews, many of which had deeply moved me. To fracture these conversations into discrete pieces of information seemed like taking a pair of scissors and cutting up family photographs. However, as I started coding I soon realized what a powerful tool it was. To my amazement, I found connections between the interviews that I hadn't previously suspected. Not only did my informants share similar experiences, they sometimes used the same language to discuss those experiences. This was exciting, for I began to see that what had at first seemed like a mass of incoherent, intractable material did, indeed, have pattern and shape—and that in spite of the unique personalities and circumstances of my informants' lives, there were commonalities in both their experiences and the way they looked at things. (Huang, 1991)

An exclusive emphasis on connecting strategies can create what another student called an "imprisonment in the story" of a particular narrative—a failure to see alternative ways of framing and interpreting the text or situation in question. Wieviorka argued that comparison "may help deconstruct what common sense takes to be unique or unified" (1992, p. 170) and generate alternative perspectives.

Displays as Categorizing and Connecting Strategies

Displays (Miles & Huberman, 1994), as techniques for data analysis, can also be divided into similarity-based and contiguity-based forms. Miles and Huberman described a wide variety of displays, but most of these fell into two basic types: matrices and networks (or figures). Matrices are essentially tables formed by the intersection of two or more lists of items; the cells in the table are filled with data, either raw or summarized, allowing comparison of the similarities and differences among the cells. The lists forming the matrix can be of individuals, roles, sites, topics, or properties of these, and can be organized in numerous ways, creating a large number of different types of matrices. Networks, on the other hand, are visual maps of the relationships (for Miles and Huberman, usually temporal or causal relationships) among individuals, events, states, or properties of these.

We see matrices and networks as, respectively, similarity-based and contiguity-based displays. Matrices are a logical extension of coding; they are created by constructing lists of mutually exclusive categories and then crossing these to create cells. Networks, on the other hand, are a logical extension of narrative or causal analysis, organizing events or concepts by time and by spatial or causal connection; they capture the contiguity-based relationships that are lost in creating matrices. Miles and Huberman provided examples of networks that link specific events, as well as those linking more abstract categories, although none were included that link actual data segments. They also presented a substantial number of hybrid forms that involve both categorizing and connecting strategies, such as time-ordered matrices and segmented causal networks.

Integrating Categorizing and Connecting Strategies

We have alluded to some of the advantages of combining categorizing and connecting strategies for analyzing qualitative data. However, even authors who explicitly discussed both types of strategies, such as Seidman (1998) and Atkinson (1992; Coffey & Atkinson, 1996), rarely address how to combine these. Implicitly, they seem to see the two as alternatives, or as parallel but separate analytic approaches.

While the separate use of the two approaches is legitimate and often productive, there are other possibilities as well. The most common is the sequential use of the two types of strategies, beginning with one and then moving to the other. For example, most qualitative researchers who employ coding strategies eventually develop a model of the connections or relational patterns among the categories, as mentioned earlier. However, this final step rarely involves direct analysis of data, and usually receives little explicit discussion. (Prominent exceptions are the work of Strauss, discussed shortly, and Miles and Huberman.)

Researchers who employ initial contextual or narrative strategies, on the other hand, often conclude by discussing similarities and differences among the analyzed phenomena. (This is the reverse of the previous strategy of connecting categories into a relational sequence or network.) For example, Erickson describes the final step in ethnographic microanalysis as the "comparative analysis of instances across the research corpus" to determine how typical these analyzed units of interaction are (1992, p. 220). Again, however, this final categorizing step generally receives little explicit attention; an important exception is Miles and Huberman's discussion (1994, pp. 204–205; Huberman, 1989/1993) of a technique they called "composite sequence analysis," in which individuals' career trajectories are derived through connecting analysis of interviews, and these trajectories are then compared to identify common features and generate phases, subgroups, and modal sequences.

We suggest that it may be useful to think of this process in terms of categorizing and connecting "moves" in an analysis, rather than in terms of alternative or sequential overall strategies. At each point in the analysis, one can take either a categorizing step, looking for similarities and differences, or a connecting step, looking for actual (contiguity-based) connections between things.

A widely used approach to qualitative analysis that seems to us to employ this strategy is the "grounded theory" method (Strauss, 1987; Strauss & Corbin, 1990), although this aspect of Strauss's method of analysis has never, to our knowledge, been explicitly recognized. The initial step in analysis, which Strauss calls "open coding," involves segmenting the data, attaching conceptual labels to these segments, and making comparisons among the segments. However, the subsequent steps are predominantly connecting ones, despite being described as forms of coding; Strauss used "coding" to mean "the process of analyzing data" (Strauss & Corbin, 1990, p. 61). Thus, the next step, "axial coding," consists of

> specifying a category (*phenomenon*) in terms of the *conditions* that give rise to it; the *context* . . . in which it is embedded; the action/interactional *strategies* by which it is handled, managed, carried out; and the *consequences* of these strategies. (Strauss & Corbin, 1990, p. 97, italics in original)

This is almost a definition of what we mean by connecting analysis; the main difference is that these connections are to *categories*, rather than to data segments. The analytical steps subsequent to open coding involve making connections among categories, developing a "story line" about the central phenomena of the study, and identifying "conditional paths" that link actions with conditions and consequences. Confusingly, Strauss and Corbin referred to these connections as "subcategories," stating that "they too are categories, but because we relate them to a category in some form of relationship, we add the prefix 'sub'" (1990, p. 97).

Strauss continually integrated categorizing steps into these later stages, stating, for example, that "having identified the differences in context, the researcher can begin systematically to group the categories. . . . This grouping again is done by asking questions and making comparisons" (Strauss & Corbin, 1990, p. 132). However, Strauss said very little about the grouping of *data* by category. Categorization, in the grounded theory approach, is manifested primarily in the development and comparison of concepts and categories. Nor does he deal with the analysis of specific contextual relations in the data, operating mostly in terms of relations among concepts.[2]

A similar alternation of strategies, but one that stayed much closer to the actual data, was employed by Miller (1991) in her study of adolescent friendships. We will therefore present an extended account of this study in order to illustrate one way in which these two strategies can be integrated.

We also have a second goal in presenting this example. The preceding account of the two different approaches to data analysis has been essentially categorizing rather than contextualizing; it classifies and compares the two types of strategies, rather than portraying them in any real context or discussing actual concurrent or sequential combinations of strategies. To complement this account, then, the following is a narrative or case presentation by Miller of her analysis. We hope that it will illustrate by example the difference between a contiguity-based account and a similarity-based one, and how to decide when to use categorical strategies and when to use connecting strategies. The account is written in the first person because it is a narrative of Miller's own struggle to make sense of her data.

A NARRATIVE EXAMPLE

"Once upon a time. . . ." While this account of data analysis is no fairy tale, it is nonetheless a story set in time and shaped by particular questions. Working with interviews with adolescents about their friendships, it seemed important to look closely at the features of the friendships, to understand in specific terms what they mean for the adolescents involved. In short, this seemed to call for a categorizing analysis, a close investigation of the components that seem to make up a relationship, for the purpose of investigating similarities across the friendships of different adolescents.

---

[1] Gerson (1991) addressed these issues in grounded theory research, using a distinction between heterogeneity heuristics and compositional heuristics that is similar to that between categorizing and connecting relations. Heterogeneity heuristics analyze similarities and differences among phenomena within a category, while compositional heuristics address the relationships among categories and between phenomena and categories. However, Gerson's compositional heuristics include relations that involve similarity as well as contiguity, such as taxonomic relations; the ones that most closely resemble what we call connecting relations are his part-whole and sequential relations.

I therefore began my analysis by formulating coding categories, coding the data, and constructing matrices. I coded the data for such elements as closeness, talk among friends, and dependence. These codes, for each interview, were then collected in matrices so that I could look across interviews for each concept. This helped me to focus on specific features of the data, informed by my research agenda as well as by the comments made by the adolescents themselves. With the completion of the matrices, though, two pressing issues emerged.

The first was that there was extensive overlap of data between the cells of the matrices. For example, many adolescents explained that part of being close to their friends involved talking with them. The matrix for closeness did not, however, capture the complexity of that talk, which involved information from other cells. These matrices seemed too simplistic for the complex, interconnected data I felt I had.

The second issue was that an essential aspect of the data was missing; namely, the narrative nature of the adolescents' accounts of their friendships. In their interviews, the adolescents did not offer isolated bits of information about their friends. Instead, what I heard were the stories of their relationships with their friends. As adolescents talked about their friends and explained why their friendships were important, they described their shared past and created a context from which to understand their relationship. This narrative quality of the data, and its implications for understanding their relationships, were lost in the process of coding and of creating the matrices.

To deal with the limitations of the matrices, and to capture the narrative quality of the data, I moved to what became the second phase of the analysis: the construction of narrative summaries. These summaries are narrative in that they seek to preserve the context and story of the relationship, yet they are summaries since they are my analytic abridgements of the narratives heard. These narrative summaries made use of extensive quotes from the data, but often involved a reorganization of the data to achieve what I, as the reader, perceived to be a concise account of the friendship narrative.

These narrative summaries were effective in holding on to the context as well as the story of the friendship. They did not, however, directly help me understand more clearly the meaning of that friendship experience for these adolescents. For that, I needed to look more closely at their relationships in light of my understanding of the larger context of that friendship. The next phase of my analysis, therefore, was to integrate the results of my categorizing and contextualizing strategies. This led to more depth within the concepts represented in the matrices; the category of closeness between friends, for example, was contextualized. By holding the narrative summaries against the matrices, I could track the meaning of closeness across different friendships for a particular adolescent or between adolescents, or trace its significance throughout a particular friendship.

Data analysis had become, for me, an iterative process of moving from categorizing to contextualizing strategies and back again. My understanding of the narrative context of the friendships informed my interpretation of the particular concepts and categories I had identified as important in these adolescents' friendships. At the same time, the particular concepts I focused on in the categorizing analysis allowed me to look at the narratives in new ways, and to see contextual relationships that were more complex than the temporal ordering of events within the narratives. My understanding of the meaning and experience of friendship for these adolescents was not stripped of the context, which the adolescents provided, nor was it locked into and limited to individual friendship stories. Coding and matrices were combined with narrative summaries to achieve an understanding of the interviews that neither could have provided alone.

A final example of a strategy that we see as combining categorizing and connecting "moves" in analysis is the "listening guide" strategy (Gilligan, Spencer, Weinberg, & Bertsch, 2003) for analyzing interviews. This strategy, which the authors describe as a "voice-centered relational method," involves a sequence of readings (the authors use the term "listenings") of the interview transcript, each focused on a different aspect of the speaker's expression of her experience within the context of the research relationship. This approach is premised on the idea that a person's voice is polyphonic rather than monotone, that different "voices" can be identified within an interview.

The first listening is typically for the "plot" of the interview—what stories are being told, and in what contexts—and the researcher's response to these. The second listening is for the voice of the "I" who is speaking—how does this person speak about himself or herself? This involves underlining all passages containing an "I," along with the associated verb and any other important words, and creating a separate text with only these segments, keeping them in their original order. Subsequent listenings depend on the specific purposes and questions of the research, but are typically "contrapuntal," focusing on contrasting issues and "voices." In Gilligan's original use of this method, the focus was on differences between men's and women's moral judgment, and the listenings were for the voices of justice and of care, and of a separate and a connected self. These later listenings are not necessarily specified in advance; they may be inductively developed. The final step is to pull together an interpretation of this person's perspective on these issues.

The listening for different "voices" is clearly a categorizing move in that it identifies segments that are similar in some way—that they are first-person statements, or deal with a particular issue. However, in contrast to traditional coding, these segments are not fragmented and reorganized by topic; they are kept in sequential order. In the case of "I" statements, these segments are used to create an "I poem" that captures the "associative stream of consciousness" (Gilligan et al., 2003) running through the interview; this is a connecting step in analysis. As in Miller's example, the analysis is composed of a mix of categorizing and connecting moves, with each strategy compensating for the deficiencies of the other. For example, the "I poem's" initial categorizing step allows the listener to focus specifically on the voice of "self" without the interference of extraneous material, foregrounding this aspect of the narrative, while the connecting step of preserving the chronological order of the statements allows the listener to follow the sequential links between these statements.

Like Atkinson (1992; Coffey & Atkinson, 1996), we see categorizing and connecting approaches as inherently complementary strategies for data analysis. The complementarity of similarity and contiguity relations in language is generally recognized, and is a central theme in the paper by Jakobson (1956) cited earlier. Jakobson, who played a major role in developing the similarity/contiguity distinction with reference to language, also applied this distinction to aphasia, the loss of ability to understand or express speech, caused by brain damage. He identified two types of aphasia, which he labeled *similarity disorder* and *contiguity disorder*, each reflecting a loss of one of these two essential components of language. A key point in Jakobson's argument is the *complementarity* of the two dimensions; he argued that the loss of either dimension resulted in an inability to use language effectively.

It seems to us that the defects in qualitative analysis that result from ignoring one or the other of these relationships among qualitative data are analogous to the communicative disturbances Jakobson (1956) described in these two types of aphasic patients. The use of computers in qualitative research is a case in point.

Computers and Qualitative Data Analysis

Computer programs for analyzing qualitative data have had a major influence on how analysis is done (Hesse-Biber & Leavy, 2011; Richards, 2005; Weitzman & Miles, 1995), and will undoubtedly have even greater impact in the future. However, so far computers have been used primarily for categorizing rather than connecting types of initial data analysis, due to the ease and power with which computers can perform similarity-based functions such as sorting and comparison.

There is thus a danger that, following what Kaplan (1964, p. 28) called "The Law of the Instrument," the ease of using computers for categorizing analysis will reinforce this approach and lead to the neglect of connecting strategies. Pfaffenberger argued that a technology is like a colonial power—it tells you that it is working in your best interests and, all the while it is functioning insidiously to dim your critical perception of the world around you. You will remain its victim so long as you fail to conceptualize adequately what it's up to. (1988, p. 20)

Against this view, Tesch claimed that "computers, like scissors, are tools. In themselves, they have no influence on the research process" (1993, p. 279). This claim neglects the ways in which the *decision to use* particular tools, such as the decision to use scissors rather than some other technique, involves assumptions, often unconscious ones, about the nature of analysis (for example, that it begins with "cutting up" the data). Such tools privilege certain analytic strategies and inhibit others.

For example, Agar (1991, p. 181) was once asked by a foundation to review a report on an interview study that it had commissioned, investigating how historians worked. The researchers had used the computer program "The Ethnograph" to segment and code the interviews by topic and collect together all the segments on the same topic; the report discussed each of these topics, and provided examples of how the historians talked about these. However, the foundation felt that the report hadn't really answered its questions, which had to do with how individual historians thought about their work—their theories about how the different topics were connected and the relationships they saw between their thinking, actions, and results.

Answering the latter question would have required an analysis that elucidated these connections in each historian's interview. However, the categorizing analysis on which the report was based fragmented these connections, destroying the contextual unity of each historian's views and allowing only a collective presentation of shared concerns. Agar argued that the fault was not with The Ethnograph, which is extremely useful for answering questions that require categorization, but with its misapplication. As he commented,

I don't mean to pick on The Ethnograph. On the contrary, later I describe a study where, if The Ethnograph had been available, I would have been the first in line. I do mean to say that a program like The Ethnograph represents a *part of* an ethnographic research process. When the part is taken for the whole, you get a pathological metonym that can lead you straight to the right answer to the wrong question. (1991, p. 181)

Connecting uses of computer software do exist. So-called "theory-building" programs (Weitzman & Miles, 1995) can use connections between categories to assist in testing hypotheses about relationships and establishing typical sequences. However, these uses are almost always based on a previous categorizing analysis, and the connecting functions focus on linkages between concepts, as in Strauss's "grounded theory" approach to analysis, rather than on linking actual data. An exception is Richards's (2005) description of software for establishing links among data and data files. However, she focused mainly on links between different *types* of data, such as between fieldnotes and memos, and on links between *different* interviews or observations, as well as links between data categories. Her emphasis was almost entirely on categorizing analysis, and she did not discuss linking data *within* a specific context, or identifying relationships of contiguity rather than similarity/difference.

Despite this, there are ways that computers can be used to assist in the direct connecting analysis of qualitative data. One way is to mark, extract, and compile selected data from a longer text, simplifying the task of data reduction in producing case studies, profiles, and narratives. This is a function that any word processor can perform, but one that could be improved by software specifically designed for this purpose. Another is to use graphics programs (such as Inspiration) to develop network displays of events and processes (Miles & Huberman, 1994). So-called "hypertext" programs (Coffey & Atkinson, 1996, pp. 181–186; Dey, 1993, pp. 180–191) allow the user to create electronic links among any segments, within or between contexts; a few of the more structured "theory-building" programs, such as ATLAS/ti and HyperRESEARCH, will not only do this, but will display the resulting networks. Software that is designed to facilitate such strategies could move case-oriented, connecting analysis beyond what Miles and Huberman (1994) call "handicraft production," and could help to prevent the "pathological metonym" that Agar warns against.

In summary, we have argued that the distinction between similarity-based (categorizing) and contiguity-based (connecting) analytic strategies, which we see as grounded in a realist understanding of relationship types, is a useful theoretical tool, both for understanding how qualitative researchers analyze data and for improving our analyses. The two strategies, rather than being antagonistic and mutually exclusive alternatives, are best seen as complementary and mutually supporting, each having its own strengths and limitations. We think that Wieviorka's statement about sociological and historical analyses (which we see as analogous to categorizing and connecting strategies) also applies to qualitative data analysis: that "research will advance not by confusing but by combining these approaches" (1992, p. 163).

8

Understanding, Validity, and Evidence

U nderstanding, validity, and evidence are aspects of qualitative research for which realism has obvious and important implications. If there is a reality that our theories and conclusions enable us to better understand and deal with, then the nature of this reality is critical for assessing the sorts of understandings that we can attain, the conclusions that embody these understandings, and the evidence we use to reach these. Conversely, if there is no reality beyond the constructions and theories we create, then the very concepts of evidence and validity become suspect, and "understanding" takes on a quite different meaning.

Thus, "numerous conceptions of (and values for) validity are described in the field of qualitative research . . . [and] it is overly simplistic—indeed inaccurate—to describe global qualitative criteria for validity" (Miller, 2008, p. 909). Many constructivist qualitative researchers have argued that the idea of a "real world" to which our accounts refer is a modernist position that is incompatible with constructivism, and that we need criteria for the quality of qualitative research that do not depend on this idea (e.g., Denzin & Lincoln, 2005a). They avoid any explicit reference to a "reality" outside of the constructions of the people studied, and "many social constructivists describe the validity of studies as being dependent on the resonance of their findings with communities' common discourses" (Miller, 2008, p. 909).

For this reason, some of these researchers reject the term "validity" (or even any analogous concept), seeing it as too closely tied to positivist ideas of a singular, objectively knowable reality. Denzin and Lincoln stated that in the constructivist paradigm, "terms such as credibility, transferability, dependability, and confirmability replace the usual positivist criteria of internal and external validity, reliability, and objectivity" (2005a, p. 24). Other researchers have argued for a number of other alternative concepts, including trustworthiness and authenticity, that they feel better represent the standards that qualitative researchers employ in evaluating the quality of their and others' work.

Ironically, however, there are important similarities between positivist/quantitative and constructivist approaches to issues of quality, trustworthiness, or validity. These derive from the very similar views held by prominent positivists and qualitative researchers on the relationship between ontology and epistemology. As discussed in Chapter 1, logical positivists rejected the idea that there was anything other than our sense data that could be the object of scientific investigation; in this way, positivism was staunchly antirealist in denying that there was a "real world" beyond the reach of our senses, one to which our theories referred. This position, known as instrumentalism or operationalism, insisted that theoretical concepts must be defined in terms of the actual procedures used and the sense data these generated, and that theories should be judged only by how well they predicted observations, not by their relationship to any external reality (Boyd, 2010; Niiniluoto, 2007; Norris, 1983). This stance was quite compatible with the positivists' regularity concept of causation, discussed in Chapter 3—that causality simply *is* the regular, observable association of events or variables.

This position essentially reduced ontology to epistemology—any reference to something beyond our senses (such as "a real world" that could only be inferred rather than directly observed) was labeled "metaphysical" and not a legitimate object of science. Danermark et al. (2001, p. 8) cited this rejection of any reference to real, but unobservable, entities and phenomena as a "fundamental error" of logical positivism, and the criticism of this position, discussed in Chapter 2, was an important cause of positivism's downfall. However, it has remained central to much quantitative research practice, and is enshrined in the concept of "operational definitions." As a result, quantitative researchers' conceptions of validity and rigor have largely avoided any reference to things that must be inferred, rather than directly observed.

As a result, and despite the realist assumptions that informed Donald Campbell's development of the widely used categories of validity in quantitative research (Campbell, 1988; Cook & Campbell, 1979; Maxwell, 1990a, 1990b), judgments of validity have largely been based on the *methods* used in the research; validity is seen as "increased by researchers' use of specifically prescribed and well-entrenched procedures and strategies" (Miller, 2008, p. 909). This is particularly apparent in the movement for "science-based" or "evidence-based" research, which relies on a hierarchy of designs and methods ranked by their validity, with randomized controlled trials (RCTs) as the "gold standard" for causal research.[1]

While most qualitative researchers have rejected the positivist conceptions of scientific investigation that are embodied in much quantitative research practice, and the instrumentalism on which these are based, many of them have held a similar view of the relationship between ontology and epistemology. The constructivist stance that they adopted implied that there was no "reality" independent of our own constructions, and thus no role for ontology that is not subsumed in a constructivist epistemology, as discussed in Chapter 1.

As a result, qualitative researchers have also relied mainly on the methods used in a study to assess its trustworthiness or validity. Lincoln and Guba's influential formulation (1985) of criteria for trustworthiness in qualitative research, based on "the assumption of multiple constructed realities" (p. 295), relied heavily on the use of specific procedures, such as member checks, prolonged engagement in the setting studied, peer review, rich description, and an "audit trail" of the research. Guba and Lincoln later (1989) added a fifth criterion, authenticity, which was somewhat more oriented toward the outcomes of the research, such as fairness in representing different realities, empowering members of the groups studied, and helping them to develop "more sophisticated" understandings. However, the latter are firmly grounded in a "relativist view that research accounts do no more than represent a sophisticated but temporary consensus of views about what is considered to be true" (Seale, 1999, p. 46), rejecting any reference to something beyond these views.

Despite the prevalence of these views in both qualitative and quantitative research, there is widespread agreement among philosophers, and shared by some researchers, that procedural criteria for validity or trustworthiness are seriously flawed. Phillips stated what seems to be a consensus: "In general it must be recognized that there are *no* procedures that will regularly (or always) yield either sound data or true conclusions" (1987, p. 21, italics in original). Brinberg and McGrath made the same point: "Validity is not a commodity that can be purchased with techniques. . . . Rather, validity is like integrity, character, and quality, to be assessed relative to purposes and circumstances" (1985, p. 13;

---

[1] One likely reason for the persistence of procedural criteria for validity is that procedures are much easier to identify and evaluate in publications or manuscripts than are the validity threats to the study's conclusions, and their plausibility in the specific context of the study. Unfortunately, this resembles the joke about the person who had lost his keys at night and was looking for them under the streetlight, rather than in the middle of the block where he dropped them, because the light was better there (Kaplan, 1964, p. 11).

see also Briggs, 2008). Similarly, Shadish et al., in what is currently the definitive work on experimental and quasi-experimental research, stated that

> validity is a property of inferences. It is *not* a property of designs or methods, for the same designs may contribute to more or less valid inferences under different circumstances. . . . No method guarantees the validity of an inference. (2002, p. 34; emphasis in original)

Validity thus pertains to the accounts or conclusions reached by using a particular method in a particular context for a particular purpose, not to the method itself. This is essentially a realist approach to validity (Hammersley, 1992a; House, 1991; Maxwell, 1992; Norris, 1983; Porter, 2007; Seale, 1999, p. 157) that sees the validity of an account as inherent, not in the procedures used to produce and validate it, but in its relationship to those things that it is intended to be an account of.

This rejection of validity or quality as a property of methods is even more relevant for qualitative than for quantitative research, since qualitative research is less "procedure bound" and codified than quantitative research. Mishler, in a critique of procedure-based approaches to validity, argued that "validation has come to be recognized as problematic in a deep theoretical sense, rather than as a technical problem to be solved by more rigorous rules and procedures" (1990, p. 417). He asserted that, while the concept of validity is indeed applicable to what he calls "inquiry-guided" research, the demonstration by Campbell and Stanley (1963) and Cook and Campbell (1979) that validity assessments are not assured by following procedures, but depend on investigators' judgments of the relative importance of the different threats, is fatal to any approach to validity in qualitative research that is based on abstract rules or a typology of procedures (Mishler, 1990, p. 418).

Mishler's alternative approach to validity relied on the use of particular studies that are recognized by the community of researchers in a particular field or specialty as "exemplars" of quality research. He focused not on "validity" as a static property, but on "validation" as the processes by which claims are assessed. He argued that

> those of us engaged in inquiry-guided and interpretive forms of research have the task of articulating and clarifying the features and methods of our studies, of showing how the work is done and what problems become accessible to study. Although they cannot serve as "standard" rules, a context-based explication is required of how observations are transformed into data and findings, and of how interpretations are grounded. (Mishler, 1990, p. 423)

This shifts the assessment of validity or quality from the application of a generic typology of procedures to a contextualized examination of studies that the community regards as exemplary. Mishler provided a detailed examination of three such cases, specifically of narrative research.

However, Mishler didn't clarify how one should apply this approach to assess the validity of a *different* study from the exemplars, unless this involves taking the characteristics of the exemplars and using these as *standards* for evaluating the study in question, which would seem to violate the "context-based" requirement and to fall back on a procedure-based strategy. Mishler identified three common characteristics of his exemplars that he seems to suggest as appropriate standards: display of the primary texts, the specification of analytic categories in terms of features of these texts, and theoretical interpretation based on structures rather than variables. Consistent with Mishler's constructivism, he based his approach on assessing the interpretation of the "text"—an interview or document—itself, rather than on its relationship to any assumed "reality," despite his claim that the key issue in interpretive research is "understanding how individuals interpret events and experiences" (1990, p. 427).

The main challenge for a realist approach to validity is to explain how, if our understandings are inevitably our own fallible constructions rather than "objective" perceptions or interpretations of actual phenomena, one can possibly have any basis for making validity judgments that go beyond procedures and attempt to engage with these real phenomena. Thus, Smith (2008b) argued that the absence of any theory-free knowledge "mean[s] that there is no possibility that reality itself can be an independent referent point for judging the quality of research and for adjudicating among different knowledge claims" (pp. 752–753). For this reason, Smith stated that "for relativists, the issue of criteria should be thought of as a list of characteristics that define what is considered good or bad inquiry" (p. 753), although he insisted that such lists are always subject to revision. Similar to Mishler, this falls back on what is ultimately a procedural approach to validity.

Smith is certainly correct that realism provides no "objective" or definitive measure of the validity or invalidity of any study, or more accurately of the conclusions of such a study. However, this does not entail that reality has *no* role in assessing the validity (trustworthiness, quality) of these conclusions. The reason for this is central to what is called the "scientific method": the possibility of *testing* one's conclusions against both existing and potential evidence, with the goal of evaluating the plausibility of alternative interpretations or "validity threats" to these conclusions (Platt, 1964). It involves identifying the plausible alternatives to the proposed explanation, interpretation, or conclusion, deciding what data exist or could be obtained that would count as evidence for or against this conclusion or the plausible alternatives, and then collecting or examining these data to determine the plausibility of these possible conclusions.

There are numerous specific strategies that can be used for these purposes in qualitative research (Maxwell 2004c; Miles & Huberman, 1994), but the important point for this argument is that any assessment of the "validity" of a study's conclusions is not simply a matter of determining *whether* specific procedures have been used, or even of how carefully or rigorously they have been applied, but of considering the actual *conclusions* drawn by using these procedures in this particular context. The evaluation of these conclusions depends not simply on the appropriate use of the procedures, but on what the data generated by these procedures allow the researcher to conclude. These data are a consequence of the *interaction* of the procedures with the actual phenomena being studied (Barad, 2007).

In taking such a realist position, I am not rejecting the importance of methods, only arguing that methods must be themselves assessed in terms of the purposes for which they are used, the context of this use, the data, conclusions, and understandings that are drawn from them, and, in particular, the ways that these understandings and conclusions could be wrong—the potential validity threats that must be addressed in order to give these conclusions credibility.

The unfortunate implication of this stance toward validity is that there can be no generic criteria for definitively assessing validity, no checklist of characteristics or procedures that can be used to adequately evaluate a study in terms of the credibility or trustworthiness of its conclusions. As with qualitative research in general, "it depends"—on the actual use of these procedures, in the context of this particular study, to address the validity threats that are most salient for these conclusions, and the evidence that these generate regarding these threats.

The existing framework for evaluating the quality of a qualitative study that comes closest to what I am proposing here is that of Seale, which is informed by Martyn Hammersley's "subtle realism" (Seale, 1999, p. 26 ff.). Seale provides a detailed list of criteria for the evaluation of qualitative research papers, including the methods, analysis, presentation, and ethics of the study. However, the purpose of these criteria is not simply to enable a reader to evaluate each component of the study in isolation. Instead, Seale emphasizes three other issues that are consistent with the realist approach presented here. First, many of the criteria focus on the *relationships* among the components (e.g., "Are the methods of the research appropriate to the nature of the question being asked?," p. 189, and "Is the selection of cases or participants theoretically justified?," p. 191), which I discussed in Chapter 5. Second, he addresses the *context* of the study (e.g., "Are the variables [or events and meanings!] being studied integrated in their social context?," p. 191). Third, he addresses the use of data as *evidence* for assessing the conclusions (e.g., "Do the conclusions follow from the data?" and "Is there adequate discussion of the evidence both for and against the researcher's arguments?," pp. 190–191).

Later in this chapter, I discuss the issue of "evidence": what counts as evidence, for whom, in the context of a specific study. Before doing this, however, I want to address the kinds of understandings that qualitative research aims at, and the implications that these have for the types of validity with which qualitative researchers must deal.

Understanding and Validity in Qualitative Research

In adopting a realist approach to validity, I am in basic agreement with the main point of Wolcott's critique of "validity" in qualitative research—that understanding is a more fundamental concept for qualitative researchers than validity (Wolcott, 1990, p. 146). I see the types of validity that I present here as derivative from the kinds of understanding gained from qualitative inquiry; my typology of validity categories is also a typology of the kinds of understanding that qualitative research aims at (see Runciman, 1983), which is in turn related to the ontological and epistemological issues involved in these understandings.

As discussed in Chapter 1, I am not assuming that there is only one correct, "objective" understanding—what Putnam (1990) refers to as the "God's eye view"—of the phenomena that we study. As observers and interpreters of the world, we are inextricably part of it; there is no way for us to step outside our own experience to obtain some observer-independent account of what it is that we experience. My approach, therefore, does not depend on a correspondence theory of truth, at least not in the usual sense of a "mirroring" or isomorphism between account and reality, a sense that has been criticized by Barad (2007), Callinicos (1995), Keller (1992), and Rorty (1979). The applicability of the concept of validity presented here does not depend on the existence of some absolute "truth" or "reality" to which an account can be compared, but only on the fact that there exist ways of assessing accounts that do not depend entirely on features of the account itself, or the methods used to produce it, but in some way relate to those things that the account claims to be about.[2] It specifically differs from positivism and instrumentalism in that it does not take these methods as the sole *criteria* for assessing validity, but only as fallible means for generating evidence about the relationship between the account and its object (Cook & Campbell, 1979).

An important point about this approach to validity is that it uses "validity" to refer primarily to accounts, conclusions, or inferences, not to data. For qualitative research, Hammersley and Atkinson (1983) stated that "data in themselves cannot be valid or invalid; what is at issue are the inferences drawn

---

[2] To apply the distinction presented in Chapters 4 and 7, between paradigmatic (similarity-based) and syntagmatic (contiguity-based) relationships, I am conceptualizing the relationship between an account and its object as based not on similarity or resemblance (the traditional "correspondence theory"), but on contiguity, on the implications and consequences of adopting and acting on a particular account. This approach obviously resembles "pragmatist" approaches in philosophy (Kaplan, 1964, pp. 42–46; Rorty, 1979); it is analogous to Helmholz's view of experience as a sign rather than an image or reflection of the world (Manicas, 1987, p. 176 ff.), to Keller's position, presented in Chapter 1, and to Barad's "agential realism" (2007). In Chapter 9, I address some of the implications, for research and social theory, of such a "nonreflectionist" view.

from them" (p. 191). It is possible to construe data as a kind of account—a description at a very low level of inference and abstraction—and in this sense it is sometimes legitimate to speak of the "validity" of data, but this use is derivative from the primary meaning of validity as a property of accounts.

I argued earlier that validity pertains to the kinds of understanding that accounts can embody. I see three broad categories of understanding that are relevant to qualitative research, and three corresponding types of validity that qualitative researchers are concerned about, which I will refer to respectively as descriptive validity, interpretive validity, and theoretical validity. I see generalizability (what quantitative researchers call "external validity") as a different issue from validity proper, particularly for qualitative research, and will discuss this separately.

The typology that I present has been influenced by others' work, particularly Cook and Campbell (1979), Erickson (1986), Kirk and Miller (1986), and Seale (1999). However, my primary debt is to the detailed analysis by Runciman (1983) of the types of understanding involved in social theory (though I depart significantly from his definitions of these), and to the discussion of description, interpretation, and explanation by Kaplan (1964). I believe that the distinctions made by Runciman, Kaplan, and others are simply explicit codifications and elaborations of a widespread commonsense conceptual structure, and that this structure is implicit in the work of many qualitative researchers. My account of validity is an attempt, in part, to explicate this implicit "theory-in-use."

I am not arguing that the categories I define are clearly and explicitly demarcated, or that every instance of a validity concern falls neatly into one and only one category. The entire approach to categorization that depends on precise and uniform criteria for determining category boundaries and assigning membership has been challenged by Lakoff (1987; Lakoff & Johnson, 1999) and Rosch (1978), and it has become increasingly apparent that ambiguity and fuzzy boundaries are the rule rather than the exception in categorization. I do not accept such cases as evidence *per se* for the inadequacy of the typology. Instances that do not fit my categories *may*, of course, challenge the validity of these categories, but they do so as a result of their implications, not simply because they can't be assigned unambiguously to a single category.

DESCRIPTIVE VALIDITY

The first concern of most qualitative researchers is with the factual accuracy of their account—that is, that they are not making up or distorting the things they saw and heard. If you report that an informant made a particular statement in an interview, is this correct? Did she really make that statement, or did you mishear, mistranscribe, or misremember her words? Did a particular student in a classroom throw an eraser on a specific occasion? These matters of descriptive accuracy are emphasized by almost every introductory qualitative-methods textbook in their discussion of the recording of field-notes and interviews. All of the subsequent validity categories I will discuss are dependent on this primary aspect of validity. As Geertz put it, "Behavior must be attended to, and with some exactness, because it is through the flow of behavior—or, more precisely, social action—that cultural forms find articulation" (1973, p. 17).

And Wolcott, holding that "description provides the foundation upon which qualitative research rests" (2009, p. 27), stated that

> Whenever I engage in fieldwork, I try to record as accurately as possible, and in precisely their words, what I judge to be important of what people do and say. (1990, p. 128)

I will refer to this first type of validity as descriptive validity; it corresponds, to some extent, to the category of understanding that Runciman (1983) calls "reportage" or "primary understanding." Insofar as this category pertains to humans (or other animals), it refers to what Kaplan (1964, p. 358) calls "acts" rather than "actions"—activities seen as physical and behavioral events, rather than in terms of the meanings that these have for the actor or others involved in the activity.

The previous quotes from Geertz and Wolcott refer mainly to what I will call primary descriptive validity: the descriptive validity of what the researcher reports having seen or heard (or touched, smelled, and so on.). There is also the issue of what I call secondary descriptive validity: the validity of accounts of things that could in principle be observed, but which were in fact inferred from other data (for example, what happened in the classroom when the researcher wasn't present. This secondary description is also included in Runciman's concept of "reportage.") Secondary descriptive validity can pertain to accounts for which the inference involved is highly complex and problematic; for example, the claim that the person known as William Shakespeare actually wrote *Hamlet*, or that a particular stone object was used as a cutting tool by a member of an early human population.

What makes these issues of descriptive validity is that they pertain to physical and behavioral events that would in principle be observable. However, the boundary between secondary descriptive validity and my third category, theoretical validity, is not rigid, since what is "in principle" observable is dependent on the methods and instruments available for such observation. Claims that were once theoretical (such as that a specific physical object is composed of atoms) are now matters of descriptive observation, using a scanning tunneling microscope (Barad, 2007, pp. 39–40).

There are several characteristics of these sorts of descriptive concerns that I want to emphasize. First, they all refer to specific events and situations. There is no issue of generalizability or representativeness involved. Second, they are all matters on which intersubjective agreement could in principle be achieved, given the appropriate data. For example, an audio recording of adequate quality could be used to determine if a person made a particular statement during an interview; a video recording could be used to decide if the student threw the eraser, and so on.

Put another way, the *terms* of the description are not problematic for the participants in the discussion; their meaning—how they ought to be applied to events and actions—is not in dispute, only the accuracy of the application. This is quite different, for example, from an account claiming that a student *assaulted* another student, in which it is possible that no amount of videotape or other data, or consensus on the behavior that took place, could resolve disagreements about the applicability of the term "assault" to this behavior. This latter dispute is not about descriptive validity, but concerns the interpretive, theoretical, and/or evaluative validity of the account.

Descriptive validity is by no means independent of theory; all observation and description is theory-laden, even if this theory is implicit or common-sense. However, it is free from *disagreement* about the theory in question. This doesn't mean that there can't be disagreement about the descriptive validity of an account, only that such disagreement could in principle be resolved by the appropriate data. Of course, the theory could be *made* problematic by one of the participants in the discussion, for example, by challenging the applicability of "throwing" to what the student did with the eraser. However, this would change the nature of the validity questions involved, making them no longer an issue of descriptive validity for participants in that discussion.

It is also quite possible that available data may not be adequate to resolve questions of descriptive validity; this is clear from the use of instant replay in sports. However, what is also clear from the increasing development and application of instant replay is that such data often *are* adequate to resolve these issues *beyond a reasonable doubt*—the everyday standard for such decisions (Scriven, 2008). This situation is quite consistent with the constructivist epistemology of critical realism—that all accounts are in principle fallible, and there is no possibility of absolute certainty.

In framing descriptive validity in this way, I am not seeking to revive the positivist view that all disagreements in science ought to be resolvable in principle by means of the appropriate evidence. In my opinion, this view has been convincingly criticized by Bernstein (1983), Kuhn (1970), Rorty (1979), and others. Instead, I am attempting to incorporate in my typology one of Kuhn's fundamental insights: that in normal practice many scientific disagreements *are* resolved in this way. Descriptive understanding pertains, by definition, to matters for which we have a framework for resolving such disagreements, a framework provided in large part by taken-for-granted assumptions about time, space, physical objects, behavior, and our perception of these. Raising questions about the definition or applicability of these categories changes the type of validity at issue from descriptive to theoretical, in particular to that aspect of theoretical validity generally known as construct validity.

Descriptive validity can refer to issues of omission as well of commission; no account can include everything, and "accuracy is a criterion relative to the purposes for which it is sought" (Runciman, 1983, p. 97). For example, a "verbatim" interview transcript might be descriptively invalid in omitting features of the informant's speech, such as stress and pitch, that are essential to understanding the interview. The omission of things that participants in the discussion feel are significant to the account (for the purposes at issue) threatens the descriptive validity of that account.

Descriptive validity can also pertain to numerically descriptive aspects of accounts. A claim that a certain phenomenon was frequent, typical, or rare in a specific situation at the time it was observed—for example, that few students raised their hands in response to the teacher's question—is also a descriptive claim. This is an issue for which Becker (1970; cf. Maxwell, 2010b, and Seale, 1999) advocated the use of what he called "quasi-statistics"—simple counts of things to support claims that are implicitly quantitative. What makes this a matter of descriptive validity is that it does not involve *inference* to some larger set of phenomena than those directly studied, but only the numerical description of the specific object of the claim.

Reliability, in my view, refers not to an aspect of validity, or to a separate issue from validity, but to a particular type of threat to validity. If different observers or methods produce descriptively different data or accounts of the same events or situations, this puts in question the descriptive validity (and other types of validity as well) of the accounts. This problem could be resolved either by modification of the accounts, so that different researchers come to agree on their descriptive accuracy, or by ascertaining that the differences were due to differences in the perspectives, situations, and purposes of the researchers, and were both descriptively valid given those perspectives, situations, and purposes. Both of these outcomes are common results of efforts to assess reliability in qualitative research (Miller, 2008), and neither should be given priority over the other.

INTERPRETIVE VALIDITY

However, qualitative researchers are not concerned solely, or even primarily, with providing a valid description of the physical objects, events, and behaviors in the settings they study. They are also concerned with what these objects, events, and behaviors *mean* to the people engaged in and with them. In this use of the term "meaning," I include intention, cognition, affect, belief, evaluation, and anything else that could be encompassed in what is broadly termed the "participants' perspective," as well as communicative meaning in a narrower sense. As argued in Chapter 2, these phenomena are just as real as physical ones, and our interpretations of these can be valid or invalid, given our purposes and perspectives. However, because the language and concepts used for these are inherently ideational or mental, rather than physical, the nature of the understanding, validity, and validity threats that pertain to them are significantly different from those involved in descriptive validity.

I will call this sort of understanding "interpretive," and the type of validity associated with it "interpretive validity," following Erickson (1986). The term "interpretive" is appropriate primarily because it is the aspect of understanding that is most central to interpretive research. This approach seeks to comprehend phenomena not on the basis of the researcher's perspective and categories, but from those of the participants in the situations studied, i.e., from an "emic" rather than an "etic" perspective (Fetterman, 2008). This is different from another common use of "interpretive" (e.g., Wolcott, 2009, p. 30 ff.), which refers to "making sense of things" in general. The latter meaning is closer to what I describe as theoretical understanding.

Thus, while the terms involved in descriptive validity can be either etic or emic, interpretive validity necessarily pertains to aspects of an account for which the terms are emic. This is because, while accounts of physical and behavioral phenomena can be constructed from a variety of perspectives, accounts of meaning must be based initially on the conceptual framework of the people whose meaning is in question. These terms are often derived to a substantial extent from the participants' own language. The terms are also necessarily, to use Kohut's phrase (Geertz, 1973), "experience-near"—based on the immediate concepts employed by participants (e.g., "love"), rather than on theoretical abstractions (e.g., "object cathexis"). Like descriptive validity, then, interpretive validity, while not atheoretical, refers to aspects of accounts for which the terms of the account are not themselves problematic. Interpretive accounts are grounded in the language and thought of the people studied, and rely as much as possible on their own words and concepts.[3]

Unlike descriptive validity, however, for interpretive validity there is not even "in principle" access to data that could unequivocally address the validity threats involved. Because mental phenomena and events can't be directly observed, interpretive understanding is inherently a matter of inference from the words and actions of participants in the situations studied. The

---

[3] In providing a valid account of individuals who lack such an accessible language, such as preverbal children or nonhuman animals, interpretive validity merges with the following category, theoretical validity. This is consistent with Putnam's analysis of the mind/body issue, discussed in Chapter 2.

development of accounts of these participants' meanings is usually based to a large extent on the participants' own statements, but it is essential not to treat these latter accounts as incorrigible; participants may be unaware of their own thoughts or feelings, may recall these inaccurately, and may consciously or unconsciously distort or conceal their views. Accounts of participants' meanings are never a matter of direct access, but are always *inferred* by the researcher(s) on the basis of participants' accounts and other evidence.

The realist approach to validity that I'm adopting here has been held by some interpretive researchers to be incompatible with a concern for interpretive understanding. For example, Lincoln argued that

> critical realism's assumption that there is a singular reality "out there" . . . ignores the issue of whether that reality is recognized or rejected by those who may be disadvantaged by that construction. (1990)

This critique misses the point that the meanings and constructions of actors are part of the reality that an account must be tested against in order to be interpretively as well as descriptively valid, as discussed in Chapter 2. It is, I think, generally accepted by social theorists that any valid account or explanation of a social phenomenon must respect the perspectives of the actors in that situation, although it need not be centered on that perspective (Bohman, 1991; Harre, 1978; Menzel, 1978). My inclusion of interpretive validity in this typology is a recognition of this consensus: that a key part of the realm "external to" an account is the perspectives of those actors whom the account is about (House, 1991; Manicas, 2009, p. 33).

Interpretive validity doesn't apply only to the conscious concepts of participants; it can also pertain to the unconscious intentions, beliefs, concepts, and values of these participants, and to what Argyris and Schoen (1974) call "theory-in-use" as opposed to "espoused theory." What makes these "interpretive" is not simply that they aren't descriptive, in the sense of being potentially verifiable with adequate observational data, but that they are framed in mental rather than physical terms, as described in Chapter 2, which precludes a purely "descriptive" account.

THEORETICAL VALIDITY

There is also a third category of understanding and validity, which, following Kirk and Miller (1986), I will call "theoretical validity." There are two major differences between theoretical understanding, and theoretical validity, and the two types discussed previously. The first is the degree of abstraction of the account in question from the immediate physical and mental phenomena studied. The reason for calling this sort of understanding "theoretical" is that it goes beyond concrete description and interpretation, which assume a shared theoretical perspective, and explicitly addresses the theoretical constructions that the researcher brings to, or develops during, the study.

This theory can refer to either physical events or mental constructions. It can also incorporate participants' concepts and theories, but its purpose goes beyond simply describing these concepts and theories. This distinction comprises the second major difference between the theoretical validity of an account and the descriptive or interpretive validity of the same account: that theoretical understanding refers to an account's function as an *explanation*, as well as a description or interpretation, of the phenomena.

Theoretical validity thus refers to an account's validity as a *theory* of some phenomenon. Any theory has two components: the concepts or categories that the theory employs, and the relationships that are thought to exist among these concepts. Corresponding to these two aspects of a theory are two aspects of theoretical validity: the validity of the concepts themselves as they are applied to the phenomena, and the validity of the postulated relationships among the concepts. The first refers to the validity of the blocks from which the researcher builds a model, as these are applied to the setting or phenomenon being studied; the second refers to the validity of the way the blocks are put together, as a theory of this setting or phenomenon.

For example, one could label the student's throwing of the eraser as an act of resistance, and connect this act to the behavior or values of the teacher, the social structure of the school, and class relationships in American society. The identification of the throwing as "resistance" constitutes the application of a theoretical construct to the descriptive and interpretive understanding of the action; the connection of this to other aspects of the participants, the school, or the community constitutes the postulation of theoretical relationships among these constructs.

The first of these aspects of theoretical validity closely matches what is generally known as construct validity, and is primarily what Kirk and Miller (1986) mean by theoretical validity. The second aspect includes, but is not limited to, what is commonly called internal or causal validity (Cook & Campbell, 1979); it corresponds to what Runciman calls "explanation" and in part to what Erickson calls "critical validity." It is not limited to causal validity, because theories or models can be developed for other things besides causal explanation—for example, for semantic relationships, narrative structure, and so on—that nevertheless go beyond description and interpretation. Theories can, and usually do, incorporate both descriptive and interpretive understanding, but in combining these they necessarily transcend either of them.

What counts as theoretical validity, rather than descriptive or interpretive validity, depends on whether there is consensus, within the community concerned with the research, about the terms used to characterize the phenomena.

Issues of descriptive and interpretive validity focus on the accuracy of the application of these terms (Did the student really throw the eraser? Was the teacher really angry?) rather than their appropriateness (Does what the student did count as "resistance"?). Theoretical validity is concerned with problems that don't disappear with agreement on "the facts" of the situation; the issue is the legitimacy of the application of a given concept or theory to established facts, or indeed whether any agreement can be reached about what the "facts" are.

The distinction between descriptive or interpretive and theoretical validity is not an absolute one, because (contrary to the assumptions of positivism) there do not exist objective "sense data" that are independent of the researcher's perspective, purposes, and theoretical framework. My distinction between the two types is not based on any such assumption, but on the presence or absence of agreement within the community of inquirers about the descriptive or interpretive terms used. Any challenge to the meaning of the terms, or the appropriateness of their application to a given phenomenon, shifts the validity issue from descriptive or interpretive to theoretical.

These three types of understanding and validity are the ones that are most directly involved in assessing a qualitative account as it pertains to the actual situation on which the account is based. There are, however, two additional categories of validity issues that I want to raise. The first of these deals with the generalizability of an account, what is often labeled "external validity"; the second pertains to the evaluative validity of an account.

GENERALIZABILITY

Generalizability refers to the extent to which one can extend the account given of a particular situation or population to other persons, times, or settings than those directly studied. This issue plays a different role in qualitative research than it does in quantitative and experimental research, because qualitative studies are usually not designed to allow systematic generalizations to some wider population. Generalization in qualitative research usually takes place through the development of a theory that not only makes sense of the particular persons or situations studied, but also shows how the same process, in different situations, can lead to different results (Becker, 1990, p. 240; Pawson & Tilley, 1997, pp. 119–120; Yin, 2003).

This is not to argue that issues of sampling, representativeness, and generalizability are unimportant in qualitative research. They are crucial whenever one wants to draw inferences from the actual persons, events, or activities observed, to other persons, events, or situations, or to these at other times than the ones when the observation was done. (The particular problems of interviewing will be dealt with shortly.) Qualitative research almost always involves some of this sort of inference, because it is impossible to observe everything even in one small setting. The sort of sampling done in qualitative research is usually what is called "purposeful" (Patton, 2001) or "theoretical" (Strauss, 1987) sampling, as discussed in Chapter 6, rather than random sampling or some other method of attaining statistical representativeness. The goal of the former types of sampling is twofold: to make sure one has adequately understood the variation in the phenomena of interest in the setting, and to test developing ideas about that setting by selecting phenomena that are crucial to the validity of those ideas.

In qualitative research, there are two aspects of generalizability: generalizing *within* the setting, group, or institution studied to persons, events, and settings that were not directly observed or interviewed, and generalizing to other settings, groups, or institutions. I will refer to the former as "internal generalizability," and to the latter as "external generalizability" (Maxwell, 2005). The distinction is analogous to Cook and Campbell's distinction (1979) in quasi-experimental research between statistical conclusion validity and external validity. This is not a clear-cut or absolute distinction in qualitative research. A researcher studying a school, for example, can rarely visit every classroom, or even gain information about these classrooms by other means, and the issue of whether to consider the generalizability of the account for those unstudied classrooms "internal" or "external" is moot. However, it is important to be aware of the extent to which the times and places actually observed may differ from those that were not observed, either because of sampling or because of the effect of the observation itself.

Internal generalizability in this sense is far more important for most qualitative researchers than external generalizability, since qualitative researchers rarely make explicit claims about the external generalizability of their accounts. Indeed, the value of a qualitative study may depend on its *lack* of external generalizability in a statistical sense; it may provide an account of a setting or population that is illuminating as an extreme case or "ideal type." Freidson, discussing his qualitative study of a medical group practice, noted that

> there is more to truth or validity than statistical representativeness. . . . In this study I am less concerned with describing the range of variation than I am with describing in the detail what survey questionnaire methods do not permit to be described—the assumptions, behavior, and attitudes of a very special set of physicians. They are interesting *because* they were special. (1975, pp. 272–273)

He argued that his study makes an important contribution to theory and policy precisely because this was a group for whom social controls on practice should have been most likely to be effective. The failure of such controls in this case not only elucidates a social process that is likely to exist in other groups, but also provides a more persuasive argument for the unworkability of such controls than would a study of a "representative" group.

Interviewing poses some special problems for internal generalizability, because the researcher usually is in the presence of the person interviewed for only a brief period, and must necessarily draw inferences from what happened during that brief period to the rest of the informant's life, actions, and perspective. An account based on interviews may be descriptively, interpretively, and theoretically valid as an account of the person's actions and perspective in that interview, but may miss other aspects of the person's perspectives that were not expressed in the interview, and can easily lead to false inferences about his or her actions outside the interview situation. Thus, internal generalizability is a crucial issue in interpreting interviews, as is widely recognized (e.g., Dexter, 1970), and has been (although not in these terms) a central focus of post-modernism. The interview is itself a social situation, and inherently involves a relationship between the interviewer and the informant. Understanding the nature of that situation and relationship, how it affects what goes on in the interview, and how the informant's actions and views could differ in other situations, is crucial to the validity of accounts based on interviews (Briggs, 1986; Mishler, 1986).

EVALUATIVE VALIDITY

Beyond all of the validity issues just discussed, there are validity questions about statements such as saying the student was wrong to throw the eraser at the teacher, or that the teacher was illegitimately failing to recognize minority students' perspectives. This aspect of validity differs from the types discussed previously in that it involves the application of an evaluative framework to the objects of study, rather than a descriptive, interpretive, or explanatory one. It corresponds to Runciman's "evaluation" as a category of understanding (1983), and is an important component of what Erickson (1986) terms "critical validity."

I have little to say here about evaluative validity that has not been said more cogently by others, and critical realism, as I use the term, has little to contribute to this type of understanding and validity. My purpose here is twofold: to acknowledge it as a legitimate category of understanding and validity in qualitative research, and to suggest how it relates to the other types of validity discussed. Like external generalizability, evaluative validity is not as central or essential in qualitative research as are descriptive, interpretive, and theoretical validity; many researchers make no claim to evaluate the things they study. Furthermore, issues of evaluative understanding and evaluative validity in qualitative research do not seem to me to be intrinsically different from those in any other approach to research; debates about whether the student's throwing of the eraser was legitimate or justified do not depend on the methods used to ascertain that this happened or to decide what interpretive or theoretical sense to make of it, although they do depend on the particular description, interpretation, or theory one constructs. To raise questions about the evaluative framework implicit in an account, however, as many critical theorists do, *creates* issues of evaluative validity for an account, and no account is immune to such questions.

IMPLICATIONS

In summary, I have presented a model of the types of validity that I believe are relevant to, and often implicit in, qualitative research. I have approached this task from a realist perspective, and have argued that this realist approach, which bases validity on the kinds of understanding we can have of the phenomena we study, is more consistent and productive than prevailing positivist typologies based on research procedures. A realist view of validity both avoids the philosophical and practical difficulties associated with positivist approaches and seems to me to better represent what qualitative researchers actually do in assessing the validity of their accounts.

However, having presented this typology, I must add that validity categories are of much less direct use in qualitative research than they are (or are assumed to be) in quantitative and experimental research. In the latter, many validity threats are addressed in an anonymous, generic fashion, by prior design features (such as random assignment and statistical controls); random assignment is held to deal with both anticipated and unanticipated validity threats.

In qualitative research, however, such prior elimination of validity threats is less possible, both because qualitative research is more inductive and because it focuses primarily on understanding particulars rather than generalizing to universals (Erickson 1986). Qualitative researchers deal primarily with specific threats to the validity of particular features of their accounts, and they generally address such threats by seeking evidence that would allow them to rule out each of these threats.

This strategy of addressing particular validity threats, or "alternative hypotheses," *after* a tentative account has been developed, rather than by attempting to eliminate such threats through prior features of the research design, is in fact more fundamental to scientific method than is the latter approach (Campbell, 1988; Platt, 1964). It is accepted by qualitative researchers from a wide range of philosophical positions (e.g., Eisner, 1991; Hammersley & Atkinson, 1983; Miles & Huberman, 1984; Patton, 2001). Its application to causal inference has been labeled the "generalized elimination model" by Scriven (2008, pp. 21–22), but the method has received little formal development in the qualitative research literature, although it is implicit in many substantive qualitative studies.

Thus, as argued earlier, researchers cannot use the typology presented here to directly and mechanically eliminate particular threats to the validity of their accounts. Qualitative researchers already have many methods for addressing validity threats, and although there are ways that the state of the art could be improved (see Maxwell, 2004c; Miles & Huberman, 1984; Seale, 1999), that is not my main goal here. Instead, what I am trying to do is to clarify the validity concepts that many qualitative researchers are using, explicitly or implicitly, in their work, to tie these concepts into a systematic model, and to reduce the discrepancy between qualitative researchers' "logic-in-use" and their "reconstructed logic" (Kaplan, 1964, pp. 3–11), a discrepancy that I think has been responsible for both some misunderstanding of qualitative research, and some shortcomings in its validation practices. I see this typology as being useful in two ways. The first is as a framework for thinking about the nature of validity issues in qualitative research and possible threats to validity. The second is as a checklist of the *kinds* of understanding qualitative research can aim at, and of the kinds of validity issues that one needs to consider in qualitative research. Gawande (2009) has argued that checklists are extremely useful in avoiding error in dealing with complex situations, and qualitative research certainly would seem to fit this description. A checklist of some of the most important ways in which qualitative researchers can deal with the validity issues that they face is included in my book *Qualitative Research Design: An Interactive Approach* (Maxwell, 2005).

Evidence

The previous discussion of validity and understanding, in contrast to most treatments of validity in qualitative research, gives a central role to the concept of evidence. Schwandt (2007, p. 98) defines evidence as "information that bears on determining the validity (truth, falsity, accuracy, etc.) of a claim or what an inquirer provides, in part, to warrant a claim." From a different perspective, Chandler, Davidson, and Harootunian, discussing Collingwood's view of evidence in history, likewise argue that "question and evidence are therefore 'correlative' in the sense that facts can only become evidence in response to some particular question" (1994, p. 1).

Schwandt's definition and Collingwood's argument point to the inextricable connections between evidence, claim, and validity. A key property of evidence (as opposed to data) is that it does not exist in isolation, but only in relation to some claim (theory, hypothesis, interpretation, etc.).

Evidence is thus in the same position as validity—it can't be assessed in context-independent ways, but only in relation to the particular question and purpose to which it is applied.

In particular, evidence can't be evaluated solely in terms of the methods used to obtain it, as argued earlier for validity. Any attempt to establish a context-free hierarchy of kinds of evidence based entirely on the methods used to create that evidence, as proponents of "evidence-based" approaches typically do, is inevitably flawed. While this emphasis on the context-dependence of evidence and conclusions is a key feature of critical realist approaches, it is shared by a much broader community of scholars.

The philosopher Peter Achinstein, who has probably done the most to systematically critique and reformulate the traditional philosophical view of evidence (2001, 2005), made the related point that evidence isn't a single thing, but several; there is no essential property that all uses of "evidence" possess (2001, p. 15).

However, there is a key difference between the uses of evidence in quantitative and qualitative research, or between what Mohr (1982) called "variance theory" and "process theory," discussed in Chapter 3. To recapitulate, variance theory deals with variables and the relationship between them, and the main use of evidence is to show *that* a particular relationship exists between different variables. Process theory, in contrast, is primarily concerned with events and processes, rather than variables, and the main use of evidence (and the primary strength of qualitative research) is to support claims about these events and processes—to get inside the "black box" of variance theory and to argue for what is actually happening in specific cases.

By "what is happening," I (and critical realists in general) include participants' meanings, intentions, beliefs, and perspectives, which are essential parts of these events and processes, as discussed in Chapter 2. Claims about meanings and perspectives, which fall under the general category of "interpretive" claims, require quite different sorts of evidence from claims about behavior, let alone claims about the relationships between variables. Thus, the kinds of claims, and the nature and evaluation of the evidence for these claims, is very different in qualitative research from that in quantitative research, and evidential standards appropriate for quantitative and experimental research can't uncritically be applied to qualitative research.

Achinstein drew a number of other conclusions from this claim-dependence and context-dependence of evidence. First, whether some fact is evidence for a particular claim depends on how the fact is obtained or generated (Achinstein, 2001, p. 8). This does not conflict with the previous point, that evidence can't be assessed strictly in terms of the methods used to obtain it. It simply asserts that how the evidence was obtained is often *relevant* to the support it lends to a particular claim, since the methods used may address (or create) certain validity threats that could threaten the support that the evidence provides for the claim.

Second, the degree of support that a particular piece of evidence provides for a particular claim depends on the plausibility of (and evidence for) *alternative* claims regarding the phenomena in question (Achinstein, 2001, pp. 7–10). Achinstein provided several examples from different sciences in which a finding that was once believed to be convincing evidence for a particular claim was no longer thought to be so when new evidence was produced or alternative explanations were proposed. Thus, part of the context that evidence for a particular claim depends on is that of alternative possible theories and explanations for the phenomenon in question.

Third, the previous point entails that whether a fact or observation is evidence for some claim is an empirical question, not a logical one (Achinstein, 2001, p. 9). The evidence can only be assessed in the context of the particular claim that the evidence is asserted to support, the way the evidence was generated, and the epistemic situation in which these claims are made. This context is not given a priori, but needs to be empirically discovered. Achinstein argued that one of the main reasons that researchers have paid so little attention to philosophical work on evidence is that this work usually presumes that the link between claim and evidence is strictly logical, semantic, or mathematical, something that can be established by calculation rather than empirical investigation.

Finally, Achinstein argued that for a fact to be evidence for some claim, the fact's simply increasing the probability that the claim is true isn't enough; there must be some *explanatory connection* between the fact and the claim (2001, p. 145 ff.). This is an essential component of realist approaches to explanation in general—that a valid explanation does not simply support the view *that* x causes y, but must address *how* it does so (Manicas, 2006; Salmon, 1998; Sayer, 1992, 2000). The lack of attention to the processes by which a causal influence takes place is a major flaw in most "evidence-based" approaches to research (Maxwell, 2004a; Pawson, 2006). Pawson argued that

> the nature of causality in social programmes is such that any synthesis of evidence on whether they work will need to investigate how they work. This requires unearthing information on mechanisms, contexts, and outcomes. The central quest is to understand the conditions of programme efficacy and this will involve the synthesis in investigating for whom, in what circumstances, and in what respects a family of programmes work. (2006, p. 25)

These are issues for which qualitative research can make a significant contribution. However, the theory of causation on which the "evidence-based" movement relies, and the bias toward quantitative and experimental methods that this produces, have largely excluded qualitative evidence from the research syntheses that this movement has generated, as discussed in Chapter 3. In part because of this bias, qualitative researchers have long been either defensive about their use of evidence, or dismissive of the entire concept of evidence. I argue that there is no good reason for either of these reactions. A realist reformulation of the concept of evidence can provide a strong justification for the value of the evidence generated by qualitative research, and qualitative researchers have their own ways of obtaining and using such evidence that are just as legitimate for their purposes as quantitative researchers' are for theirs (Maxwell, 2004c).

A realist understanding of validity leads to a quite different approach to issues of quality, credibility, or trustworthiness than those normally employed in qualitative (or, for that matter, quantitative) research. Rather than relying only on the designs or procedures used in a study to assess its quality, a realist perspective focuses attention on the credibility of the *interpretations* and *conclusions* drawn from the study, and the ways in which the researcher used the study's data to assess these interpretations and conclusions in light of plausible alternatives. While the methods and approaches used are obviously an important issue in this assessment, they must themselves be assessed in terms of the actual context and purposes of their use. Rather than being employed as context-independent criteria for quality, their real value is as a means of obtaining evidence that can deal with plausible threats to the validity of the study's interpretations and conclusions.

Part III

Applications of Realism in Qualitative Research

Introduction

In the final section of this book, I present two extended examples of qualitative research that incorporated a realist perspective, taken from my own research in anthropology. I had originally planned to include a third example, based on a series of studies in medical education that I conducted, in the belief that this research would be more familiar to most qualitative researchers. However, in writing the first two chapters of this section, I realized that these adequately covered the main implications of a realist stance, and that the intended third chapter would add little to what I had already presented. There are discussions of more typical qualitative studies undertaken from a realist perspective in Pawson and Tilley (1997).

Chapter 9 deals with a long-term study of Plains Indian social organization. It is relevant to this book mainly because my philosophical stance shifted during the course of this research, from a basically positivist approach, to an interpretivist and significantly constructivist approach, and finally to a realist approach. At each stage of this research, I describe how the approach I followed shaped my methods and conclusions, and my reasons for ultimately abandoning both positivism and ontological constructivism. A major issue for this study was how to integrate causal explanation with a concern for meaning and context.

Chapter 10 is based on a year of ethnographic fieldwork in an Inuit community in northern Canada. In contrast to the previous example, I began this research from a realist stance, which became more elaborated as I continued my work, but didn't shift significantly. The main goal for this study was to integrate a fundamentally interpretive and cultural account of this community's understanding of kinship and social relationships with my commitment to a realist approach to meaning and diversity.

9

Explaining Plains Indian Social Organization

In this chapter, I describe a long-term research project of mine that illustrates the differences among three "paradigmatic" approaches to social research: positivism/postpositivism, interpretivism/constructivism, and realism. I chronicle how my own thinking evolved through these three perspectives, and the implications that each perspective had for my attempts to understand the changes that took place in Plains Indian social organization when these tribes acquired horses from the Spanish after 1650 and adopted mounted bison hunting as their main subsistence strategy. In this extended example, I hope to show what differences each of these three approaches makes for understanding a social and cultural phenomenon, and the advantages of a realist perspective in explaining what happened and why.

There are some significant disadvantages to using this as an example of different approaches to qualitative research. The study was based entirely on published, and a few unpublished, sources; because I was trying to understand a social and cultural process that had largely been completed by the beginning of the twentieth century, I could not interview or observe participants who had been part of that process. I was able to draw on more recent anthropological fieldwork with members of these societies, mainly to understand their social organization and their conceptualizations of this, but often this fieldwork was not focused on the same issues that I was concerned with. In most cases, I had only the results of these researchers' analyses, rather than the original data. As a result, I was not able to use some of the most important strategies for assessing the validity of qualitative conclusions, such as member checks and deliberately attempting to elicit data that would test my theories.

However, there were corresponding advantages to this situation. I was able to draw on a wide range of sources, and data collected by researchers with a variety of theoretical perspectives, many of which were different from my own. This acted to some extent as a check on my imposing my own theories of cultural and social change on the data. I was also able to take advantage of ethnographic fieldwork with the entire range of tribes in this area by other researchers, providing data and interpretations that would have been impossible for a single researcher to produce.

I didn't select this research as an example because I think it's an ideal model for doing qualitative research from a realist (or any other) perspective. I encountered lots of problems in the research, many of which I discuss. I have two main reasons for using this example. First, I've been through it—I can talk about my struggles with using each of the approaches, and the actual reasons for the shifts in my perspective. Second, it emphasizes the central importance of the philosophical and theoretical approach, rather than simply the data collection and analysis methods, of each of the three approaches. The data sources for my application of each of the perspectives were largely the same; all of the data were obtained from existing publications and other documents, including ethnographic accounts and fieldnotes, linguistic and historical research, and comparative analyses. In addition, all of the data were initially qualitative, though some were subjected to later quantitative analysis by other researchers.

The fundamental research problem that I was dealing with was succinctly stated by Eggan: "Tribes coming into the Plains with *different* backgrounds and social systems ended up with *similar* kinship systems" (1937, p. 93, italics in original). He later added, "I think it is now clear that they achieved a common pattern of social structure as well" (1966, p. 72). As reconstructed from historical records, comparison with related tribes, and archeological and linguistic evidence, the historic Plains tribes exhibited considerable diversity in their former subsistence patterns, social structures, and kin terminologies. However, by the time these tribes were first described by Europeans, most of them possessed similar subsistence activities, social structures, and patterns of kin terminology. The question that I was trying to answer was, how and why did this happen?

I came to this problem as an undergraduate anthropology major, and although my interest in this problem has continued for over 40 years, my thinking about it has gone through three distinct phases.

A Positivist Approach

After discovering Eggan's work on Plains kinship, my first step in pursuing this problem was to review existing theories of change in kinship and social systems. When I began this research, in 1964, the dominant approach to this problem was to explain aspects of kinship and social organization in terms of other aspects of social organization and, ultimately, of factors external to social organization, primarily the type of subsistence pattern and the division of labor between men and women that this entailed. A major exemplar of this approach was George Peter Murdock's book *Social Structure* (1949), which presented a general theory of the processes of change in social systems of traditional (what were then often called "primitive") societies. Murdock's strategy was described by the *New World Encyclopedia* as follows:

> Murdock was interested in making scientific generalizations about culture. . . . He first identified key variables, and then made causal and functional relationships between them. In order to keep his method scientific, Murdock created databases for cross-cultural comparisons, coding them for statistical analysis. With this approach he was able to make global generalizations about cultures. In his most important book, *Social Structure* (1949), he was able to identify "natural laws" of social organization by means of cross-cultural statistical comparisons. (Accessed 11/19/2010 at http://www.newworldency clopedia.org/entry/George_Peter_Murdock)

Murdock developed the Human Relations Area Files (HRAF), a massive compilation of ethnographic data on all societies for which such data had been recorded, and he used data from 250 of these societies to develop and test his theory.

Murdock's approach was essentially positivist in all of its main features. First, it involved an abstraction from actual human beings, events, and processes to variables that could be analyzed using inferential statistics. Second, his goal was to discover universal laws of social change that correlated particular features of social structure with other factors, through cross-cultural comparison of societies.[1] Murdock's approach was evolutionary, but in the sense of Steward's "multilinear evolution" (1955); he did not believe that there was a single evolutionary sequence that all societies followed, but that different societies could follow different sequences, depending on changes in the primary causal variables—subsistence patterns and the male/female division of labor that these generated.

Third, his strategy was to use his theoretical model of social evolution to generate predictions about the relationships among different variables, which were then tested against data from the HRAF, using statistical significance as the main criterion. Finally, cultural aspects of kinship and social organization, in particular the kin terms and their meanings, were seen as simply reflecting the social and behavioral features of these societies, though with a lag when

---

[1] At the conclusion of his book *Social Structure*, Murdock stated that "cultural forms in the field of social organization reveal a degree of regularity and of conformity to scientific law not significantly inferior to that found in the so-called natural sciences" (1949, p. 259). In hindsight, this statement stands as a classic example of positivist overreaching.

changes occurred in the latter. This lag was assumed to account for any incon-sistencies between the terminological pattern and the actual structure "on the ground"—primarily the organization of kin groups and where couples resided after marriage. No serious attention was given to the mechanisms for the relationships between cultural and physical or behavioral features.

Other theories were also being seriously considered at the time I began this work. The primary competitor to Murdock's approach was that of Service (1962). This approach was also evolutionist and universalist, but unilinear, presenting a single sequence of evolutionary change, although one that could be affected by environmental and demographic factors. (This theory was sub-stantially influenced by the evolutionary theories of Leslie White, and through him of Engels and Marx.) However, it was still essentially positivist in its meth-ods, creating variables and developing a theory of the relations among these, testing these relations through statistical analysis of cross-cultural data, and seeking universal laws of social change.

The main criticisms of these theories were that they didn't work for the specific societies that the critic had studied. In particular, Eggan claimed that Murdock's theory didn't fit the historical evidence for change in Plains social organization. This critique rejected the universalism, but not the other prem-ises, of the dominant theories, and did not propose any alternative general theory of changes in social organization. Eggan's explanation of the particular pattern of kinship and social organization found in most Plains tribes was that this was a creative and adaptive response to the conditions of Plains life, the result of the need for greater social solidarity resulting from the increased importance of cooperation between men in warfare and bison hunting, rather than a reflection of particular features of social structure or the results of demographic change. (Eggan had been a student of the British social anthro-pologist A. R. Radcliffe-Brown, whose structural-functional theory of society emphasized the ways in which particular features of social organization met the functional needs of the society.) Eggan argued that

> Plains life required a flexible type of organization that could adjust both to the seasonally varying habits of the buffalo and to the requirements of pro-tection and warfare. The amorphous and composite bands were well adapted for such purposes and could change in size and leadership as the situation demanded. A successful leader attracted new members, while those of a poor leader were lost or melted away. (1966, p. 56)

However, Eggan did not challenge the basic methodology that Murdock employed, although he paid more attention to specific historical and ecologi-cal circumstances and to other influences, such as acculturation, that he saw as important in specific societies (1966, p. 172 ff.).

As a result, my approach to explaining the patterns of kin terminology and social organization in Plains tribes was largely positivist, although incorporating aspects of Eggan's structural-functionalism. (The title of my undergraduate thesis was "The Determinants of Plains Kinship," a phrase that I assume I borrowed from the title of one of Murdock's chapters, "Determinants of Kinship Terminology.") I took four prominent existing theories of kinship change, generated predictions from each, and tested these against the Plains data. My strategy was variable-oriented, creating tables of tribes' "values" for specific social and terminological variables and looking for overall patterns, although the small number of societies precluded the use of inferential statistics. It also implicitly accepted the positivist lack of attention to mechanisms; I primarily attempted to correlate the changes that had occurred with particular social variables. However, it was particularistic in that it focused not just on general patterns, but also on developing an explanation for specific Plains tribes that didn't fit this pattern, incorporating the unique subsistence patterns, features of social structure, and intertribal relations of these tribes.

My conclusion was that Murdock's predictions were frequently contradicted by the ethnographic and historical data, as well as by linguistic reconstructions of the proto-kinship systems of particular language families. Service's theory was also flawed, but mainly because of the absence of the causal factors that he had used to explain the social and kinship patterns found in these tribes, or their presence in other tribes that did not undergo these changes. Eggan's theory was best supported by the data, which is not surprising since it was designed specifically to deal with the Plains tribes, but it didn't explain the pattern of terms for a person's uncles, aunts, nieces, and nephews. I explained the latter as the result of a combination of three social variables, ones that Murdock had showed were correlated with this pattern, and the existence of which was supported by Plains data.

From a critical realist perspective, several things were wrong with this positivist approach. First, it reified the theoretical concepts involved, treating variables as causal entities in a Humean, regularity sense, without thinking in terms of the processes involved in actual human behavior. This was less true of Eggan's approach, but his structural-functional perspective still paid little attention to the actual mechanisms of change, simply assuming that social structures were adaptive. Second, it did not consider individuals' perspectives or intentions as having a causal role in the changes identified. Eggan's concern with solidarity might seem to be an exception, but Eggan saw solidarity as a social phenomenon, more or less equivalent to "social integration," rather than as an individual and symbolic one.

My thinking was thus trapped in the categories and assumptions of prevailing theory and research. In this, it is a good example of what Becker (1986, pp. 146–149) called the "deforming power" of established theory—how accepting the prevailing views of the phenomena you're studying can prevent you from seeing different and more productive ways of conceptualizing these.

However, my explanation was a departure from positivist approaches in that my theory was not intended to be applicable to traditional societies in general; I was critical of universal theories of changes in kinship, although I did suggest the possible applicability of my explanation of Plains kin terminology to other societies having similar terminological patterns. The explanations I proposed were specific to Plains tribes, and in some cases to particular tribes. From a strict positivist perspective, this particularism was illegitimate, since it was "ad hoc" and not subject to rigorous testing. However, it involved a commonsense realism in its implicit recognition of the legitimacy of causal explanations of unique situations.

I have no clear memory of how or why I used this approach. The only social science courses I had taken outside of anthropology (economics and sociology) had been quantitatively oriented, but I had never studied statistics or research design. I assume that I simply followed the model presented by Murdock and others doing cross-cultural research, reinforced by the quantitative sociology I had learned, which was variable-oriented and dominated by regularity approaches to causation. However, I had also read a fair number of ethnographies by the time I began my research on Plains kinship, and so was open to the idea of specific interpretations of particular societies' social structures. I had also read Eggan's classic paper on "controlled comparison" (1954) in anthropology, in which he advocated a more qualitative and case-oriented approach—selecting societies for comparison that were historically or geographically related—and this paper undoubtedly influenced my thinking as well.

When I enrolled in the graduate program in anthropology at the University of Chicago the following year, I gave a copy of my thesis to Eggan. He returned this with a few critical comments on specific details, but did not challenge the overall approach that I had taken; he wrote next to my explanation of the terminology for uncles and aunts, which simply invoked Murdock's variables, "This sounds like you are on the right track."

Rejection of Positivism, Incorporation of Interpretivism

After completing three years of coursework in anthropology and passing my comprehensive exams, I took a leave of absence from graduate school, and during this leave I tried to extend my analysis of Plains kinship in writing my master's paper at Chicago. This involved an enormous amount of library research; I included other tribes in areas adjacent to the Plains, making comparisons between linguistically related tribes in the Plains and adjoining areas, and gathered a great deal more information about the history (using archeological and linguistic, as well as ethnographic, data), economy and ecology, and social organization of each tribe. (In doing this, I was working entirely on my own, with no guidance from faculty at Chicago.) I submitted this paper in 1971; it was substantially expanded from my previous paper (from 50 to 170 pages).

There were several major changes in my approach to the explanation of Plains kinship systems from my original analysis. First, I abandoned the deductive strategy of making predictions from general theories of kinship and then using the data to test these. I first presented the data on 22 Plains and surrounding tribes, then discussed how well different theories made sense of these data. While I included summary tables of these data, the presentation treated the categories less as variables and more as descriptions, with brief narrative summaries of many of the categories and more attention to the individual diversity of each tribe. I no longer assumed that general theories of change in kinship and social organization, and the variables on which these were based, would necessarily identify the appropriate influences and changes that were involved in particular cases.

In line with this, the analysis was less comparative, and involved more of a "case study" approach. I attempted to explain *particular* tribes' kinship systems and social structures, rather than simply seeing if the data fit into a general pattern. This involved a greater awareness of the uniqueness of each tribe's social system, and the need for context-specific explanations of these. As a result, my presentation shifted toward process and away from variance explanations. Not only were the explanations more contextualized, but they also focused on the specific processes by which the change occurred. I also sought data that would allow me to assess whether these processes were in fact operative, rather than simply seeing if a theory's predictions fit the data.

In addition, I incorporated a cultural approach to kinship, which I had learned in courses with David Schneider and from his book *American Kinship: A Cultural Account* (1968). This involved recognizing that the meaning of kinship and kin terms was a different phenomenon from social structure and behavior, and required a different approach to understanding. As a consequence, I began to treat Eggan's "solidarity" theory as a cultural interpretation in its own right, rather than simply a functional need of the society, and considered individuals' motives as involved in the explanation of particular cases.

Third, I recognized, partly as a result of Schneider's influence, that kin terminology could not be "explained" as simply a reflection of the social structure. The key to my incorporation of this idea, however, was a statement in a paper on Mohawk kinship (Voget, 1953) that "a number of informants have suggested . . . that these usages [of particular kin terms] are attempts to emphasize a degree of relationship which in fact does not exist" (p. 391); Voget further argued that "all of [these usages] emphasize group solidarity" (p. 391).

The idea that the relationship between meaning and behavior was one of contradiction (the terminological meaning contradicted the actual behavior) became the cornerstone for a new way of thinking about the relationship between the meanings of kin terms and social/behavioral change. Applying Voget's insight, I argued that

> in this light, it seems possible that, instead of sibling terms having been extended to cousins in most Plains tribes as a result of the extension of the [behavioral] sibling relationship, the wider use of the sibling terms was an important and to some extent structurally independent part of the change toward a greater range of solidarity and integration. (Maxwell, 1971, p. 151)

I then argued that several features of Plains social organization could be better understood by seeing the meaning of kin terms and the behavioral norms between relatives as partially independent factors in the changes that occurred (see Example 9.1).

Example 9.1

A Simplified Model of the Causal Processes of Change in Blackfeet Kinship

The map in Figure 9.1 displays some of the events and influences leading to the widespread use of "brother" terms in Blackfeet society by the late 1800s. More than any other Plains tribe, the Blackfeet were involved in the fur trade. This led to increased wealth (including guns), a greater value of women's work in preparing bison hides for trade, a highly unequal distribution of wealth that favored men who had many horses for bison hunting, and a massive increase in polygyny, as wealthy men acquired large numbers of wives to process hides. The acquisition of guns and horses allowed the Blackfeet to move westward into the Plains, driving out the tribes that had previously lived there. The increase in warfare and bison hunting created a greater need for male solidarity and led to the widespread use of brother terms between men of the same generation to enhance this solidarity. However, the increased polygyny led to a wider range of ages within a man's generation and to the extension of brother terms to men of other generations who were of about the speaker's age. This proliferation of the use of brother terms eventually diluted their solidarity value, generating a new term, "comrade," which was often used in close relationships between men.

Figure 9.1   A Simplified Model of the Causal Processes of Change in
Blackfeet Kinship

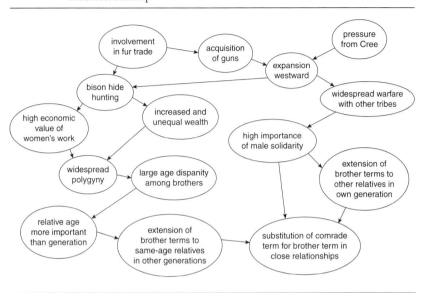

Finally, I applied this view of partial independence to the structure of the kin terminology itself. The pattern of terminology in most Plains tribes was logically "inconsistent" in that the distinctions made in a person's parents' and children's generations were not the same as those made in that person's own generation. A person's parents' opposite-sex siblings were labeled by a different terms from that used for their parents and their same-sex siblings, but this distinction was *not* made in the person's own generation: all cousins were called by the same terms as one's brothers and sisters. (This was the inconsistency that I had previously tried to explain using Murdock's variables.) Essentially all general theories of kin terminology to that time had treated such "inconsistencies" as an anomaly, and as evidence that the system was unstable and in transition from one "consistent" pattern to another. This was a key feature of Murdock's theory of social change, since he held that the pattern of terminology was a reflection of general social distinctions that affected all generations, although not necessarily at the same rate. Even Eggan had held that the Plains tribes were in the process of shifting to a "Generation" pattern in which these distinctions in a person's parents' and children's generations were being lost, making them consistent with the pattern for siblings and cousins.

I argued that this was an unwarranted assumption, and that there is no reason to believe that such "inconsistent" systems could not exist as stable patterns, pointing out that some linguistic reconstructions of the prototerminologies of particular language groups have been "inconsistent," and that other "inconsistent" systems were widespread in native North America. I concluded that different terms and sets of terms can be affected by different influences. One of the main conclusions of the present work is that this is true of all aspects of kinship, although this should not be taken to deny its systemic nature. The holistic theories of Murdock, Dole, and Service have contributed significantly to our understanding of kinship systems, but there remain many exceptions to their generalizations which require limited, intensive work in order to be understood, and this understanding of specific problems is essential to the general advancement of kinship theory. (Maxwell, 1971, p. 159)

However, despite the insights that I gained from Schneider's perspective, I was uncomfortable with some aspects of his interpretive approach, although I didn't explicitly address these in my master's paper. First, Schneider held a radical constructivist view of culture, stating that "I do not take the position that culture is *sui generis*, a thing in and of itself, or that it has any existence outside the construction of the anthropologist who builds that structure of abstractions" (1980, p. 128). As I described in Chapter 2, Schneider held that it constituted "cheating" to take participants' statements, or descriptions of their behavior, as "evidence" for any claims about culture, since "culture" is not a real entity, but an analytical abstraction.

Second, a purely cultural understanding (particularly a constructivist one) did not seem to provide a plausible *process* for understanding change in terminological systems. Schneider denied not only that the meanings of kin terms were a reflection of the social structure, but also that there was *any* causal relationship between social structure and kin terminology. In conversation, Schneider appeared to argue that kinship systems *didn't* change, claiming that a student of his found the same kin terminology in use on the island of Yap, in the South Pacific, that Schneider himself had described decades earlier. This position was inconsistent with my main premise, that the kin terminologies of the Plains tribes *had* changed, based on extensive linguistic and comparative evidence, and that there was good reason to believe that these changes were a response to their moving into the Plains physical and social environment.

This phase of my Plains research thus embodied the tension between naturalism and constructivism that Hammersley and Atkinson described (2007, pp. 10–11)—that between a realist approach to social phenomena and a constructivist understanding of people's perspectives and actions. However, at the time I saw no way out of this dilemma.

Developing a Critical Realist Approach

Shortly after completing my master's paper, however, I discovered a number of works that developed more systematically the idea of a relationship between terminology and behavior that was not one of reflection (Bloch, 1971; Cottrell,

1965; McKinley, 1971a, 1971b; Murphy, 1967; Tambiah, 1967). All of these authors argued that neither cultural/cognitive nor social factors can be given precedence *a priori*, but that both must be integrated into a single causal explanation. Kin terminology, as a cultural system of terms and meanings, is neither a reflection nor a determinant of behavior; it can serve as a charter (Tambiah) or ideology (McKinley, Murphy) for behavior while allowing that behavior to deviate substantially from it, including tactical or metaphoric uses of the terms that are inconsistent with their literal meaning (Bloch).

While none of these authors explicitly employed a realist perspective, all were implicitly making the realist point that meaning, behavior, and social structure are all real phenomena, and that the relationships among them are not ones of reflection or strict determination of one by the other, but of interaction and interdependence. All of these authors viewed kin terminology as a cultural phenomenon that is grounded in social life but that may "contradict" the social order as manifested behaviorally. The meanings of kin terms can have important ideological and symbolic functions separate from the representation of social relationships, and these meanings may independently contribute to group functioning and adaptation. Both stability and change involve an interaction between ideas and behavior.

This insight gave me the final piece that I needed in order to transcend the either/or dichotomy between positivism and constructivist interpretivism, and to systematically make sense of the changes in Plains kinship. I continued working on this issue while developing my dissertation plans, writing two long papers that served both as preparation for my dissertation proposal and field research, and as further development of my ideas on Plains kinship. The first of these papers was a review of theories of kin terminology, incorporating work in linguistics and philosophy on the relationship between meaning and use and the processes by which changes in meaning occur. The second was an investigation of the philosophy of mind and its relevance for cultural theory (the basis for Chapter 2 of this book); this was a major influence on my understanding of a realist approach to mental phenomena, and led to my development of a concept of culture as both mental and real, and as interacting with social/behavioral phenomena in ways that were not captured by a hierarchical, one-way determinist view of this relationship.

Drawing on these two papers, I then prepared a paper on Plains kinship for publication (Maxwell, 1978), revising the argument of my master's paper. The theory I presented in this paper went beyond my previous versions in explicitly incorporating the *meanings* of kin terms, and the ways in which these meanings influenced and were influenced by the ways the terms were used tactically. I claimed that kin terms, as linguistic symbols, inform and motivate the behavior of individuals, and are employed in social situations to influence the behavior of other actors in these situations. However, this behavior and its consequences in turn influence the use and meaning of the terms, and thus the structure of the terminology. Patterns of terminology must be explained not by what they reflect, but by what they accomplish in social life (McKinley, 1971a), and "no explanation of change can ignore either the motives of individuals or the functions of the terminology in the sociocultural system as a whole" (Maxwell, 1978, p. 17).

This idea was central to my revised explanation of the changes in Plains kinship systems. I argued that in the context of Plains subsistence patterns (bison hunting) and intertribal relationships (frequent warfare and raiding), the perceived need for a wider range of cooperation and solidary relationships, and a relative absence of formal institutions for achieving this, would lead to the broader tactical use of terms with solidary value—most importantly, the terms for "brother"—for relatives (particularly male cousins) to whom the meaning could easily be extended. This use, in the context of the recognized value of greater solidarity, would have facilitated the development of solidary relationships.

However, it also influenced the *meaning* of these terms, as the wider tactical or metaphoric use eventually became incorporated into the literal meaning of the terms, leading to the loss of the separate "cousin" terms and thus changing the pattern of terminology. (This incorporation of usage into the meaning of the terms was not a necessary consequence of the tactical or metaphoric extension of the use of the terms, as Murphy, Bloch, and others showed, but in the Plains situation it was a plausible one, since it would have contributed both to individual support and security and to tribal solidarity and integration.) I applied this explanation not only to Plains kinship in general, but also to specific instances that on the surface seemed to be exceptions to the general pattern of Plains kin terms, showing how, in the context of these tribes' economies, prior social organizations, and cultural patterns, the theory explained these differences. (Example 9.1 illustrates some of these factors for the kin terminology of the Blackfeet Indians.) In doing this, I was unconsciously applying the view of generalization in qualitative research discussed in Chapter 8, subsequently published by Becker and Yin.

At this point I became involved in other research projects, and did not return to this topic until Eggan asked me, in the late 1980s, for permission to incorporate the argument of my paper in a chapter that he had been invited to write, on Plains kinship and social organization, for the *Handbook of North American Indians*, Plains volume. I agreed, and Eggan eventually asked me to be a coauthor for the chapter; I ended up completing the chapter when Eggan died after finishing only a draft of the first part of the chapter, on the Prairie Plains tribes. My main argument in this chapter (Eggan & Maxwell, 2001) didn't change substantially from that in the previous paper, although I was able to draw on more recent research to support that argument. In addition, I was clearer that I was proposing a *causal* explanation; one section of the chapter was labeled "Causes of Terminology Patterns." Finally, I linked my emphasis on the diversity of tribes' responses to moving onto the Plains with evolutionary theory in biology, arguing that "there was more than one way of adapting to the Plains environment," and citing Gould (1989, 1996) on the centrality of variation for evolutionary theory generally (see Chapter 4). Such an evolutionary model was an important part (although not a well-developed one) of my theory of social change, which assumed that *individual* variations in behavior and terminological use, if beneficial to these individuals, would likely be noticed, copied, and spread, leading in this situation to more general social change.[2]

The changes in my approach to this research topic exhibit a clear progression from a largely positivist framing of the problem, to a conflict between a positivist and an interpretive/constructivist understanding, to an implicitly, although not explicitly, critical realist analysis. The realism, though implicit, was manifested in several aspects of the final argument. First, I described an explicit *process* by which the changes could have occurred, outlining a plausible sequence of events that could have led to the documented outcome. (This was a major change from my first approach to this topic, which paid essentially no attention to process, simply appealing to associations between variables.) I provided some evidence supporting this process, and other evidence that was inconsistent with competing explanations for this outcome. My argument thus constituted a realist mechanism for Eggan's theory that the changes were an adaptation to the Plains environment, a result of the need for increased solidarity and cooperation.

Second, I treated both meanings and behaviors, as well as the physical and social environment, as real phenomena that causally influence one another. This acceptance of both physical and mental phenomena as real was a critical piece of my argument against reflectionist theories of kinship, since

---

[2] This is *not* an endorsement of the biologist Richard Dawkins's idea of "memes," which he saw as the cultural analogue of genes, using this idea to develop a selectionist theory of cultural evolution that was modeled on biological evolution (1976). Aside from problems with the selectionist approach as a general model of social and cultural change (Fracchia & Lewontin, 1999, 2005), I have serious ontological concerns about memes. While we have a fairly adequate idea of what genes are, ontologically, and how they function, we have no such understanding of memes; the entire theory rests on an IOU that there really is something that this concept stands for, and that memes are "transmitted" from one individual to another in some meaningful sense. (My realist treatment of the acquisition of meaning, in Chapter 10, seriously challenges this view.) While I see individual learning and behavior change as potentially adaptive, and capable of generating social and cultural change, I am skeptical that what has come to be called "memetics" can constitute the basis for a general theory of such change (cf. Atran, 2002; Atran & Medin, 2008, p. 155 ff.).

the recognition of meanings as causally interacting with other phenomena challenged any automatic assumption that they were simply a reflection of social-structural and behavioral realities. This opened up the possibility for multiple sorts of interaction between the two, which could be context-specific rather than general. It also led to my conclusion that the ideological or tactical uses of kin terms (employing their designative meanings as social tools) could have led to both behavioral and social-structural changes in kin relationships and, eventually, to changes in the designative meanings of the terms.

Third, I assumed that each tribe's situation was potentially unique, requiring an understanding of the actual conditions and processes that were involved in the changes that occurred in this tribe's transition to a Plains way of life. In this, I implicitly accepted the validity of causal explanation in single cases, and anticipated Pawson and Tilley's realist principle (1997) that mechanism + context = outcome. My argument was also an example of Becker's account (1990) of how qualitative findings can be generalized—not by simply applying these findings to a wider range of phenomena, but by developing a theory of the processes involved, one that applies to other settings, but may result in different outcomes when the contextual influences differ. I also rejected the implicit Platonism of much quantitative social research, which saw common patterns and general laws, rather than individual diversity, as the fundamental reality.

Finally, in the argument in my paper (Maxwell, 1978) I frequently invoked the logic of testing a theory against the available evidence and competing theories. This included testing both my own theory ("An important test of the theory proposed here. . . ," p. 18; "Several implications follow from this hypothesis. . . . Blackfoot kin terminology bears out these predictions," p. 22) and competing explanations ("Contrary to Murdock's argument, the differences between Plains and surrounding tribes are not correlated with differences in marital residence, descent, kin group exogamy, or forms of marriage," p. 14).

These four aspects of my final approach to explaining Plains Indian social organization embodied the realist concepts that I described in Chapters 2–4 and 8: meanings, causal processes, and diversity as real phenomena, and validity as a matter of using available evidence to test proposed conclusions. It was not until much later that I understood all of these *as* implications of a critical realist perspective, but it is clear that my "logic-in-use," if not my "reconstructed logic" (Kaplan, 1964, p. 8) was essentially realist. Eventually, like the character in Moliere's play *Le Bourgeois Gentilhomme* who was delighted to discover that all his life he had been speaking prose, I was delighted to learn that there was a term for the way I was thinking: critical realism.

10

Meaning and Diversity in Inuit Kinship and Culture

In this chapter, I present a second example of how realism has informed my approach to a qualitative study. This example differs from the previous one in a number of important ways:

1. Rather than depending entirely on written sources, this research was a year-long ethnographic study, conducted in an Inuit community in northern Canada, which was the basis for my doctoral dissertation.

2. The focus of the study was primarily on the meaning that the Inuit in this community attached to social relations, particularly to kinship, rather than on explaining patterns of meaning and social structure across different cultural groups.

3. Because I was able to collect data on individuals' conceptualizations of kinship and social relations, I was particularly interested in the diversity of meanings within this community, an issue (addressed in Chapters 2 and 4) for which the data sources used in the first study were rarely applicable.

4. The major focus of Chapter 9 was on my development of a realist understanding of causation in social processes, although a realist approach to meaning and diversity played significant secondary roles in my account. In contrast, this chapter is mainly concerned with a realist understanding of meaning, culture, and diversity, although I connect these to possible causal processes that may have been involved.

5. In contrast to the first study, in which a realist approach only emerged toward the end of the research and was somewhat implicit even then, a realist perspective was present at the beginning of this study, although not well developed, and had an increasingly important influence on my analysis of the data as I completed my dissertation.

One goal of this chapter is to show how a realist approach to qualitative research is compatible with an interpretive understanding of meaning. A second goal is to show how the nature of, and reasons for, significant diversity in the conceptions of kinship held by these Inuit support a realist understanding of meaning and diversity.

My original plan when I entered graduate school had been to study Inuit adaptations to the Arctic environment. This was an outgrowth of my undergraduate interest in cultural ecology, an interest that also informed my study of Plains Indian social organization. Although my theoretical focus shifted to kinship and cultural theory, I had by then invested considerable time in learning about Inuit society and culture, and I was able to build on previous dissertation research on Inuit kinship conducted by several students at Chicago. As I described in Chapter 9, in preparing for my dissertation I did extensive library research on the philosophy of mind and on the theory of culture; this was my first encounter with explicitly realist ideas, and these helped shape my conception of culture.

This exposure to realist work in philosophy was strongly reinforced after I returned to Chicago from my field research, when I became acquainted with the philosopher William Wimsatt, with whom I had many discussions on the philosophy of the social sciences. In particular, Wimsatt introduced me to the work of Donald Campbell, whose advocacy of critical realism I discussed in Chapter 1.

My fieldwork situation in the community I studied was not ideal. I made a number of mistakes in my initial establishment of relations with the inhabitants of this community, and the resulting relationships both constrained and facilitated my data collection, in ways similar to those described by Briggs (1970) and Abu-Lughod (1986); I addressed this issue in general terms in Chapter 6. An additional factor was my own personality. I am basically shy, and do not interact easily with strangers. Since these traits are described in the literature as characteristic of Inuit as well, I had thought that I might fit in better in this culture than in others that emphasized a more outgoing and talkative norm of interaction. This proved not to be the case.

My first explicit recognition of this was about three months after I arrived, when the man in whose house I was living at the time (who spoke fairly good English) asked me if I knew why people don't like someone. When I said I didn't understand, he said, "You! Do you know why people don't like you?" He explained that Inuit like people who are cheerful and talkative, make jokes, and kid around a lot; I don't do this, and therefore people are uncomfortable around me. He also said that people don't like someone who's unhappy, and that people think I'm unhappy. This attitude was confirmed by others; someone who is *uqadluriktuq*, "he speaks easily and well," tends to be well liked. I was repeatedly chided for not being talkative and outgoing, but was only partly successful in trying to correct this. Briggs, who conducted her research in a nearby region (and one from which many Inuit in my community had immigrated) quoted one of her informants as saying, "People who joke are not frightening," and went on to explain that

> the feeling [he] was expressing is one that is very characteristic of Eskimos: a fear of people who do not openly demonstrate their good-will by happy (*quvia*) behavior, by smiling, laughing, and joking. Unhappiness is often equated with hostility. . . . A happy person, on the other hand, is a safe person. (1970, pp. 47–48)

Later in my stay, the man who had explained to me why people didn't like me commented that people seemed to want me to live with them, that I was happier now than before.

This incident was significant for my development of a theory of community that challenged the traditional view that solidarity and community are necessarily based on similarities, as discussed in Chapter 4. As I argue there, the actual processes of interaction, and the relationships created by these, are also important, and these relationships may be based on complementarity rather than similarity. I was told by several Inuit that they generally liked Whites who were talkative and outgoing, because they removed the burden of sustaining conversation from the Inuit themselves.

This theory also informed my conceptualization of research relationships as a key component of research design, described in Chapter 6. Key factors in my establishing relationships with members of this community were based on complementarity rather than similarity: playing my banjo, giving guitar lessons to many younger Inuit, teaching classes in English, and the additional income that I provided for the families with whom I stayed.

My methods were the usual anthropological strategies of participant observation and interviewing. I lived with a series of different families while I was there, paying for room and board on a monthly basis, so I had many opportunities to observe interactions among kin and relations between parents and children. My proficiency in Inuktitut was not particularly good when I arrived, due mainly to the absence of available tapes for learning the language. However, as a result of some tapes and workbooks given to me by a linguist with the government of the Northwest Territories whom I met on my way to this community, and my immersion in Inuktitut-speaking families, I eventually became proficient enough to carry on a conversation in Inuktitut with someone who was willing to speak somewhat more slowly than was typical and to repeat words that I missed. I was also able, toward the end of my stay, to follow a good part of everyday conversation between Inuit when situational cues were available. I ended up doing virtually all of my interviewing in Inuktitut. (For details on my situation and methods, see Maxwell, 1986.)

My investigation of Inuit kin terminology was based on Schneider's approach, focusing primarily on their understanding of kinship, and not on their attitudes and behavior toward kin. My goal was to elucidate the conceptual system underlying behavior ("underlying" in the sense that the immediate cause of all behavior is the system of concepts, beliefs, values, intentions, and perceptions held by the actor), which had been much less adequately studied than behavioral norms and attitudes.

This investigation was strongly influenced by a major controversy in the theory of kinship at the time of my study, a dispute between two groups of anthropologists with conflicting views on the nature of kinship. One group, prominently represented by Harold Scheffler (e.g., 1972), held that kin terms in all societies fundamentally referred to biological relationships (as these were understood by the members of the society in question), and that other, nonbiological meanings of these terms were a metaphoric extension of the biological meanings. The other group, mainly consisting of David Schneider (e.g., 1968) and his former students, argued that biological meanings were only one possible meaning of kin terms, and that other meanings could be equally, if not more, fundamental.

My research questions for this study were the following:

1. What are the meanings of the terms that these Inuit use for relatives?

2. How are these meanings related to one another?

3. What roles do these meanings play in the social life of the community?

The term "relatives" is critical here, since many anthropological studies of kinship have used the researcher's prior, etic definition of "relative" (usually based on biological relationship) as a starting point for the investigation. In contrast, following Schneider (1968), I sought to discover how these Inuit themselves conceptualize "relatives," and to gain an emic understanding not only of particular terms, but of their entire conceptualization of relatedness.

For this reason, a key focus of my investigation was the concept of *ila*, the term regularly used for relatives. Although the meaning of this term substantially overlaps with the English term "relative," it has a wider range of meanings (Example 10.1), and this full set of meanings is important for understanding the ways in which these Inuit think about relationship. My definition of "kin term," therefore, was not based on my own prior theory, but was drawn from the answers I received to the question *qanuq ilagiviuk*, "How do you have him/ her as an *ila*?" This approach was based on my premise that meaning is a real phenomenon that is not definable in terms of, or reducible to, behavior, as explained in Chapter 2, and that requires an investigative strategy that does not impose the researcher's own assumptions and definitions.

Example 10.1

The Meanings of *Ila*

The central term in the Inuit conception of kinship is *ila*. It has a range of meanings that are not confined to kinship, and an understanding of the significance and implications of the term in the area of kinship requires an analysis of both the kinship and nonkinship meanings that it possesses.

In its most general sense, *ila* means "part" or "piece." It is most commonly used, not for a part of a homogeneous mass or for one of a number of objects that simply happen to be together, but for something that has a separable identity yet is a necessary or functioning part of a larger whole, such as a part of a motor or harpoon. *Ila* forms the base for numerous words such as *ilaku*, "something with a part missing," *ilaaqtuq*, "he repairs (something with a piece missing)," and *ilaksaq*, "potential *ila*," used for material for mending or for a new part to repair something.

When used to refer to persons, *ila* has the general meaning of "partner" or "companion." It is the standard term for someone who accompanies one on a trip; one of the two verbs regularly used to mean "he accompanies," *ilauvuq*, means literally "he is an *ila*," and *ila* in this sense is synonymous with *piqati*, "companion." It also is used for any coparticipant in some activity, in particular for persons on the same side in a fight or in a game involving two teams, who are termed *ilagiit*. In these contexts, this meaning of *ila* takes precedence over the use of *ila* to mean "relative." One woman, referring to her former companions in an English class that I conducted during part of my stay in this community, used the term *ilaviniit*, "former *ilait*"; her husband laughed, because *ilaviniit* is commonly used in Christian hymns to refer to deceased relatives.

When talking about the uses of the term in this broader sense, informants emphasized not the physical proximity of the individuals classed as *ilagiit*, but the cooperation and assistance involved. For example, one informant gave *ikajuqtigiit*, "those who help one another," as synonymous with *ilagiit*, in the sense of people on one side in a game. Informants often gave as examples of ilagiit situations in which one person was more capable than another, and thus able to help the other.

(Continued)

(Continued)

Thus, one informant, discussing religion with me, said, "Jesus has me as an *ila*," elaborating on how God will take care of him.

The use of *ila* to designate genealogical relatives shares much of the meaning of these more general uses of the term. In kinship contexts, *ila* often is opposed to *adlaq*, "stranger, nonrelative." In discussing these two terms, informants emphasized the importance of helping, love, being "mindful" and concerned, and not being afraid or uneasy as distinguishing *ilait* from *adlait*.

However, the meaning of *ila* also involves the concept of genealogical connection. Informants would discuss in abstract genealogical terms which kinsmen were one's *ilait* and which were not. One informant, speaking of a third person who was present and participating in the conversation, said, "Although I love him, he's not my *ila*, but my *adlaq*," explaining that his (the speaker's) relatives were here, while the other person's relatives were in another settlement.

The salience of both genealogical connection and social relationship for whether someone is considered a relative is exemplified by an incident that occurred when I was collecting genealogies. The informant had been adopted when he was an infant, and had "biological" brothers in another settlement whom he had never seen, but with whom he corresponded, sent pictures, and kept up a connection. When I asked how he was related to his brothers' wives (whom he also had never seen), he immediately and unequivocally replied that he wasn't related to them; then, after thinking about this, he retracted his statement and gave an "in-law" term.

Source: Adapted from Maxwell (1986).

However, I was also interested in understanding the relationship between conceptualization and behavior, and how behavior (including the use of kin terms) is influenced by the actual context in which it occurs, as well as by the conceptual model held by the person. This issue was important in my development of a theory of the changes that occurred in Plains Indian kinship, as described in Chapter 9, but here, in contrast, I was more concerned with the diversity of meanings and uses, and how meaning and use were interrelated. I also paid attention to behavior insofar as it constituted evidence regarding the conceptual system(s) held by these Inuit. This was most directly employed in one chapter of my dissertation, in which I provided an analysis of my observations on the treatment (and mistreatment) of children, and how these supported my theory of these Inuit's conceptualization of social relationship.

The Meaning of Kinship

As Example 10.1 illustrates, the term *ila* has multiple meanings. Is it plausible to argue, as some kinship theorists claimed, that biological relationship is the primary, "real" meaning of *ila* in a kinship context, and that other meanings are secondary and metaphorical? This was the central theoretical issue that my study was intended to address. A key type of evidence for answering this question is the meaning of the suffixes *dlataaq* and *mmarik*, which are generally translated as "real" and "really." Like the English terms, these suffixes can mean both "truly" and "very." Thus, *inummarik*, "a real Eskimo," can mean both a true Eskimo, biologically, or a person who is very Eskimo either in physical features or in maintaining a traditional way of life.

When used with kin terms, *dlataaq* and *mmarik* have a number of different meanings. They are most commonly used to distinguish natal relatives (members of the family into which one was born) from adoptive or step relationships. For example, one's natal father is one's *ataatadlataaq*, while one's stepfather is not one's *ataatadlataaq*, but one's *ataataksaq*. However, the former is not the same as biological relationship. In cases of spouse-exchange, *ataatadlataaq* is used for the speaker's natal father (one's mother's husband), rather than for the speaker's mother's exchange-partner (and one's presumed biological father), who is one's *ataataksaq*. In contrast, in a polyandrous marriage, both husbands of one's mother are one's *ataatadlataaq*.

However, *dlataaq* and *mmarik* can mean other things besides natal relationship. These meanings are much less common in normal conversation, but many informants readily used them in explaining particular terms to me. For example, they can be used for close rather than distant genealogical relatives denoted by the same term (e.g., first rather than second cousins), for relationships based on a first marriage as opposed to those resulting from remarriage, and to distinguish biological relationships from purely social ones. The last of these is uncommon, and was limited to a few informants. Most people would accept my use of the terms in this sense, but did not spontaneously use *dlataaq* to refer to a person's biological father in discussing situations in which the person's biological father and social father were different, such as having a White biological father.

Which of these different meanings of *dlataaq* is intended by the speaker, and understood by the hearer, depends on the speech context, and the term is therefore a "shifter" (Silverstein, 1976), indexing features of the speech situation as well as communicating situation-independent referential meanings.

This point was also made by Kelley (1982, p. 74) with respect to the English term "real"; he stated that "real" does not in itself designate a particular sufficiency condition for the use of a kin term, but simply denotes the sufficiency condition that is considered to be critical to a given conversation. He argued that the statistical predominance of references to biological ties for American kin terms is a result of Americans' belief that the social order derives from the natural order rather than vice versa. This belief is not present to the same extent in Inuit culture.

If *dlataaq* derives part of its meaning in a specific use from the context of that use, different persons would be expected to interpret these meanings differently when these terms are used without any particular context, as in abstract discussion of the meaning of terms. This is in fact what happens. For example, I asked a number of people if one's cousin of the opposite sex (*ani* or *najak*, the same term as is used for brother or sister) is one's *anidlataaq* or *najadlataaq*. Most of them replied that these cousins would be *dlataaq*, as long as they were not adopted or step relatives, although several said that if asked about the relationship they would explain that they had different parents. A minority of my informants, however, employed the criterion of genealogical distance rather than natal relationship; they denied that opposite-sex cousins are *dlataaq*, saying that *dlataaq* refers only to *nangminiik* (one's own siblings).

As was often the case in my investigation of alternative cognitive models, informants would usually give only one interpretation, without recognizing that there were other possibilities; only if I raised these other possibilities would they become aware of them. Some informants used different models at different times without being aware of the discrepancy, but when I pointed out the difference they would agree that there were different "correct" ways of answering the question. Other informants maintained that their model was the "correct" one, and that others were incorrect.

When used with *ila* rather than with particular kin terms, informants would often use *dlattaq* and *mmarik* to distinguish narrower and more focal meanings from peripheral and more inclusive ones. Two criteria can be identified in these "focal" meanings marked by *dlataaq* and *mmarik*: genealogical closeness and social closeness. There is a term, *ilammarigiit*, "those who are real relatives to one another," that is used for one's genealogically closest kin. Whenever I was given a genealogical definition of this term, it was limited to the children and grandchildren of a single couple.

However, informants also used *iladlattaq* and *ilammarik*, usually the latter, to mark social rather than genealogical closeness. The explanations of social closeness given for this term invoked the concepts of love, concern, "proper" attitude, and assistance mentioned previously as part of the meaning of *ila*. One informant defined *ilammarigiit* as *ikajuqpaktut*, "those who frequently help (one another)," explaining that if your relatives treated you well and loved you, they would be *ilammariit*, while if they didn't they would be *adlait*. When I asked about the relative importance of genealogical connection and proper behavior for the meaning of *ilammarigiit*, he replied that one's attitude and behavior were most important, that in principle anyone in the world could be one's *ilammarik* if that person acted and thought in the right way (*pitsiaqpat, isumatsiaqpat*) toward one.

The conclusion that I drew from this analysis of the meanings of *dlataaq* and *mmarik* in kinship contexts is that these suffixes can be used to convey a variety of distinctions, and that these distinctions fall into two categories, genealogical and social. This supports the earlier analysis of the term *ila* itself, which concluded that the term has two central meanings, genealogical connection and social relatedness.

The Treatment of Children

This conclusion is supported by my investigation of the treatment of children in this community. The central concept pertaining to the relationship between parents and children is *nagli*, which was translated by my English-speaking informants as "love." The term appears frequently in my interviews regarding proper behavior, not only between parents and children, but also between relatives in general. It is also frequently used in everyday conversation to and about children; the expression *naglingnaqtuq*, "causes one to feel *nagli*," is particularly common (see Briggs, 1970). The affection that Inuit show to small children is legendary, and although there are exceptions to the rule that children are always deeply loved (to be discussed shortly), this affection is a striking feature of Inuit family life (Briggs, 1970).

However, for these Inuit, the bond between parent and child is not felt to be something that exists, even in potential form, at birth, but something that develops as a result of the love and affection that the child is given by its parents. A child's mind (*isuma*) is believed to be unformed at birth, and develops gradually during the first few years of life, as a result of the care and attention that it is given by its parents. It is one of the reasons given by Inuit for their indulgence of children and their extreme reluctance to directly thwart their wishes or interfere with their actions; because small children lack *isuma*, they say, it is no use trying to get them to conform to socially acceptable behavior. The relationship between parent and child is not felt to be the result of any biological connection between them but develops from their interaction.

This belief is consistent with the high rate of adoption of children in this community. The relationship that exists between a child adopted as an infant and its adoptive parents not only is stronger, but is felt naturally to be stronger, than that with its natal parents. (The terms *tiguaq*, "adopted child," and *tiguaqsi*, "adoptive parent," are kin terms in the strict sense; that is, they are accepted answers to the question *qanuq ilagiviuk?*, "How are you related to him or her?") The child's relationship to its natal parents, in contrast, involves a considerable degree of optionality on the part of both the parents and child, ranging from a close and friendly relationship, almost a "second family," to a nearly complete lack of contact or concern. (This possibility was not present for the relationship of *illegitimate* children with their fathers, where the relationship was not natal, but only biological; in no case that I know of did the father attempt to maintain a relationship with the child.) This predominance of adoptive over natal ties was also reflected in the genealogical information I collected. In listing their children, informants frequently forgot to mention natal children who had been given away in adoption, while this never occurred for children whom they had adopted. I knew of several families who had adopted children but also given away natal children of their own. It seems likely that one reason why an adopted child's relationship to its natal parents is frankly and openly accepted by Inuit, in comparison to the views of many Americans, is that the natal relationship is not seen as a serious threat to the child's ties to its adoptive parents.

It is, however, well established that some Inuit children *are* mistreated—in particular, orphans (*iliarjuk*), that is, children whose parents die after they are past infancy. The nature of the mistreatment varies, ranging from ridicule, teasing, and lack of affection to serious beating. Several children in this community, during or shortly before my fieldwork there, were injured seriously enough that the nurse took official action to have them removed from the families they were living with.

The most striking thing, to me, about such mistreatment was the almost complete absence of any attempt to conceal it from me (at least initially) or from other Inuit, and the extent to which others accepted and even participated in it. This was not universally the case for all children; some children were mistreated by their parents, but were treated normally by at least some other people. However, in at least one case (the one I happen to be most familiar with) the child was teased and tormented by virtually everyone in the settlement. Furthermore, the child's siblings were encouraged to do this. This was admittedly an extreme case, a child who was mentally challenged and had severe behavior problems. However, the pattern was repeated to a lesser degree with other children.

When I asked, in general terms, about the treatment of children, the explanations that I was given were in terms of the characteristics of the parents; some people do not love their children as much as others. This clearly is not an adequate account; parents who mistreated one child invariably were indulgent and affectionate toward their other children. In fact, one man who was extremely caring and protective toward his children, and forthright in his disapproval of the father of the child just mentioned, was the head of a family from whom one child was removed by Social Services because of beatings and neglect. While it is true that Inuit parents vary in their treatment of children, this cannot account for the instances of mistreatment that I documented.

Rousseau (1970, pp. 106–107) gave as the explanation for this treatment the fact that an orphan has become attached to its own parents, and thus cannot be assimilated into the family as a child adopted as an infant could. It is the care given to the child, he argues, rather than the biological relationship, that is the determining factor. His informants said that for orphans, and other stepchildren, there has been no opportunity to become attached to the child. The data I collected on specific cases of mistreatment support this interpretation. In all instances but two, the mistreated child was adopted, and the exceptions are the classic ones that prove the rule: children who had a serious illness during infancy, and had been out of the community in a hospital for a good part of the first several years of life. These children never established a normal bond with their parents on their return, and were treated similarly to children who are adopted after infancy.

The normal treatment of children thus depends on the establishment of a relationship of love, affection, and caring between parent and child, and not primarily on community norms or a definition of biological relatedness. When this relationship between parent and child fails to establish itself, either because of innate characteristics of the child or of contingencies affecting contact between parent and child during childhood, the treatment of the child suffers. Children are treated well if they are loved; if they are not loved, there is little to enjoin their care beyond the provision of physical needs, and equally little to prevent their abuse.

A number of features of the meaning and use of kin terms can be seen as consequences of this understanding of the parent-child bond. First, it explains why adoptive relatives are considered genealogically related; that is, these kin are considered *ilait* in abstraction, to the same extent as natal kin, regardless of their actual social relationship to the speaker. It also explains why the "adoptive" terms are not used for orphans and other children adopted later in life. In such cases the normal bond between parent and child has not been established, and the relationship usually lacks the closeness and affection that typically exist when the child is born into the family or adopted at birth.

Thus, the conceptualization of the parent-child bond parallels my analysis of kin terms in its emphasis on love rather than putative biological connection as the basis for the relationship between parents and children. Although natal ties (but not biological relationships in the strict sense) are recognized as socially significant, they are often overridden by social relationship as a determinant of behavior. Along with other evidence, this explanation supports the fundamental importance of *nagli* (love) in the Inuit worldview, and thus makes more plausible my analysis of Inuit kin terminology, in which *nagli* is of at least equal importance to biology in the meaning of the kin terms and of the term *ila.*

A Realist Theory of Inuit Kinship

The central issue that I sought to resolve was the relative importance of bio-logical and nonbiological criteria in the meaning and use of kin terms in this community. I concluded that my analysis did not support Scheffler's claim (1972) that "most, perhaps all" systems of social classification that have been considered kin terminologies are based on presumed connection through pro-creation and birth, with other meanings being secondary. I argued that *both* natal relationship and the concept of *nagli*, which is similar to what Schneider (1968) called "diffuse, enduring solidarity," are centrally involved in the mean-ing of kin terms in this community.

In order to test this theory, I constructed the strongest "Schefflerian" alternative explanation for my data that I could, one that treated all non-biological meanings as metaphorical and not part of the signification of the term (Maxwell, 1986, pp. 197–198). As a result, I accepted some aspects of Scheffler's analysis, in particular that many of the meanings of kin terms *are* genealogical extensions from a "primary" meaning. However, I found several types of evidence that were not compatible with this analysis as a general char-acterization of kinship in this community. As described earlier, some mean-ings of the term *ataata*, "father," emphasize natal rather than procreational relationship—a person's mother's husband, not the presumed biological father, is the person's *ataatadlataaq*, "real father." In addition, my analysis of the term *ila* showed that many people held that the classification of individuals as *ilamariit*, "real relatives," was determined as much by the social relationship one had with them as by any biological or natal connection.

I also argued, similarly to my account of Plains Indian kinship described in Chapter 9, that this emphasis on attitudinal and behavioral criteria in the definition of relatives, rather than a strictly genealogical definition, would have been of considerable adaptive value in the Arctic environment, providing wide-ranging ties and considerable flexibility in social organization. The ecological reasons for the value of this extended support network and flexibility cannot be discussed in detail here, but are connected to the uncertainty of resources, the consequent frequent need to move to new locations, and the importance of sharing. (I was told repeatedly that the difference between Whites and Inuit was that Inuit share everything and Whites don't.) These Inuit place consider-able importance on creating and extending kin ties, and the "negotiability" of Inuit social organization has been noted by many researchers. In contrast, for the Inuit of Northwest Alaska, where environmental resources were more stable, settlements were larger, and social organization more complex and formalized, a "Schlefflerian" analysis of the kin terminology seems more valid (Burch, 1975, pp. 9–26).

This analysis was informed by a realist perspective in several ways. First, I treated the meanings of kin terms, and of terms such as *ila* and *dlataaq*, as real phenomena that are causally related to behavior, and I saw both meaning and behavior as influenced by the particular context in which these occurred, as well as by the abstract meanings of the terms. The meanings held by the members of this community form a cultural system, but one that is deeply interconnected with behavioral and physical phenomena, rather than constituting a separate and independent realm. Second, I argued that these Inuit have what Guemple (1972) called a "social metaphysic" that emphasizes locality and actual participation as the primary bases for social connection, rather than virtual relationships such as shared biological substance (see Chapter 4), and that this metaphysic is intrinsic to the meaning of kinship, which is the main form of relationship in these communities. (This is an example of what I called, in Chapter 4, a contiguity-based, rather than a similarity-based, ideology for solidarity.) This metaphysic is embodied in the general meaning of the term *ila*, described earlier, as well as in Inuit values regarding sharing and cooperation.

The other issue that I sought to investigate was the nature and extent of intracultural diversity in the meanings attached to kinship, and I now turn to this issue.

Diversity of Meanings in Inuit Culture

As I argued in Chapters 2 and 4, diversity of meaning within a culture is an almost unavoidable implication of a realist concept of culture, an implication that sharply contrasts with the traditional view of culture, which has taken sharing and social transmission as the defining features of culture. I therefore set out to deliberately look for individual differences in meanings, and not to assume commonality. This did not entail any differences from normal qualitative data collection procedures (primarily interviewing and observation), but it required a different approach to analysis, by not prioritizing a search for, and categorizing of, similar statements or behaviors in my data, and by paying equal attention to differences and to the particular contexts in which these occurred (Chapter 8).

A striking example of the kind of diversity that I was looking for emerged entirely by accident. I had been interested in Berlin and Kay's cross-cultural analysis of color terms (e.g., 1991), and conducted some preliminary investigation of the meanings of color terms with a few Inuit in this community. Berlin and Kay argued that the meaning of color terms in most languages involves a specific "focal" color that is seen as the best exemplar of each term, and a much broader region of the color spectrum for which the term is seen as appropriate. I cut out a large number of different-colored squares of construction paper (that I got from the community school), and sat down one evening with two Inuit (an older man who spoke no English, and his son), to see how they would classify these.

The Inuit language has five basic color terms, for black, white, red, yellow, and a term that includes both blue and green (*tungujuktuq*), plus other terms that are modifications of these. After a few minutes of sorting my paper squares by terms, the son said that there were really only five colors, picking a square for each term. For red and yellow, he picked what we would call a fairly "pure" example. For the term *tungujuktuq*, he picked up a blue square. His father looked at him with surprise and said, "No, *this* is *tungujuktuq*," picking up a bright green square. The son, looking equally surprised, replied, "No, *this* is *tungujuktuq*," pointing to the blue square. This exchange continued a few more times, and then the father said, "Huh, we disagree," and the topic was completely dropped.

This example illustrates several key points. First, diversity of conceptualizations may be largely invisible when this diversity pertains to the focal meaning of a term, rather than to the range of things to which it may appropriately be applied. Second, these Inuit do not see diversity as inherently problematic, something that needs to be "resolved" in order to maintain a relationship.

The latter point was reinforced in numerous ways during my research. These Inuit did not assume shared meanings or consensus among themselves, or even presume to know what another person thought about some issue. When I asked one man, whom I had been talking with (in Inuktitut) about kinship, whether other people held the same view that he had expressed, he replied that he didn't know; pointing to his wife, who was sitting nearby, he said, "I've been married to her for 20 years, and I have no idea what she thinks." Often, when I asked about the meaning of a term, the person would reply, "To me, it means. . . ."

Diverse responses to my questions about the meaning of kin terms, and diverse uses of these terms in people's genealogies, were frequent. Some of this diversity was due to the fact that the inhabitants of this community consisted of people from two different locations, with slight dialectal differences. However, other differences were not associated with this division, and some were idiosyncratic. In some cases, informants differed on the precise genealogical meaning of a term, but said that it could be used for a wider range of relatives; this is similar to the situation for *tungujuktuq* described earlier. For example, one woman, who had denied that a particular usage was correct, backtracked when I pointed out just such a usage in her own genealogy, saying that such terms could be used to make the relationship clearer to someone. This is reinforced by the high degree of optionality that exists in the use of many kin terms.

The way in which the meaning of kin terms (and of words in general) is learned in this community suggests a plausible process for the development of such diversity. Terms are not learned through abstract definition, but through observing usage. Since usage doesn't specify the core meaning of a term, it is understandable that individuals would construct different understandings of this, which would not always affect their use of the terms. For example, there are two sets of grandparental terms in use in this community, which most people considered to be alternate, synonymous terms. However, one woman held that one set correctly referred only to one's mother's parents, while the other referred to one's father's parents. An examination of this woman's genealogy showed that she in fact used the terms consistently with this distinction. In her case, an accidental difference in usage in her family became incorporated in her cognitive model of the terminology.

In this model, the meanings of terms are not "transmitted" in any direct sense, but are *constructed* by individuals based on their observation of usage. There is no necessity that there be agreement among the meanings held by individuals, only that these meanings result in congruent usage, as I argued in Chapter 2. To the extent that terminological usage is contextually variable, it is not only possible, but likely, that different individuals will develop different meanings for these terms.

The extended example presented in this chapter illustrates several important aspects and implications of a realist approach to qualitative research. First, such an approach is completely compatible with an interpretive perspective on the understanding and analysis of meaning. Interpretive analysis is in fact necessitated, and supported, by a view of meanings as real phenomena, separate from behavior or social structure. Meaning is not reducible to, definable in terms of, or based in an ontological sense on, observations of people's actions, although the latter actions (including people's verbal statements) constitute the *evidence for* any inferences about meaning. This approach contrasts sharply with Geertz's (1973) concept of "thick description," which essentially takes statements about meaning to ultimately *refer to* observable action (Maxwell & Mittapalli, 2008), and denies that in cultural analysis we are making inferences to anything unobservable.

Second, a realist approach to meaning problematizes the traditional definition of culture as inherently shared, as argued in Chapter 2, and directs attention to the ways in which meaning may be distributed rather than shared (Atran & Medin, 2008; Hannerz, 1992; Kronenfeld, 2008; Maxwell, 1999; Wallace, 1970). An understanding of meaning as distributed and diverse also connects to a key premise of postmodernism: the danger of ignoring diversity and creating "totalizing metanarratives" that impose uniformity on the phenomena we study. A realist understanding of meaning entails that the methods of data collection and analysis that we use must be able to discover potentially hidden forms of diversity, and to adequately characterize these, as argued in Chapter 4.

Third, a realist perspective emphasizes the pervasive interconnectedness of meaning, social action, and the physical world, and the influence that each of these has on the others. This influence is in principle two-directional, although the actual degree of influence in each direction depends on the particular situation. This perspective thus leads to a focus on the actual processes of mutual influence. One instance of this, described earlier, is the argument that these Inuit *construct* the meanings they attach to terms on the basis of the actual uses of the terms to which they are exposed, rather than having these meanings somehow immaculately transmitted, individually or socially.

Finally, critical realism incorporates a constructivist epistemology, as described in Chapter 1, in the sense that the understandings and theories we create, although they pertain to a reality outside of our constructions, are never a reflection or "objective" rendition of the phenomena we study. For this reason, our data collection and analysis should be guided by the need not only to make theoretical sense of our data, but also to test our own theories against the most plausible alternative theories and the entire range of data we collect, as argued in Chapter 8. My construction of a "Schefflerian" alternative theory of kinship for this community, and testing my theory against this alternative, is an example of the kind of systematic assessment that a realist approach to qualitative research requires. However, unlike in many of the physical sciences, the outcome will usually not be a clear determination of a single "best" theory. As was the case for my evaluation of Scheffler's and Schneider's theories of the meaning of kinship, it will often be the case that each theory captures some aspect of the reality we are studying, and that a more complex understanding, drawing from multiple theories, is required (Maxwell, 2010a).

Conclusion

My goal in writing this book has been to show how a realist approach can help qualitative researchers design and conduct research that will be more insightful, valid, and useful. I believe that a realist approach can do this by enabling researchers to develop more relevant and insightful theories about the things they study, to plan their strategies and methods to be more productive, valuable, and ethical, and to develop conclusions that more validly indicate what is actually happening in the situations they study. In addition, I also believe that realist approaches are compatible with the research strategies, and methods of data collection and analysis, used by most qualitative researchers.

I suggested that there are four theoretical concepts, ones of considerable importance for qualitative research, for which realism can contribute to better, more useful theorizing: meaning, culture, causation, and diversity. A realist perspective provides a quite different understanding of these issues from either postpositivism or constructivism.

For meaning and culture, a realist approach assumes that these terms refer to real phenomena, not abstractions from observations or constructions with no actual referent. In addition, a realist conception of culture challenges several widely held beliefs about culture, most importantly that culture is by definition shared. The view that culture is a group property, rather than something that is possessed by individuals, and that beliefs and values are differentially distributed in social groups, rather than shared, consequently challenges the widespread assumption that social groups are united by their members' shared beliefs, values, and experiences, and that differences are inherently inimical to social solidarity, as argued in Chapter 4.

Similarly, a realist concept of causality sees actual processes, rather than regularities, as central to this concept. A realist approach can not only get inside the "black box" of typical quantitative approaches to causality, but can provide important support for qualitative researchers' explanations of events and outcomes, and justify the claim that qualitative research is able to credibly identify causal relationships. The understanding of causality as fundamentally local, rather than general, also supports the argument for contiguity, and not simply similarity, as a source of social solidarity.

For qualitative practice, realism can contribute to better strategies for designing a research study and understanding how to modify that design as the study develops. This requires seeing a research design as a real entity, not simply an abstract plan, and paying close attention to what is going on in your research and how to best adapt your design to the context in which it is situated. It also involves seeing your goals, beliefs, and research questions from a realist stance.

It can also inform the selection of settings and participants in ways that contribute to answering research questions; relating to participants in ways that are both ethical and productive; collecting and analyzing data to both answer research questions and generate new questions; and credibly addressing issues of quality and validity for a wider audience.

For data analysis, I have focused on the real relationships manifested in your data, and not simply on the virtual relationships of similarity and difference that are the outcome of coding and thematic analysis. The former require different approaches to analysis (what I call "connecting" analysis), but these have not been systematically developed to the extent that coding has, and are often neglected in textbook presentations of qualitative analysis.

For validity, I have criticized procedural criteria for quality or validity, and presented a realist alternative that focuses on the relationships between your conclusions and the phenomena that these refer to. The latter relationships are more difficult to use in assessing a study's conclusions, but they are ultimately what we want to know, and although evaluating the methods used is one type of relevant evidence about the validity of the conclusions, when employed as the only strategy, it is indirect, incomplete, and unreliable.

I have provided two detailed examples of how some of these ideas have played out in my own research. The Plains example illustrates how realist strategies, in contrast to both positivism and constructivism, can provide credible *explanations* for particular sociocultural phenomena and outcomes, explanations that incorporate meaning, behavior, and social structure and the interactions among these in a specific context. The Inuit example shows how a realist approach to meaning is compatible with interpretive approaches, provides important insights into intracultural diversity and why this exists, and suggests that theories of social solidarity based exclusively on commonalities may be seriously incomplete. In both of these studies I employed a realist strategy of testing my conclusions against alternative interpretations.

I am not advocating realism either as the "correct" approach for qualitative research, or as one that can guarantee better results; no approach can do the latter. I *am* presenting it as a useful conceptual strategy for qualitative researchers, one that can have substantial value for many research projects.

References

Abbott, A. (1992). What do cases do? Some notes on activity in sociological analysis. In C. C. Ragin & H. S. Becker (Eds.), *What is a case? Exploring the foundations of social inquiry* (pp. 53–82). Cambridge, England: Cambridge University Press.

Abbott, A. (2001). *Chaos of disciplines.* Chicago: University of Chicago Press.

Abbott, A. (2004). *Methods of discovery: Heuristics for the social sciences.* New York: W. W. Norton.

Aberle, D. F. (1960). The influence of linguistics on early culture and personality theory. In G. Dole & R. Carneiro (Eds.), *Essays in the science of culture in honor of Leslie A. White* (pp. 1–29). New York: Thomas Y. Crowell.

Abu-Lughod, L. (1986). *Veiled sentiments: Honor and poetry in a Bedouin society.* Berkeley: University of California Press.

Achinstein, P. (2001). *The book of evidence.* Oxford, England: Oxford University Press.

Achinstein, P. (Ed.). (2005). *Scientific evidence: Philosophical theories and applications.* Baltimore: Johns Hopkins University Press.

Agar, M. (1991). The right brain strikes back. In N. G. Fielding & R. M. Lee (Eds.), *Using computers in qualitative research* (pp. 181–194). Thousand Oaks, CA: Sage.

Anyon, J. (2009). *Theory and educational research: Toward critical social explanation.* New York: Routledge.

Archer, M. (1996). *Culture and agency: The place of culture in social theory* (Rev. ed.). Cambridge, England: Cambridge University Press.

Archer, M. (2007). *Making our way though the world: Human reflexivity and social mobility.* Cambridge, England: Cambridge University Press.

Archer, M., Bhaskar, R., Collier, A., Lawson, T., & Norrie, A. (Eds.). (1998). *Critical realism: Essential readings.* London: Routledge.

Argyris, C., & Schoen, D. A. (1974). *Theory in practice: Increasing professional effectiveness.* San Francisco: Jossey-Bass.

Atkinson, P. (1992). The ethnography of a medical setting: Reading, writing, and rhetoric. *Qualitative Health Research, 2,* 451–474.

Atran, S. (2002). *In gods we trust: The evolutionary landscape of religion.* New York: Oxford University Press.

Atran, S., & Medin, D. (2008). *The native mind and the cultural construction of nature.* Cambridge, MA: MIT Press.

Baert, P. (1998). *Social theory in the twentieth century.* New York: New York University Press.

Baldwin, J. R., Faulkner, S. L., Hecht, M. L., & Lindsley, S. L. (2005). *Redefining culture: Perspectives across the disciplines.* Mahwah, NJ: Lawrence Erlbaum.

Barad, K. (2007). *Meeting the universe halfway: Quantum physics and the entanglement of matter and meaning.* Durham, NC: Duke University Press.

Barone, T. (1990). Using the narrative text as an occasion for conspiracy. In E. Eisner & A. Peshkin (Eds.), *Qualitative inquiry in education: The continuing debate* (pp. 305–326). New York: Teachers College Press.

Barth, F. (1987). *Cosmologies in the making: A generative approach to cultural variation in inner New Guinea.* Cambridge, England: Cambridge University Press.

Barthes, R. (1968). *Elements of semiology* (A. Lavers & C. Smith, Trans.). New York: Hill and Wang.

Bates, R. H., Greif, A., Levi, M., Rosenthal, J-L., & Weingast, B. R. (1998). *Analytic narratives.* Princeton, NJ: Princeton University Press.

Bateson, G. (1971). The cybernetics of "self": A theory of alcoholism. *Psychiatry 34*(1), 1–18. Reprinted in Bateson, *Steps to an ecology of mind* (pp. 309–337). San Francisco: Chandler, 1992.

Bateson, M. C. (1989). *Composing a life.* New York: Penguin Books.

Becker, H. S. (1966). The life history and the scientific mosaic. Introduction to C. Shaw, *The jack-roller,* reprinted edition. Chicago: University of Chicago Press. Reprinted in H. Becker, *Sociological work: Method and substance.* New Brunswick, NJ: Transaction Books, 1970.

Becker, H. S. (1970). *Sociological work: Method and substance.* New Brunswick, NJ: Transaction Books.

Becker, H. S. (1986). *Writing for social scientists.* Chicago: University of Chicago Press.

Becker, H. S. (1990). Generalizing from case studies. In E. W. Eisner & A. Peshkin (Eds.), *Qualitative inquiry in education: The continuing debate* (pp. 233–242). New York: Teachers College Press.

Becker, H. S. (1996). The epistemology of qualitative research. In R. Jessor, A. Colby, & R. A. Shweder (Eds.), *Ethnography and human development: Context and meaning in social inquiry* (pp. 205–216). Cambridge, England: Cambridge University Press.

Becker, H. S. (2008). *How to find out how to do qualitative research.* Retrieved February 18, 2011 from http://home.earthlink.net/~hsbecker/articles/NSF.html

Becker, H. S., & Geer, B. (1957). Participant observation and interviewing: A comparison. *Human Organization, 16*(3), 28–32.

Becker, H. S., Geer, B., Hughes, E. C., & Strauss, A. L. (1961). *Boys in white: Student culture in medical school.* Chicago: University of Chicago Press. Reprinted by Transaction Books, 1977.

Bensimon, E. M., & Neumann, A. (1993). *Redesigning collegiate leadership: Teams and teamwork in higher education.* Baltimore: The Johns Hopkins University Press.

Berg, D. N., & Smith, K. K. (1988). *The self in social inquiry: Researching methods.* Thousand Oaks, CA: Sage.

Berkhofer, R. (1973). Clio and the culture concept: Some impressions of a changing relationship in American historiography. In L. Schneider & C. M. Bonjean (Eds.), *The idea of culture in the social sciences* (pp. 77–100). Cambridge, England: Cambridge University Press.

Berlin, B., & Kay, P. (1991). *Basic color terms: Their universality and evolution*. Berkeley: University of California Press.

Bernard, J. (1973). *The sociology of community*. Glenview, IL: Scott, Foresman and Company.

Bernstein, R. J. (1983). *Beyond objectivism and relativism*. Philadelphia: University of Pennsylvania Press.

Bernstein, R. J. (1992). *The new constellation: The ethical-political horizons of modernity-postmodernity*. Cambridge, MA: MIT Press.

Bhaskar, R. (1978). *A realist theory of science* (2nd ed.). Brighton, England: Harvester.

Bhaskar, R. (1986). *Scientific realism and human emancipation*. London: Verso.

Bhaskar, R. (1989). *Reclaiming reality: A critical introduction to contemporary philosophy*. London: Verso.

Bhaskar, R. (2011). *Critical realism: A brief introduction*. London: Routledge.

Bishop, B. (2008). *The big sort: How the clustering of like-minded America is tearing us apart*. Boston: Houghton Mifflin Harcourt.

Bloch, M. (1971). The moral and tactical meaning of kinship terms. *Man, 6*, 79–87.

Blumer, H. (1956). Sociological analysis and the "variable." *American Sociological Review, 22*, 683–690. Reprinted in H. Blumer, *Symbolic interactionism: Perspective and method* (pp. 127–139). Berkeley: University of California Press.

Blumer, H. (1969). The methodological position of symbolic interactionism. In H. Blumer, *Symbolic interactionism: Perspective and method* (pp. 1–60). Berkeley: University of California Press.

Blumstein, P., & Schwartz, P. (1983). *American couples*. New York: Simon and Schuster.

Boaler, J., & Staples, M. (2008). Creating mathematical futures through an equitable teaching approach: The case of Railside school. *Teachers College Record, 110*(3), 608–645.

Bogdan, R., & Biklen, S. K. (2003). *Qualitative research for education: An introduction to theory and methods* (4th ed.). Boston: Allyn & Bacon.

Bohman, J. (1991). *New philosophy of social science*. Cambridge, MA: MIT Press.

Bosk, C. (1979). *Forgive and remember: Managing medical failure*. Chicago: University of Chicago Press.

Boulding, K. (1956). *The image: Knowledge in life and society*. Ann Arbor: University of Michigan Press.

Boyd, R. (2010). Scientific realism. In E. N. Zalta (Ed.), *The Stanford encyclopedia of philosophy (summer 2010 edition)*, http://plato.stanford.edu/archives/sum2010/entries/scientific-realism/

Briggs, C. (1986). *Learning how to ask*. Cambridge, England: Cambridge University Press.

Briggs, D. (2008). Comments on Slavin: Synthesizing causal inferences. *Educational Researcher, 37*(1), 15–22.

Briggs, J. (1970). *Never in anger: Portrait of an Eskimo family*. Cambridge, MA: Harvard University Press.

Brinberg, D., & McGrath, J. E. (1985). *Validity and the research process*. Newbury Park, CA: Sage.

Britan, G. (1978). Experimental and contextual models of program evaluation. *Evaluation and Program Planning, 1*, 229–234.

Brown, L. M., & Gilligan, C. (1992). *Meeting at the crossroads: Women's psychology and girls' development*. Cambridge, MA: Harvard University Press.

Bruner, J. (1986). Two modes of thought. In J. Bruner, *Actual minds, possible worlds* (pp. 11–43). Cambridge, MA: Harvard University Press.

Burbules, N. C., & Rice, S. (1991). Dialogue across differences: Continuing the conversation. *Harvard Educational Review, 61*(4), 393–416.

Burch, E. S., Jr. (1975). *Eskimo kinsmen: Changing family relationships in Northwest Alaska. American Ethnological Society monograph 59*. St. Paul, MN: West.

Burman, E. (2001). Minding the gap: Positivism, psychology, and the politics of qualitative methods. In D. L. Tolman & M. Brydon-Miller (Eds.), *From subjects to subjectivities: A handbook of interpretive and participatory methods* (pp. 259–275). New York: New York University Press.

Callinicos, A. (1995). *Theories and narratives: Reflections on the philosophy of history.* Durham, NC: Duke University Press.

Campbell, D. T. (1974). Evolutionary epistemology. In P. A. Schilpp (Ed.), *The philosophy of Karl Popper* (pp. 413–463). Reprinted in Campbell, D. T. (1988). *Methodology and epistemology for social science: Selected papers* (S. Overman, Ed.) (pp. 393–434). Chicago: University of Chicago Press.

Campbell, D. T. (1986). Science's social system of validity-enhancing collective belief change and the problems of the social sciences. In D. W. Fiske & R. A. Shweder (Eds.), *Metatheory in social science: Pluralisms and subjectivities* (pp. 108–135). Chicago: University of Chicago Press.

Campbell, D. T. (1988). *Methodology and epistemology for social science: Selected papers* (S. Overman, Ed.). Chicago: University of Chicago Press.

Campbell, D. T., & Stanley, J. (1963). Experimental and quasi-experimental designs for research on teaching. In N. L. Gage (Ed.), *Handbook of research on teaching* (pp. 171–246). Chicago: Rand McNally.

Carruthers, P. (2009). Invertebrate concepts confront the generality constraint (and win). In R. Lurz (Ed.), *The philosophy of animal minds* (pp. 89–107). Cambridge, England: Cambridge University Press.

Carter, B., & New, C. (2004). *Making realism work: Realist social theory and empirical research.* London: Routledge.

Cartwright, N. (1999). *The dappled world: A study of the boundaries of science.* Cambridge, England: Cambridge University Press.

Cartwright, N. (2007). *Hunting causes and using them.* Cambridge, England: Cambridge University Press.

Chambers, E. (2000). Applied ethnography. In N. K. Denzin & Y. S. Lincoln (Eds.), *SAGE handbook of qualitative research* (2nd ed.) (pp. 851–869). Thousand Oaks, CA: Sage.

Chandler, J., Davidson, A., & Harootunian, H. (1994). *Questions of evidence: Proof, practice, and persuasion across the disciplines.* Chicago: University of Chicago Press.

Clark, A. M. (2008). Critical realism. In L. Given (Ed.), *The SAGE encyclopedia of qualitative research methods* (pp. 167–170). Thousand Oaks, CA: Sage.

Coffey, A., & Atkinson, P. (1996). *Making sense of qualitative data: Complementary research strategies.* Thousand Oaks, CA: Sage.

Cole, M. (1991). Conclusion. In L. B. Resnick, J. M. Levine, & S. D. Teasley (Eds.), *Perspectives on socially shared cognition* (pp. 398–417). Washington, DC: American Psychological Association.

Cook, T. D., & Campbell, D. T. (1979). *Quasi-experimentation: Design and analysis issues for field settings.* Boston: Houghton-Mifflin.

Cook, T. D., Hunt, H. D., & Murphy, R. F. (2000). Comer's school development program in Chicago: A theory-based evaluation. *American Educational Research Journal, 37*, 535–597.

Corlett, W. (1989). *Community without unity: A politics of Derridean extravagance.* Durham, NC: Duke University Press.

Cottrell, C. (1965). *Changes in Crow kinship.* Unpublished master's thesis, University of Chicago.

Coventry, A. (2006). *Hume's theory of causation: A quasi-realist interpretation.* London: Continuum.

D'Andrade, R. (1984). Cultural meaning systems. In R. A. Shweder & R. A. LeVine (Eds.), *Culture theory: Essays on mind, self, and emotion* (pp. 88–119). Cambridge, England: Cambridge University Press.

Danermark, B., Ekstrom, M., Jakobsen, L., & Karlsson, J. (2001). *Explaining society: An introduction to critical realism in the social sciences.* London: Routledge.

Davidson, D. (1975). Hempel on explaining action. *Erkenntnis, 10,* 239–253. Reprinted in D. Davidson, *Essays on actions and events* (pp. 261–275). Oxford, England: Oxford University Press.

Davidson, D. (1980). *Essays on actions and events.* Oxford, England: Oxford University Press.

Davidson, D. (1993). Thinking causes. In J. Heil & A. Mele (Eds.), *Mental causation* (pp. 3–17). Oxford, England: Clarendon Press.

Davidson, D. (1997). Indeterminism and antirealism. In C. B. Kulp (Ed.), *Realism/antirealism and epistemology* (pp. 109–122). Lanham, MD: Rowman and Littlefield.

Dawkins, R. (1976). *The selfish gene.* New York: Oxford University Press.

Denzin, N. K., & Lincoln, Y. S. (2000). Introduction: The discipline and practice of qualitative research. In N. K. Denzin & Y. S. Lincoln (Eds.), *SAGE handbook of qualitative research* (2nd ed.) (pp. 1–28). Thousand Oaks, CA: Sage.

Denzin, N. K., & Lincoln, Y. S. (2005a). Introduction: The discipline and practice of qualitative research. In N. K. Denzin & Y. S. Lincoln (Eds.), *SAGE handbook of qualitative research* (3rd ed.) (pp. 1–42). Thousand Oaks, CA: Sage.

Denzin, N. K., & Lincoln, Y. S. (Eds.). (2005b). *SAGE handbook of qualitative research* (3rd ed.). Thousand Oaks, CA: Sage.

Dere, E., Easton, A., Nadel, L., & Huston, J. P. (Eds.). (2008). *Handbook of episodic memory.* Amsterdam: Elsevier.

Devitt, M. (2005). Scientific realism. In F. Jackson & M. Smith (Eds.), *The Oxford handbook of contemporary philosophy* (pp. 767–791). Oxford, England, Oxford University Press.

de Waal, F. (1990). *Peacemaking among primates.* Cambridge, MA: Harvard University Press.

de Waal, F. (2007). *Chimpanzee politics: Power and sex among apes* (2nd ed.). Baltimore: Johns Hopkins University Press.

Dexter, L. A. (1970). *Elite and specialized interviewing.* Evanston, IL: Northwestern University Press.

Dey, I. (1993). *Qualitative data analysis: A user-friendly guide for social scientists.* London: Routledge.

Dickinson, A., & Shanks, D. (1995). Instrumental action and causal representation. In D. Sperber, D. Premack, & A. J. Premack (Eds.), *Causal cognition: A multidisciplinary debate* (pp. 5–25). Oxford, England: Clarendon Press.

Dobzhansky, T. (1962). *Mankind evolving.* New Haven, CT: Yale University Press.

Dressman, M. (2008). *Using social theory in educational research: A practical guide.* London: Routledge.

Dunn, J. (1978). Practising history and social science on "realist" assumptions. In C. Hookway & P. Pettit (Eds.), *Action and interpretation: Studies in the philosophy of the social sciences* (pp. 145–175). Cambridge, England: Cambridge University Press.

Durkheim, E. (1893/1984). *The division of labor in society.* New York: The Free Press.

Eckert, P. (1989). *Jocks and burnouts: Social categories and identity in the high school.* New York: Teachers College Press.

Eggan, F. (1937). The Cheyenne and Arapaho kinship system. In F. Eggan (Ed.), *Social anthropology of North American tribes* (pp. 35–95). Chicago: University of Chicago Press.

Eggan, F. (1954). Social anthropology and the method of controlled comparison. *American Anthropologist, 56,* 743–763.

Eggan, F. (1966). *The American Indian: Perspectives for the study of social change.* Cambridge, England: Cambridge University Press.

Eggan, F., & Maxwell, J. A. (2001). Kinship and social organization. In R. DeMallie (Ed.), *Handbook of North American Indians, volume 13: Plains* (pp. 974–982). Washington, DC: Smithsonian Institution.

Eisner, E. W. (1991). *The enlightened eye: Qualitative inquiry and the enhancement of educational practice.* New York: Macmillan.

Elbow, P. (1986). Methodological doubting and believing: Contraries in inquiry. In P. Elbow, *Embracing contraries: Explorations in learning and teaching* (pp. 254–300). Oxford, England: Oxford University Press.

Erickson, F. (1986). Qualitative methods. In M. Wittrock (Ed.), *Handbook of research on teaching* (pp. 119–161). New York: Macmillan.

Erickson, F. (1992). Ethnographic microanalysis of interaction. In M. D. LeCompte, W. L. Millroy, & J. Priessle (Eds.), *The handbook of qualitative research in education* (pp. 201–225). San Diego, CA: Academic Press.

Erikson, K. (1976). *Everything in its path: Destruction of community in the Buffalo Creek flood.* New York: Simon and Schuster.

Ezzy, D. (2002). *Qualitative analysis: Practice and innovation.* London: Routledge.

Falleti, T., & Lynch, J. (2009). Context and causal mechanisms in political analysis. *Comparative Political Studies, 42,* 1143–1166.

Fetterman, D. (2008). Emic/etic distinction. In L. Given (Ed.), *The SAGE encyclopedia of qualitative research methods* (p. 249). Thousand Oaks, CA: Sage.

Feyerabend, P. (1981). *Realism, rationalism, & scientific method. Philosophical papers, vol. 1.* Cambridge, England: Cambridge University Press.

Fielding, N. G. (2008). Analytic density, postmodernism, and applied multiple method research. In M. Bergman (Ed.), *Advances in mixed method research* (pp. 37–52). London: Sage.

Fielding, N. G., & Fielding, J. L. (1986). *Linking data.* Thousand Oaks, CA: Sage.

Fracchia, J., & Lewontin, R. C. (1999). Does culture evolve? *History and Theory: Studies in the Philosophy of History, 38*(4), 52–78. DOI: 10.1111/0018-2656.00104

Fracchia, J., & Lewontin, R. C. (2005). The price of metaphor. *History and Theory: Studies in the Philosophy of History, 44*(1), 1429. DOI: 10.1111/j.1468-2303.2005.00305.x

Frazer, E., & Lacey, N. (1993). *The politics of community: A feminist critique of the liberal-communitarian debate.* New York: Harvester Wheatsheaf.

Freidson, E. (1975). *Doctoring together: A study of professional social control.* Chicago: University of Chicago Press.

Gawande, A. (2009). *The checklist manifesto: How to get things right.* New York: Henry Holt.

Gee, J. P. (2005). *An introduction to discourse analysis: Theory and method.* New York: Routledge.

Geertz, C. (1959). Ritual and social change: A Javanese example. *American Anthropologist, 61.* Reprinted in C. Geertz (1973), *The interpretation of cultures* (pp. 142–169). New York: Basic Books.

Geertz, C. (1960). *The religion of Java.* London: The Free Press of Glencoe.

Geertz, C. (1963). The integrative revolution: Primordial sentiments and civil politics in the new states. In C. Geertz, *Old societies and new states.* New York: The Free Press of Glencoe. Reprinted in C. Geertz (1973), *The interpretation of cultures* (pp. 255–310). New York: Basic Books.

Geertz, C. (1965). The impact of the concept of culture on the concept of man. In J. R. Platt (Ed.), *New views of man.* Chicago: University of Chicago Press. Reprinted in C. Geertz (1973), *The interpretation of cultures* (pp. 33–54). New York: Basic Books.

Geertz, C. (1973). Thick description. In C. Geertz, *The interpretation of cultures* (pp. 1–31). New York: Basic Books.

Gellner, E. (1973). *Cause and meaning in the social sciences.* London: Routledge & Kegan Paul.

George, A., & Bennett, A. (2005). *Case studies and theory development in the social sciences.* Cambridge, MA: MIT Press.

Gerson, E. M. (1991). Supplementing grounded theory. In D. R. Maines (Ed.), *Social organization and social process: Essays in honor of Anselm Strauss* (pp. 285–302). Chicago: Aldine.

Giere, R. A. (1999). *Science without laws.* Chicago: University of Chicago Press.

Gilligan, C., Spencer, R., Weinberg, M. C., & Bertsch, T. (2003). On the listening guide: A voice-centered relational method. In P. M. Camic, J. E. Rhodes, & L. Yardley (Eds.), *Qualitative research in psychology: Expanding perspectives in methodology and design* (pp. 157–172). Washington, DC: American Psychological Association.

Giroux, H. (1991). Modernism, postmodernism, and feminism: Rethinking the boundaries of educational discourse. In H. Giroux (Ed.), *Postmodernism, feminism, and cultural politics: Redrawing educational boundaries* (pp. 1–59). Albany: State University of New York Press.

Given, L. (Ed.). (2008). *The SAGE encyclopedia of qualitative research methods.* Thousand Oaks, CA: Sage.

Glesne, C. (2011). *Becoming qualitative researchers: An introduction* (4th ed.). Boston: Pearson.

Glesne, C., & Peshkin, A. (1992). *Becoming qualitative researchers: An introduction.* White Plains, NY: Longman.

Goldenberg, C. (1992). The limits of expectations: A case for case knowledge of teacher expectancy effects. *American Educational Research Journal, 29*(3), 517–544.

Gould, S. J. (1985). The median isn't the message. *Discover, 6,* 40–42.

Gould, S. J. (1989). *Wonderful life: The Burgess Shale and the nature of history.* New York: W. W. Norton.

Gould, S. J. (1996). *Full house: The spread of excellence from Plato to Darwin.* New York: Crown.

Greene, J. (2007). *Mixed methods in social inquiry.* San Francisco: Jossey-Bass.

Groff, R. (Ed.). (2007). *Revitalizing causality: Realism about causality in philosophy and social science.* London: Routledge.

Guba, E. G., & Lincoln, Y. S. (1989). *Fourth generation evaluation.* Thousand Oaks, CA: Sage.

Guemple, D. L. (1972). Kinship and alliance in Belcher Island Eskimo society. In D. L. Guemple (Ed.), *Alliance in Eskimo Society. Proceedings of the American Ethnological Society 1971, supplement* (pp. 56–78). Seattle: University of Washington Press.

Haack, S. (1998). *Manifesto of a passionate moderate.* Chicago: University of Chicago Press.

Haack, S. (2003). *Defending science—within reason.* Amherst, NY: Prometheus Press.

Hammersley, M. (1992a). Ethnography and realism. In M. Hammersley, *What's wrong with ethnography? Methodological explorations* (pp. 43–56). London: Routledge.

Hammersley, M. (1992b). *What's wrong with ethnography? Methodological explorations.* London: Routledge.

Hammersley, M. (1998). Get real! A defence of realism. In P. Hodkinson (Ed.), *The nature of educational research: Realism, relativism, or postmodernism.* Crewe, England: Crewe School of Education, Manchester Metropolitan University. Reprinted in H. Piper & I. Stronach (Eds.), *Educational research: Difference and diversity* (pp. 59–78). Aldershot, England: Ashgate, 2004.

Hammersley, M. (2002). Research as emancipatory: The case of Bhaskar's critical realism. *Journal of Critical Realism, 1*(1), 33–48.

Hammersley, M. (2008). *Questioning qualitative inquiry: Critical essays.* Thousand Oaks, CA: Sage.

Hammersley, M. (2009). Why critical realism fails to justify critical social research. *Methodological Innovations Online, 4*(2), 1–11. Retrieved from http://www.pbs.plym.ac.uk/mi/pdf/12809/1.%20Hammersley_final%20August%209%200.pdf

Hammersley, M., & Atkinson, P. (1983). *Ethnography: Principles in practice.* London: Tavistock.

Hammersley, M., & Atkinson, P. (2007). *Ethnography: Principles in practice* (3rd ed.). London: Routledge.

Hannerz, U. (1992). *Cultural complexity: Studies in the social organization of meaning.* New York: Columbia University Press.

Harlow, L. L., Mulaik, S. A., & Steiger, J. H. (Eds.). (1997). *What if there were no significance tests?* Mahwah, NJ: Lawrence Erlbaum.

Harre, R. (1978). Accounts, actions, and meanings—the practice of participatory psychology. In M. Brenner, P. Marsh, & M. Brenner (Eds.), *The social contexts of method* (pp. 44–66). New York: St. Martin's Press.

Hawthorn, G. (1987). *Enlightenment and despair: A history of social theory* (2nd ed.). Cambridge, England: Cambridge University Press.

Heider, E. R. (1972). Probability, sampling, and ethnographic method: The case of Dani colour names. *Man, 7*, 448–466.

Heider, K. (1978). Accounting for variation: A nonformal analysis of Grand Valley Dani kinship terms. *Journal of Anthropological Research, 34*, 219–261.

Heil, J., & Mele, A. (Eds.). (1993). *Mental causation.* Oxford, England: Clarendon.

Heinrich, B. (1999). *Mind of the raven.* New York: HarperCollins.

Hempel, C. G. (1952). Fundamentals of concept formation in empirical science. *International Encyclopedia of Unified Science, 2*(7). Chicago: University of Chicago Press.

Hempel, C. G., & Oppenheim, P. (1948). Studies in the logic of explanation. *Philosophy of Science, 15,* 135–175.

Henry, G., Julnes, J., & Mark, M. (1998). *Realist evaluation: An emerging theory in support of practice. New directions for evaluation 78.* San Francisco: Jossey-Bass.

Hesse-Biber, S., & Leavy, P. (2011). *The practice of qualitative research* (2nd ed.). Thousand Oaks, CA: Sage.

House, E. (1991). Realism in research. *Educational Researcher, 20*(6), 2–9, 25.

House, E. (2005). Qualitative evaluation and changing social policy. In N. K. Denzin & Y. S. Lincoln (Eds.), *SAGE handbook of qualitative research* (3rd ed.) (pp. 1069–1088). Thousand Oaks, CA: Sage.

Howe, K. R. (2011). Mixed methods, mixed causes? *Qualitative Inquiry, 17,* 166–171.

Huang, B. (1991). Unpublished course paper, Harvard Graduate School of Education.

Huberman, A. M. (1989). *La vie des enseignants.* Neuchâtel, Switzerland: Editions Delachaux & Niestlé. English translation published in the United States in 1993 as *The lives of teachers.* New York: Teachers College Press.

Huberman, A. M., & Miles, M. B. (1985). Assessing local causality in qualitative research. In D. N. Berg & K. K. Smith (Eds.), *Exploring clinical methods for social research* (pp. 351–382). Beverly Hills, CA: Sage.

Huck, S. W. (2009). *Statistical misconceptions.* New York: Taylor & Francis.

Hume, D. (1739/1978). *A treatise of human nature.* Edited, with an analytical index, by L. A. Selby-Bigge (2nd ed.) Oxford, England: Oxford University Press.

Hutchins, E. (1995). *Cognition in the wild.* Cambridge, MA: MIT Press.

Ignatieff, M. (1994, April 21). Homage to Bosnia. *New York Review of Books, 41*(8).

Jakobson, R. (1956). Two aspects of language and two types of aphasic disturbance. In R. Jakobson & M. Halle, *Fundamentals of language* (pp. 55–82). 'S-Gravenhage, Netherlands: Mouton.

Jankowski, M. S. (1991). *Islands in the street: Gangs and American urban society.* Berkeley: University of California Press.

Jansen, G., & Peshkin, A. (1992). Subjectivity in qualitative research. In M. D. LeCompte, W. L. Millroy, & J. Preissle (Eds.), *The handbook of qualitative research in education* (pp. 681–725). San Diego, CA: Academic Press.

Johnson, M. (2007). *The meaning of the body: Aesthetics of human understanding.* Chicago, IL: University of Chicago Press.

Kaplan, A. (1964). *The conduct of inquiry: Methodology for behavioral science.* San Francisco: Chandler.

Keesing, R. (1974). Theories of culture. *Annual Review of Anthropology, 3,* 73–97.

Keller, E. F. (1992). *Secrets of life, secrets of death: Essays on language, gender, and science.* New York: Routledge.

Kelley, W. R. (1982). *Aspects of the meaning of American English kinterms.* Unpublished master's thesis, Department of Anthropology, University of Chicago.

Kerlinger, F. N. (1979). *Behavioral research: A conceptual approach.* New York: Holt, Rinehart & Winston.

Kincheloe, J., & McLaren, P. (2000). Rethinking critical theory and qualitative research. In N. K. Denzin & Y. S. Lincoln (Eds.), *SAGE handbook of qualitative research* (pp. 279–313). Thousand Oaks, CA: Sage.

King, G., Keohane, R. O., & Verba, S. (1994). *Designing social inquiry: Scientific inference in qualitative research.* Princeton, NJ: Princeton University Press.

Kirk, J., & Miller, M. (1986). *Reliability and validity in qualitative research.* Thousand Oaks, CA: Sage.

Kitcher, P., & Salmon, W. C. (Eds.). (1989). *Scientific explanation.* Minneapolis: University of Minnesota Press.

Knapp, N. F. (1997). Interviewing Joshua: On the importance of leaving room for serendipity. *Qualitative Inquiry, 3*(3), 326–342.

Knorr-Cetina, K. (1999). *Epistemic cultures: How the sciences make knowledge.* Cambridge, MA: Harvard University Press.

Kroeber, A. L., & Parsons, T. (1958). The concepts of culture and of social system. *American Sociological Review, 23*, 582–583.

Kronenfeld, D. B. (2008). *Culture, society, and cognition: Collective goals, values, action, and knowledge.* Berlin, Germany: Mouton de Gruyter.

Kuhn, T. (1970). *The structure of scientific revolutions* (2nd ed.). Chicago: University of Chicago Press.

Kummer, H. (1995). Causal knowledge in animals. In D. Sperber, D. Premack, & A. J. Premack (Eds.), *Causal cognition: A multidisciplinary debate* (pp. 26–36). Oxford, England: Clarendon Press.

Kvale, S. (1995). *Interviews: An introduction to qualitative research interviewing.* Thousand Oaks, CA: Sage.

Labov, W. (1972). The transformation of experience in narrative syntax. In W. Labov (Ed.), *Language in the inner city: Studies in the Black English vernacular* (pp. 354–396). Philadelphia: University of Pennsylvania Press.

Labov, W. (1982). Speech actions and reactions in personal narrative. In D. Tannen (Ed.), *Analyzing discourse: Text and talk* (pp. 219–247). Washington, DC: Georgetown University Press.

Labov, W., & Fanshel, D. (1977). *Therapeutic discourse: Psychotherapy as conversation.* New York: Academic Press.

Labov, W., & Waletzky, J. (1967). Narrative analysis: Oral versions of personal experience. In J. Helm (Ed.), *Essays on the verbal and visual arts* (pp. 12–44). Seattle: University of Washington Press.

Lakoff, G. (1987). *Women, fire, and dangerous things: What categories reveal about the mind.* Chicago: University of Chicago Press.

Lakoff, G., & Johnson, M. (1999). *Philosophy in the flesh: The embodied mind and its challenge to western thought.* New York: Basic Books.

Lave, C. A., & March, J. G. (1975). *An introduction to models in the social sciences.* New York: Harper & Row.

Lawrence-Lightfoot, S., & Hoffman Davis, J. (1997). *The art and science of portraiture.* San Francisco: Jossey-Bass.

Lawson, T. (2003). *Reorienting economics.* London: Routledge.

Layton, R. (1997). *An introduction to theory in anthropology.* Cambridge, England: Cambridge University Press.

Leach, M. S. (1992). Can we talk? A response to Burbules and Rice. *Harvard Educational Review, 62*(2), 257–263.

LeCompte, M., & Preissle, J. (1993). *Ethnography and qualitative design in educational research* (2nd ed.). San Diego, CA: Academic Press.

Lenk, H. (2003). *Grasping reality: An interpretation-realistic epistemology.* Singapore: World Scientific.

Leplin, J. (1984). Introduction. In J. Leplin (Ed.), *Scientific realism* (pp. 1–7). Berkeley: University of California Press.

Levi-Strauss, C. (1963). *Structural anthropology* (C. Jacobson & B. G. Schoepf, Trans.). New York: Basic Books.

Levi-Strauss, C. (1966). *The savage mind.* Chicago: University of Chicago Press.

Lewontin, R. C. (1973). Darwin and Mendel—The materialist revolution. In J. Neyman (Ed.), *The heritage of Copernicus: Theories "pleasing to the mind"* (pp. 166–183). Cambridge, MA: MIT Press.

Lewontin, R. C. (1974). The analysis of variance and the analysis of causes. *American Journal of Human Genetics, 26,* 400–411.

Lieblich, A., Tuval-Mashiach, R., & Zilber, T. (1998). *Narrative research: Reading, analysis, and interpretation.* Thousand Oaks, CA: Sage.

Light, R. J., Singer, J., & Willett, J. (1990). *By design: Conducting research on higher education.* Cambridge, MA: Harvard University Press.

Lincoln, Y. S. (1990). Response to "Up from positivism." *Harvard Educational Review, 60,* 508–511.

Lincoln, Y. S. (1995). Emerging criteria for quality in qualitative and interpretive research. *Qualitative Inquiry, 1,* 275–289.

Lincoln, Y. S., & Guba, E. G. (1985). *Naturalistic inquiry.* Thousand Oaks, CA: Sage.

Lincoln, Y. S., & Guba, E. G. (2000). Paradigmatic controversies, contradictions, and emerging confluences. In N. K. Denzin & Y. S. Lincoln (Eds.), *SAGE handbook of qualitative research* (2nd ed., pp. 163-188). Thousand Oaks, CA: Sage.

Linde, C. (1993). *Life stories: The creation of coherence.* Oxford, England: Oxford University Press.

Linton, R. (1936). *The study of man.* New York: Appleton-Century-Crofts.

Little, D. (1991). *Varieties of social explanation: An introduction to the philosophy of social science.* Boulder, CO: Westview Press.

Little, D. (1995). Causal explanation in the social sciences. *Southern Journal of Philosophy* (Supplement). Reprinted in D. Little, *Microfoundations, method, and causation* (pp. 197–214). New Brunswick, NJ: Transaction, 1998.

Little, D. (2010). *New contributions to the philosophy of history.* New York: Springer.

Lofland, J., & Lofland, L. (1984). *Analyzing social settings: A guide to qualitative observation and analysis.* Belmont, CA: Wadsworth.

Lundsgaarde, H. P., Fischer, P. J., & Steele, D. J. (1981). *Human problems in computerized medicine. University of Kansas publications in anthropology, no. 13.* Lawrence: University of Kansas.

Lurz, R. W. (Ed.). (2009). *The philosophy of animal minds.* Cambridge, England: Cambridge University Press.

Lyons, J. (1968). *Introduction to theoretical linguistics.* Cambridge, England: Cambridge University Press.

MacIntyre, A. (1967). The idea of a social science. *Aristotelian society supplement 41.* Reprinted in B. R. Wilson (Ed.), *Rationality* (pp. 112–130). New York: Harper & Row, 1970.

MacIntyre. A. (1993). Notes from outside the field. *Anthropology Newsletter, 34*(7), 5–6.

Manicas, P. T. (1987). *A history and philosophy of the social sciences*. Oxford, England: Basil Blackwell.

Manicas, P. T. (2006). *A realist philosophy of social science: Explanation and understanding*. Cambridge, England: Cambridge University Press.

Manicas, P. T. (2009). Realist metatheory and qualitative methods. *Sociological Analysis, 33*(1), 31–46.

Margolis, J. (1990). *Psychology of gender and academic discourse: A comparison between female and male students' experiences talking in the college classroom*. Unpublished doctoral dissertation, Harvard Graduate School of Education, Cambridge, MA.

Mark, M. M., Henry, G. T., & Julnes, G. (2000). *Evaluation: An integrated framework for understanding, guiding, and improving policies and programs*. San Francisco: Jossey-Bass.

Marshall, C., & Rossman, G. (1999). *Designing qualitative research* (3rd ed.). Thousand Oaks, CA: Sage.

Maxwell, J. A. (1971). *The development of Plains kinship systems*. Unpublished master's thesis, Department of Anthropology, University of Chicago.

Maxwell, J. A. (1978). The evolution of Plains Indian kin terminologies: A non-reflectionist account. *Plains Anthropologist, 23*, 13–29.

Maxwell, J. A. (1986). *The conceptualization of kinship in an Inuit community*. Unpublished doctoral dissertation, University of Chicago.

Maxwell, J. A. (1990a). Up from positivism (essay review of D. T. Campbell, Methodology and epistemology for social science). *Harvard Educational Review, 60*(4), 497–501.

Maxwell, J. A. (1990b). Response to Campbell's retrospective and a constructivist's perspective. *Harvard Educational Review, 60*(4), 504–508.

Maxwell, J. A. (1992). Understanding and validity in qualitative research. *Harvard Educational Review, 62*(3), 279–300.

Maxwell, J. A. (1993, March). *Rethinking homogeneity and diversity*. Keynote address, Eleventh International Forum, Harvard Graduate School of Education, Cambridge, MA.

Maxwell, J. A. (1995). Biology and social organization in the kin terminology of an Inuit community. In R. J. DeMallie & A. Ortiz (Eds.), *North American Indian anthropology: Essays on culture and society* (pp. 25–48). Norman: University of Oklahoma Press.

Maxwell, J. A. (1996a). Diversity and methodology in a changing world. *Pedagogía, 30*, 32–40.

Maxwell, J. A. (1996b, April). *Rethinking diversity and community*. Presented at the Annual Meeting of the American Educational Research Association.

Maxwell, J. A. (1999). A realist/postmodern concept of culture. In E. L. Cerroni-Long (Ed.), *Anthropological theory in North America* (pp. 143–173). Westport, CT: Bergin & Garvey.

Maxwell, J. A. (2002). Realism and the role of the researcher in qualitative psychology. In M. Kiegelmann (Ed.), *The role of the researcher in qualitative psychology* (pp. 11–30). Tuebingen, Germany: Verlag Ingeborg Huber.

Maxwell, J. A. (2004a). Causal explanation, qualitative research, and scientific inquiry in education. *Educational Researcher, 33*(2), 3–11.

Maxwell, J. A. (2004b). Re-emergent scientism, postmodernism, and dialogue across differences. *Qualitative Inquiry, 10*(1), 35–41.

Maxwell, J. A. (2004c). Using qualitative methods for causal explanation. *Field Methods, 16*(3), 243–264.

Maxwell, J. A. (2005). *Qualitative research design: An interactive approach* (2nd ed.). Thousand Oaks, CA: Sage.

Maxwell, J. A. (2006, December). Literature reviews of, and for, educational research: A commentary on Boote and Beile's "Scholars before researchers." *Educational Researcher, 35*(9), 28–31.

Maxwell, J. A. (2007, August). *The value of realism for qualitative research.* Presented at the Annual Conference of the International Association for Critical Realism, Drexel University, Philadelphia, PA.

Maxwell, J. A. (2008). The value of a realist understanding of causality for qualitative research. In N. K. Denzin (Ed.), *Qualitative research and the politics of evidence* (pp. 163–181). Walnut Creek, CA: Left Coast Press.

Maxwell, J. A. (2009). Evidence: A critical realist perspective for qualitative research. In N. K. Denzin & M. D. Giardina (Eds.), *Qualitative inquiry and social justice* (pp. 108–122). Walnut Creek, CA: Left Coast Press.

Maxwell, J. A. (2010a). Review of Jean Anyon, Theory and educational research: Toward critical social explanation. *Education Review* (online journal). Available at http://edrev.asu.edu

Maxwell, J. A. (2010b). Using numbers in qualitative research. *Qualitative Inquiry, 16*(6), pp. 475–482.

Maxwell, J. A. (2011, April). *The importance of qualitative research for causal explanation in education.* Presented at the Annual Meeting of the American Educational Research Association, New Orleans, LA.

Maxwell, J. A., & Eggan, F. (2001). Kinship and social organization. In R. DeMallie (Ed.), *Handbook of North American Indians. Volume 13: Plains* (pp. 974–982). Washington, DC: Smithsonian Institution.

Maxwell, J. A., & Loomis, D. (2003). Mixed methods design: An alternative approach. In A. Tashakkori & C. Teddlie (Eds.), *Handbook of mixed methods in social and behavioral research* (pp. 241–271). Thousand Oaks, CA: Sage.

Maxwell, J. A., & Miller, B. (2008). Categorizing and connecting strategies in qualitative data analysis. In S. Hesse-Biber & P. Leavy (Eds.), *Handbook of emergent methods* (pp. 461–477). New York: Guilford.

Maxwell, J. A., & Mittapalli, K. (2008). Thick description. In L. Given (Ed.), *The SAGE encyclopedia of qualitative research methods* (p. 880). Thousand Oaks, CA: Sage.

Maxwell, J. A., & Mittapalli, K. (2010). Realism as a stance for mixed methods research. In A. Tashakkori & C. Teddlie, *Handbook of mixed methods in social and behavioral research* (2nd ed., pp. 145–167). Thousand Oaks, CA: Sage.

Maxwell, J. A., Sandlow, L. J., & Bashook, P. G. (1986). Combining ethnographic and experimental methods in evaluation research: A case study. In D. M. Fetterman & M. A. Pitman (Eds.), *Educational evaluation: Ethnography in theory, practice, and politics* (pp. 121–143). Thousand Oaks, CA: Sage.

Mayes, A. H. (2000). Selective memory disorders. In E. Tulving & F. I. M. Craik (Eds.), *The Oxford handbook of memory* (pp. 427–440). Oxford, England: Oxford University Press.

Mayr, E. (1982). *The growth of biological thought: Diversity, evolution, and inheritance.* Cambridge, MA: Harvard University Press.

McAdam, D., Tarrow, S., & Tilly, C. (2008). Methods for measuring mechanisms of contention. *Qualitative Sociology, 31*, 307–331.

McCawley, J. D. (1982). *Thirty million theories of grammar.* Chicago: University of Chicago Press.

McGinn, C. (1991). Conceptual causation: Some elementary reflections. *Mind, 100*(4), 573–586. Reprinted in C. McGinn, *Knowledge and reality: Selected essays* (pp. 152–167). Oxford, England: Clarendon Press, 1999.

McGinn, C. (1999). *Knowledge and reality: Selected essays.* Oxford, England: Clarendon Press.

McKinley, R. (1971a). A critique of the reflectionist theory of kinship terminology: The Crow/Omaha case. *Man, 6,* 228–247.

McKinley, R. (1971b). Why do Crow and Omaha kinship terminologies exist? A sociology of knowledge interpretation. *Man, 6,* 408–426.

McMillan, J. H., & Schumacher, S. (2001). *Research in education: A conceptual introduction.* New York: Longman.

Medill, A. (2008). Realism. In L. Given (Ed.), *The SAGE encyclopedia of qualitative research methods* (pp. 731–735). Thousand Oaks, CA: Sage.

Menzel, H. (1978). Meaning—who needs it? In M. Brenner, P. Marsh, & M. Brenner (Eds.), *The social contexts of method* (pp. 140–171). New York: St. Martin's Press.

Merriam, S. (1988). *Case study research in education: A qualitative approach.* San Francisco: Jossey-Bass.

Michotte, A. E. (1946). *La perception de la causalite.* Louvain: Editions de l'Institute Superieur de Philosophie. English translation: *The perception of causality.* London: Methuen, 1963.

Miles, M. B., & Huberman, A. M. (1984). *Qualitative data analysis: A sourcebook of new methods.* Thousand Oaks, CA: Sage.

Miles, M. B., & Huberman, A. M. (1994). *Qualitative data analysis: An expanded sourcebook.* Thousand Oaks, CA: Sage.

Milgram, S. (1974). *Obedience to authority: An experimental view.* New York: Harper and Row.

Miller, A. (2010). Realism. In E. N. Zalta (Ed.), *The Stanford encyclopedia of philosophy (summer 2010 edition).* Available at http://plato.stanford.edu/archives/sum2010/entries/realism/

Miller, B. A. (1991). *Adolescents' relationships with their friends.* Unpublished doctoral dissertation, Harvard Graduate School of Education.

Miller, P. (2008). Validity. In L. Given (Ed.), *The SAGE encyclopedia of qualitative research methods* (pp. 909–910). Thousand Oaks, CA: Sage.

Mishler, E. G. (1984). *The discourse of medicine: Dialectics of medical interviews.* Norwood, NJ: Ablex.

Mishler, E. G. (1986). *Research interviewing: Context and narrative.* Cambridge, MA: Harvard University Press.

Mishler, E. G. (1990). Validation in inquiry-guided research: The role of exemplars in narrative studies. *Harvard Educational Review, 60,* 415–442.

Mohr, L. B. (1982). *Explaining organizational behavior.* San Francisco: Jossey-Bass.

Mohr, L. B. (1996). *The causes of human behavior: Implications for theory and method in the social sciences.* Ann Arbor: University of Michigan Press.

Morgan, D. L. (2008). Sample. In L. Given (Ed.), *The SAGE encyclopedia of qualitative research methods* (pp. 797–798). Thousand Oaks, CA: Sage.

Morgan, D. L., & Guevara, H. (2008). Cultural context. In L. Given (Ed.), *The SAGE encyclopedia of qualitative research methods* (pp. 181–182). Thousand Oaks, CA: Sage.

Morrison, K. (2009). *Causation in educational research.* London: Routledge.

Morse, J. M., & Tylko, S. J. (1985). *The use of qualitative methods in a study examining patient falls.* Paper presented at the annual meeting of the Society for Applied Anthropology, Washington, DC.

Morse, J. M., Tylko, S. J., & Dixon, H. A. (1987). Characteristics of the fall-prone patient. *The Gerontologist, 27*(4), 516–522.

Mulaik, S. (2009). *Linear causal modeling with structural equations.* Boca Raton, FL: Chapman & Hall/CRC Press.

Murdock, G. P. (1949). *Social structure.* New York: Macmillan.

Murnane, R. J., & Willett, J. B. (2010). *Methods matter: Improving causal inference in educational and social science research.* Oxford, England: Oxford University Press.

Murphy, R. F. (1967). Tuareg kinship. *American Anthropologist, 69,* 163–170.

Niiniluoto, I. (2002). *Critical scientific realism.* Oxford, England: Oxford University Press.

Niiniluoto, I. (2007). Scientific progress. *Stanford Encyclopedia of Philosophy.* Retrieved October 18, 2010 from http://plato.stanford.edu/entries/scientific-progress/

Nisbet, R. A. (1966). *The sociological tradition.* New York: Basic Books.

Norris, C. (2002). *Hilary Putnam: Realism, reason, and the uses of uncertainty.* Manchester, England: Manchester University Press.

Norris, S. P. (1983). The inconsistencies at the foundation of construct validation theory. In E. R. House (Ed.), *Philosophy of evaluation. New directions for program evaluation, no. 19* (pp. 53–74). San Francisco: Jossey-Bass.

Novak, J. D., & Gowin, D. B. (1984). *Learning how to learn.* Cambridge, England: Cambridge University Press.

Nyberg, L., & Cabeza, R. (2000). Brain imaging of memory. In E. Tulving & F. I. M. Craik (Eds.), *The Oxford handbook of memory* (pp. 501–520). Oxford, England: Oxford University Press.

Palys, T. (2008). Purposive sampling. In L. Given (Ed.), *The SAGE encyclopedia of qualitative research methods* (pp. 697–698). Thousand Oaks, CA: Sage.

Parsons, T. (1961). Introduction. In T. Parsons, E. Shils, K. D. Naegale, & J. R. Pitts (Eds.), *Theories of society* (pp. 30–79). New York: Free Press of Glencoe.

Parsons, T. (1966). *Societies: Evolutionary and comparative perspectives.* Englewood Cliffs, NJ: Prentice-Hall.

Pattee, H. H. (1973). *Hierarchy theory: The challenge of complex systems.* New York: George Braziller.

Patton, M. Q. (2001). *Qualitative research and evaluation methods* (3rd ed.). Thousand Oaks, CA: Sage.

Pawson, R. (2006). *Evidence-based policy: A realist perspective.* London: Sage.

Pawson, R., & Tilley, N. (1997). *Realistic evaluation.* London: Sage.

Pelto, P., & Pelto, G. (1975). Intra-cultural diversity: Some theoretical issues. *American Ethnologist, 2,* 1–18.

Perkins, D. (1992). *Smart schools: From training memories to educating minds.* New York: The Free Press.

Peshkin, A. (1991). *The color of strangers, the color of friends: The play of ethnicity in school and community.* Chicago: University of Chicago Press.

Pfaffenberger, B. (1988). *Microcomputer applications in qualitative research.* Thousand Oaks, CA: Sage.

Phillips, D. C. (1987). *Philosophy, science, and social inquiry: Contemporary methodological controversies in social science and related applied fields of research.* Oxford, England: Pergamon Press.

Platt, J. (1964). Strong inference. *Science, 146*(3642), 347–353.

Poggie, J. J., Jr. (1972). Toward control in key informant data. *Human Organization, 31,* 23–30.

Popper, K. (1934/1959). *The logic of scientific discovery.* New York: Basic Books. (Originally published in German, 1934.)

Porter, S. (2007). Validity, trustworthiness, and rigour: Reasserting realism in qualitative research. *Journal of Advanced Nursing, 60*(1), 79–86.

Portmann, A. (1961). *Animals as social beings.* New York: Harper and Row.

Pratt, M. L. (1988). Linguistic utopias. In N. Fabb, D. Attridge, A. Durant, & C. McCabe (Eds.), *The linguistics of writing: Arguments between language and literature* (pp. 48–66). Manchester, England: Manchester University Press.

Preissle, J. (2008). Subjectivity statements. In L. Given (Ed.), *The SAGE encyclopedia of qualitative research methods* (p. 844). Thousand Oaks, CA: Sage.

Premack, D., & Premack, A. J. (1995). Afterword. In D. Sperber, D. Premack, & A. J. Premack (Eds.), *Causal cognition: A multidisciplinary debate* (pp. 650–654). Oxford, England: Clarendon Press.

Putnam, H. (1987). *The many faces of realism.* LaSalle, IL: Open Court Press.

Putnam, H. (1990). *Realism with a human face* (James Conant, Ed.). Cambridge, MA: Harvard University Press.

Putnam, H. (1999). *The threefold cord: Mind, body, and world.* New York: Columbia University Press.

Rabinow, P. (1977). *Reflections on fieldwork in Morocco.* Berkeley: University of California Press.

Ragin, C. C. (1987). *The comparative method: Moving beyond qualitative and quantitative strategies.* Berkeley: University of California Press.

Rappaport, R. (1967). *Pigs for the ancestors: Ritual in the ecology of a New Guinea people.* New Haven, CT: Yale University Press.

Rappaport, R. (1971). The sacred in human evolution. *Annual Review of Ecology and Systematics, 2,* 22–44.

Regan-Smith, M. G. (1992). *The teaching of basic science in medical school: The students' perspective.* Unpublished doctoral dissertation, Harvard Graduate School of Education, Cambridge, MA.

Resnick, L. B., Levine, J. M., & Teasley, S. D. (Eds.). (1991). *Perspectives on socially shared cognition.* Washington, DC: American Psychological Association.

Richards, L. (2005). *Handling qualitative data: A practical guide.* London: Sage.

Robb, D., & Heil, J. (2003). Mental causation. *Stanford Encyclopedia of Philosophy.* Retrieved Dec. 28, 2007 from http://plato.stanford.edu/entries/mental-causation/

Robson, C. (2011). *Real world research* (3rd ed.). Oxford, England: Blackwell.

Rogers, E. M. (2003). *Diffusion of innovations* (5th ed.). New York: The Free Press.

Rorty, R. (1979). *Philosophy and the mirror of nature.* Princeton, NJ: Princeton University Press.

Rorty, R. (1989). *Contingency, irony, and solidarity.* Cambridge, England: Cambridge University Press.

Rosch, E. (1978). Principles of categorization. In E. Rosch & B. B. Lloyd (Eds.), *Cognition and categorization* (pp. 27–48). Hillsdale, NJ: Lawrence Erlbaum.

Rosenau, P. M. (1992). *Post-modernism and the social sciences*. Princeton, NJ: Princeton University Press.

Rousseau, J. (1970). L'adoption chez les Esquimaux Tununermiut Pond Inlet, T. du N.-O. *Centre d'Etudes Nordiques, Travaux Divers, 28*. Quebec, Canada: Universite Laval.

Rudestam, K. E., & Newton, R. R. (1992). *Surviving your dissertation*. Thousand Oaks, CA: Sage.

Runciman, W. G. (1983). *A treatise on social theory, vol. 1: The methodology of social theory*. Cambridge, England: Cambridge University Press.

Russell, B. (1912/1913). On the notion of cause. *Proceedings of the Aristotelian Society, 13* (New Series), 1–26.

Ryle, G. (1949). *The concept of mind*. London: Hutchinson.

Salmon, W. C. (1984). *Scientific explanation and the causal structure of the world*. Princeton, NJ: Princeton University Press.

Salmon, W. C. (1989). Four decades of scientific explanation. In P. Kitcher & W. C. Salmon (Eds.), *Scientific explanation* (pp. 3–219). Minneapolis: University of Minnesota Press.

Salmon, W. C. (1998). *Causality and explanation*. New York: Oxford University Press.

Salmon, W. C. (2005). *Reality and rationality* (P. Dowe & M. Salmon, Eds.). New York: Oxford University Press.

Sanjek, R. (1977). Cognitive maps of the ethnic domain in urban Ghana: Reflections on variability and change. *American Ethnologist, 4*, 603–622.

Sankoff, G. (1971). Quantitative aspects of sharing and variability in a cognitive model. *Ethnology, 10*, 389–408.

Sapir, E. (1929/1958). The status of linguistics as a science. In E. Sapir, *Culture, language and personality* (D. G. Mandelbaum, Ed., pp. 65–77). Berkeley: University of California Press.

Saussure, F. de (1916/1986). *Course in general linguistics*. La Salle, IL: Open Court.

Sayer, A. (1992). *Method in social science: A realist approach* (2nd ed.). London: Routledge.

Sayer, A. (2000). *Realism and social science*. London: Sage.

Scheffler, H. W. (1972). Kinship semantics. In B. J. Siegel (Ed.), *Annual review of anthropology 1* (pp. 309–328). Palo Alto, CA: Annual Reviews.

Schmid, M. (1992). The concept of culture and its place within a theory of social action: A critique of Talcott Parsons's theory of culture. In R. Münch & N. J. Smelser (Eds.), *Theory of culture* (pp. 88–120). Berkeley: University of California Press.

Schneider, D. M. (1968). *American kinship: A cultural account*. Englewood Cliffs, NJ: Prentice-Hall.

Schneider, D. M. (1976). Notes toward a theory of culture. In K. H. Basso & H. A. Selby (Eds.), *Meaning in anthropology* (pp. 197–220). Albuquerque: University of New Mexico Press.

Schneider, D. M. (1980). *American kinship: A cultural account* (2nd ed.). Chicago: University of Chicago Press.

Schwandt, T. A. (1997). *The SAGE dictionary of qualitative inquiry*. Thousand Oaks, CA: Sage.

Schwandt, T. A. (2007). *The SAGE dictionary of qualitative inquiry* (3rd ed.). Thousand Oaks, CA: Sage.

Scott, D. (2000). *Realism and educational research*. London: Routledge.

Scriven, M. (1976). Maximizing the power of causal investigations: The modus operandi method. From M. Scriven, evaluation perspectives and procedures. In G. V. Glass (Ed.), *Evaluation studies review annual 1* (pp. 108–118). Beverly Hills, CA: Sage.

Scriven, M. (2008). A summative evaluation of RCT methodology and an alternative approach to causal research. *Journal of MultiDisciplinary Evaluation, 5*(9), 11–24.

Seale, C. (1999). *The quality of qualitative research.* London: Sage.

Seidman, I. E. (1998). *Interviewing as qualitative research: A guide for researchers in education and the social sciences* (2nd ed.). New York: Teachers College Press.

Service, E. R. (1962). *Primitive social organization: An evolutionary perspective.* New York: Random House.

Shadish, W. R., Cook, T. D., & Campbell, D. T. (2002). *Experimental and quasi-experimental designs for generalized causal inference.* Boston: Houghton Mifflin.

Shaffer, C., & Anundsen, K. (1993). *Creating community anywhere: Finding support and connection in a fragmented world.* New York: Jeremy P. Tarcher/Perigee Books.

Shavelson, R., & Towne, L. (2002). *Scientific research in education.* Washington, DC: National Academy Press.

Sheldon, R. C. (1951). Some observations on theory in the social sciences. In T. Parsons & E. Shils (Eds.), *Toward a general theory of action* (pp. 30–44). New York: Harper and Row.

Shettleworth, S. (2010). *Cognition, evolution, and behavior* (2nd ed.). New York: Oxford University Press.

Shore, B. (1996). *Culture in mind: Cognition, culture, and the problem of meaning.* New York: Oxford University Press.

Shubin, N. (2008). *Your inner fish: A journey into the 3.5-billion-year history of the human body.* New York: Random House.

Shulman, L. (1986). Paradigms and programs. In M. C. Wittrock (Ed.), *Handbook of research on teaching* (3rd ed.). New York: Macmillan. Reprinted separately as *Research in teaching and learning, vol. 1.* New York: Macmillan,1990.

Silverstein, M. (1976). Shifters, linguistic categories, and cultural description. In K. H. Basso & H. A. Selby (Eds.), *Meaning in anthropology* (pp. 11–55). Albuquerque: University of New Mexico Press.

Simon, H. (1969). *The sciences of the artificial.* Cambridge, MA: MIT Press.

Smith, J. K. (2004). Learning to live with relativism. In H. Piper & I. Stronach (Eds.), *Educational research: Difference and diversity* (pp. 45–58). Aldershot, England: Ashgate.

Smith, J. K. (2008a). Interpretive inquiry. In L. Given (Ed.), *The SAGE encyclopedia of qualitative research methods* (pp. 459–461). Thousand Oaks, CA: Sage.

Smith, J. K. (2008b). Relativism. In L. Given (Ed.), *The SAGE encyclopedia of qualitative research methods* (pp. 749–753). Thousand Oaks, CA: Sage.

Smith, J. K., & Deemer, D. K. (2000). The problem of criteria in the age of relativism. In N. K. Denzin & Y. S. Lincoln (Eds.), *SAGE handbook of qualitative research* (2nd ed., pp. 877–896). Thousand Oaks, CA: Sage.

Smith, J. K., & Hodkinson, P. (2005). Relativism, criteria, and politics. In N. K. Denzin & Y. S. Lincoln (Eds.), *SAGE handbook of qualitative research* (3rd ed., pp. 915–932). Thousand Oaks, CA: Sage.

Smith, L. (1979). An evolving logic of participant observation, educational ethnography, and other case studies. *Review of Research in Education, 6,* 316–377.

Smith, M. L. & Shepard, L. A. (1988). Kindergarten readiness and retention: A qualitative study of teachers' beliefs and practices. *American Educational Research Journal, 25*(3), 307–333.

Sperber, D. (1995). Introduction. In D. Sperber, D. Premack, & A. J. Premack (Eds.), *Causal cognition: A multidisciplinary debate* (pp. xv–xx). Oxford, England: Clarendon Press.

Stake, R. (1995). *The art of case study research.* Thousand Oaks, CA: Sage.

Starnes, B. (1990). *"Save one of those high-up jobs for me": Shared decision making in a day care center.* Unpublished doctoral dissertation, Harvard Graduate School of Education, Cambridge, MA.

Steward, J. (1955). *Theory of culture change: The methodology of multilinear evolution.* Urbana: University of Illinois Press.

Strauss, A. (1987). *Qualitative analysis for social scientists.* Cambridge, England: Cambridge University Press.

Strauss, A., & Corbin, J. (1990). *Basics of qualitative research.* Thousand Oaks, CA: Sage.

Strauss, C. (1992). Models and motives. In R. G. D'Andrade & C. Strauss (Eds.), *Human motives and cultural models.* Cambridge, England: Cambridge University Press.

Strawson, G. (1989). *The secret connexion: Causation, realism, and David Hume.* Oxford, England: Oxford University Press.

Strike, K. (1994). On the construction of public speech: Pluralism and public reason. *Educational Theory, 44*(1), 1–26.

Suppe, F. (1977). Afterword. In F. Suppe (Ed.), *The structure of scientific theories* (2nd ed.). Urbana: University of Illinois Press.

Swartz, M. J. (1982). Cultural sharing and cultural theory: Some findings of a five-society study. *American Anthropologist, 84*, 314–338.

Sypnowich, C. (2010). Law and ideology. In E. N. Zalta (Ed.), *The Stanford encyclopedia of philosophy (fall 2010 edition).* Retrieved from http://plato.stanford.edu/archives/fall2010/entries/law-ideology/

Tambiah, S. (1967). Kinship fact and fiction in relation to the Kandyan Sinhalese. *Journal of the Royal Anthropological Institute, 95*(2), 131–173.

Tappan, M. (2001). Interpretive psychology: Stories, circles, and lived experience. In D. L. Tolman & M. Brydon-Miller (Eds.), *From subjects to subjectivities: A handbook of interpretive and participatory methods* (pp. 45–56). New York: New York University Press.

Tesch, R. (1990). *Qualitative research: Analysis types and software tools.* New York: Falmer Press.

Tesch, R. (1993). Personal computers in qualitative research. In M. D. LeCompte & J. Preissle (Eds.), *Ethnography and qualitative design in educational research* (2nd ed., pp. 279–314). San Diego, CA: Academic Press.

Tetzlaff, M., & Rey, G. (2009). Systematicity and intentional realism in honeybee navigation. In R. Lurz (Ed.), *The philosophy of animal minds* (pp. 72–88). Cambridge, England: Cambridge University Press.

Tilly, C. (2008). *Explaining social processes.* Boulder, CO: Paradigm.

Tinbergen, N. (1961). *The herring gull's world.* New York: Basic Books.

Toennies, F. (1887/1957). *Community and society (Gemeinschaft und Gesellschaft).* (Charles P. Loomis, Trans., Ed.). East Lansing: Michigan State University Press.

Tolman, D. L. (2001). Echoes of sexual objectification: Listening for one girl's erotic voice. In D. L. Tolman & M. Brydon-Miller (Eds.), *From subjects to subjectivities: A handbook of interpretive and participatory methods* (pp. 130–144). New York: New York University Press.

Tolman, D. L., & Brydon-Miller, M. (2001). *From subjects to subjectivities: A handbook of interpretive and participatory methods.* New York: New York University Press.

Toulmin, S. (1972). *Human understanding: The collective use and evolution of concepts.* Princeton, NJ: Princeton University Press.

Trend, M. (1978). On the reconciliation of qualitative and quantitative analyses: A case study. *Human Organization, 37,* 345–354. Reprinted in T. D. Cook & C. S. Reichardt (Eds.), *Qualitative and quantitative methods in evaluation research.* Thousand Oaks, CA: Sage, 1979.

Tulving, E. (1983). *Elements of episodic memory.* Oxford, England: Oxford University Press.

Tulving, E., & Craik, F. I. M. (Eds.). (2000). *The Oxford handbook of memory.* Oxford, England: Oxford University Press.

Urban, G. (1991). *A discourse-centered approach to culture: Native South American myths and rituals.* Austin: University of Texas Press.

Varenne, H. (2008). Culture, education, anthropology. *Anthropology and Education Quarterly, 39*(4), 356–368.

Voget, F. (1953). Kinship changes at Caughnawaga. *American Anthropologist, 55,* 385–394.

Wallace, A. F. C. (1970). *Culture and personality* (2nd ed.). New York: Random House.

Watson, J. D. (1968). *The double helix: A personal account of the discovery of the structure of DNA.* New York: Atheneum.

Wax, R. (1971). *Doing fieldwork: Warnings and advice.* Chicago: University of Chicago Press.

Webb, R. B., & Glesne, C. (1992). Teaching qualitative research. In M. D. LeCompte, W. L. Millroy, & J. Preissle (Eds.), *The handbook of qualitative research in education* (pp. 771–814). San Diego, CA: Academic Press.

Weber, M. (1905). Critical studies in the logic of the social sciences. *Archiv fuer Sozialwissenschaft und Sozialpolitik.* Reprinted in M. Weber, *The methodology of the social sciences* (pp. 113–188, E. A. Shils & H. A. Finch, Eds. & Trans.). New York: The Free Press, 1949.

Weisner, T. S. (Ed.). (2002). *Discovering successful pathways in children's development: Mixed methods in the study of childhood and family life.* Chicago: University of Chicago Press.

Weiss, R. S. (1994). *Learning from strangers: The art and method of qualitative interviewing.* New York: The Free Press.

Weitzman, E. A., & Miles, M. B. (1995). *Computer programs for qualitative data analysis.* Thousand Oaks CA: Sage.

Welch, S. D. (1990). *A feminist ethic of risk.* Minneapolis, MN: Fortress Press.

Wheeler, M. A. (2000). Episodic memory and autonoetic awareness. In E. Tulving & F. I. M. Craik (Eds.), *The Oxford handbook of memory* (pp. 597–608). Oxford, England: Oxford University Press.

Wieviorka, M. (1992). Case studies: History or sociology? In C. Ragin & H. Becker (Eds.), *What is a case?* (pp. 159–172). Cambridge, England: Cambridge University Press.

Willett, J. (1993). *Constructing difference in community.* Paper presented at the Annual Meeting of the American Educational Research Association, Atlanta, GA.

Williams, B. (1988). *Upscaling downtown: Stalled gentrification in Washington, D.C.* Ithaca, NY: Cornell University Press.

Willis, P. (1977). *Learning to labor: How working class kids get working class jobs.* Farnborough, England: Saxon House.

Wimsatt, W. (2007). *Re-engineering philosophy for limited beings: Piecewise approximations to reality.* Cambridge, MA: Harvard University Press.

Wolcott, H. F. (1990). On seeking—and rejecting—validity in qualitative research. In E. W. Eisner & A. Peshkin (Eds.), *Qualitative inquiry in education: The continuing debate* (pp. 121–152). New York: Teachers College Press.

Wolcott, H. F. (2009). *Writing up qualitative research* (3rd ed.). Thousand Oaks, CA: Sage.

Wolf, M. (1992). *A thrice-told tale: Feminism, postmodernism, and ethnographic responsibility.* Stanford, CA: Stanford University Press.

Yanagisako, S. (1978). Introduction to special section: American kinship. *American Ethnologist, 5,* 1–29.

Yin, R. K. (1993). *Applications of case study research.* Thousand Oaks, CA: Sage.

Yin, R. K. (2003). *Case study research: Design and methods* (3rd ed.). Thousand Oaks, CA: Sage.

Young, I. M. (1990). The ideal of community and the politics of difference. In L. J. Nicholson (Ed.), *Feminism/postmodernism* (pp. 300–323). New York: Routledge, Chapman & Hall.

Author Index

Abbott, A., 13, 44, 86
Aberle, D. F., 28
Abu-Lughod, L., 166
Achinstein, P., 146–147
Agar, M., 124–125
Anundsen, K., 59
Anyon, J., 86
Archer, M., 4, 21, 25
Argyris, C., 139
Atkinson, P., 46, 96, 100, 112, 114, 118, 123, 125, 133, 144, 160
Atran, S., 28–29, 31, 163n2, 179

Baert, P., 3, 8, 10
Baldwin, J. R., 21, 26, 27
Barad, K., 4, 6, 132, 133n2, 135
Barone, T., 115
Barth, K., 6
Barthes, R., 53
Bashook, P. G., 45
Bates, R. H., 45
Bateson, G., 18
Bateson, M. C., 61–62
Becker, H. S., 35, 39, 42–44, 72, 76, 86, 137, 141, 155, 162
Bennett, A., 36
Bensimon, E. M., 60
Berg, D. N., 98
Berkhofer, R., 30
Berlin, B., 177, 178
Bernard, J., 62
Bernstein, R. J., 50, 136

Bertsch, T., 122
Bhaskar, R., 1, 4, 4n1, 5n2, 11–12, 16, 24
Biklen, S. K., 104, 111
Bishop, B., 58
Bloch, M., 160–162
Blumer, H., 10–11, 19
Blumstein, P., 74
Boaler, J., 60
Bogdan, R., 104, 111
Bohman, J., 139
Bosk, C., 96
Boulding, K., 18
Boyd, R., 3, 128
Briggs, C., 143
Briggs, D., 130
Briggs, J., 46, 166–167, 173
Brinberg, D., 129
Britan, G., 37
Brown, L. M., 101
Bruner, J., 54
Brydon-Miller, M., 96, 101–102
Burbules, N. C., 52–53
Burch, E. S. Jr., 177
Burman, E., 101

Cabeza, R., 111
Callinicos, A., 12, 20, 41, 133
Campbell, D. T., 1, 4, 4n1, 5n2, 6, 12, 42, 128, 130, 133–134, 140, 144, 166
Carruthers, P., 18
Carter, B., 10

Cartwright, N., 4, 33, 36, 40, 47n4
Chambers, E., 26, 30
Chandler, J., 145
Clark, A. M., 11
Coffey, A., 110, 112, 118, 123, 125
Cole, M., 22, 30
Collier, A., 4
Cook, T. D., 4, 5n2, 128, 130, 133–134,
    140, 142
Corbin, J., 94, 103, 112, 119–120
Corlett, W., 64
Cottrell, C., 160–161
Coventry, A., 34n1
Craik, F. I. M., 110–111

D'Andrade, R. G., 22
Danermark, B., 10, 128
Davidson, A., 145
Davidson, D., 4, 19
Dawkins, R., 163n2
de Waal, F., 18
Deemer, D. K., 12
Denzin, N. K., 127
Dere, E., 110–111
Devitt, M., 3, 8
Dexter, L. A., 143
Dey, I., 125
Dickinson, A., 39
Dixon, H. A., 38
Dobzhansky, T., 23
Dole, G., 160
Dressman, M., 86
Dunn, J., 42
Durkheim, E., 58, 63

Easton, A., 111
Eckert, P., 101
Eggan, F., 46, 152, 154–156, 159, 162
Eisenhower, D., 77
Eisner, E. W., 144
Ekstrom, M., 10
Erickson, F., 37, 44, 116, 119, 134, 138,
    140, 143–144
Erikson, K., 29, 55–57
Ezzy, D., 51, 110

Falleti, T., 36
Fanshel, D., 116

Faulkner, S. L., 21
Fetterman, D. M., 138
Feyerabend, P., 8, 17
Fielding, J. L., 37, 106
Fielding, N. G., 107
Fischer, P. J., 45
Fracchia, J., 163n2
Frazer, E., 5
Freidson, E., 142

Gawande, A., 145
Gee, J. P., 116
Geer, B., 43, 76
Geertz, C., 27, 57–58, 135, 138
Gellner, E., 21
George, A., 36
Gerson, E. M., 120n1
Giere, R. A., 4, 9, 19
Gilligan, C., 101, 105, 122–123
Giroux, H., 52
Given, L., 11, 21, 35
Glesne, C., 83–84, 95, 97, 101,
    104, 113
Goldenberg, C., 40, 45
Gould, S. J., 49–50, 163
Gowin, D. B., 88
Greene, J., 66, 107
Greif, A., 45
Groff, R., 5n2, 36
Guba, E. G., 12, 35, 45, 129
Guemple, D. L., 177
Guevara, H., 21

Haack, S., 4
Hammersley, M., 3–4, 6, 10–11, 46, 65,
    96, 100, 107, 130, 132–133,
    144, 160
Hannerz, U., 28, 55, 67, 179
Harlow, L. L., 103
Harootunian, H., 145
Harre, R., 139
Hawthorn, G., 20, 63
Hecht, M. L., 21
Heider, E. R., 28, 31, 66
Heider, K., 28
Heil, J., 19
Heinrich, B., 18
Hemholz, 133n2

Hempel, C. G., 26, 34
Henry, G. T., 4
Hesse-Biber, S., 113–114, 143
Hodkinson, P., 12
Hoffman Davis, J., 100
House, E. R., 16, 35, 130, 139
Howe, K. R., 18n3, 19
Huang, B., 117
Huberman, A. M., 4, 6, 11, 16, 37, 39–40,
    46, 78, 88, 90, 94n1, 95, 111, 114,
    117–119, 125, 131, 144–145
Huck, S. W., 94n1, 108
Hughes, E. C., 76
Hume, D., 34n1, 38, 53–54
Huston, J. P., 111
Hutchins, E., 29

Ignatieff, M., 58, 61

Jakobsen, L., 10
Jakobson, R., 53–54, 123
James, W., 9, 16
Jankowski, M. S., 39
Jansen, G., 98
Johnson, M., 4, 9, 17–18, 134
Julnes, G., 4
Julnes, J., 4

Kaplan, A., 123, 129n1, 133n2,
    134–135, 145, 164
Karlsson, J., 10
Kay, P., 178
Keesing, R., 28
Keller, E. F., 6–8, 11–12, 133n2
Kelley, W. R., 172
Keohane, R. O., 41
Kerlinger, F. N., 8
Kincheloe, J., 65–66
King, G., 41
Kirk, J., 104–105, 134, 139–140
Kitcher, P., 33
Knapp, N. F., 73
Knorr-Cetina, K., 13n3
Kroeber, A. L., 22–25, 27–28
Kronenfeld, D. B., 28, 30, 179
Kuhn, T., 136
Kummer, H., 39
Kvale, S., 50

Labov, W., 116
Lacey, N., 5
Lakoff, G., 4–5, 17, 30, 109n1, 134
Lave, C. A., 88
Lawrence-Lightfoot, S., 100
Lawson, T.4, 4, 13, 36
Layton, R., 41
Leach, M. S., 50, 65
Leavy, P., 113–114, 123
LeCompte, M. D., 78, 113
Lenk, H., 6
Leplin, J., 3
Levi, M., 45
Levi-Strauss, C., 53
Levine, J. M., 29
LeVine, R. A., 29
Lewontin, R. C., 23, 49, 163n2
Lieblich, A., 44
Light, R. J., 34
Lincoln, Y. S., 6, 11–12, 35, 45,
    127, 129, 139
Linde, C., 116
Lindsley, S. L., 21
Linton, R., 28
Little, D., 4, 9, 36–37, 45
Lofland, J., 35, 115
Lofland, L., 35, 115
Loomis, D., 45, 74–75, 77, 81
Lundsgaarde, H. P., 45
Lurz, R. W., 18
Lynch, J., 36
Lyons, J., 53

MacIntyre, A., 19, 21, 102
Manicas, P. T., 4, 11, 34, 40,
    133n2, 139, 147
March, J. G., 88
Margolis, J., 96
Mark, M. M., 4, 6
Marshall, C., 76
Maxwell, J. A., 6, 8–9, 13, 27–28, 30,
    34–35, 41, 43, 45–46, 51, 66–67, 69,
    71–72, 74–75, 77–79, 81–82, 86–88,
    91, 93, 95, 99–100, 102, 103, 106,
    111, 128, 130–131, 137, 142, 145,
    147–148, 158, 160–162, 164, 167,
    170, 176, 179–180
Mayes, A. H., 111

Mayr, E., 49, 59
McAdam, D., 37
McCawley, J. D., 31
McGinn, C., 4, 19
McGrath, J. E., 129
McKinley, R., 28, 161–162
McLaren, P., 65–66
McMillan, J. H., 111–112
Mead, G. H., 42
Medill, A., 11
Medin, D., 28–29, 31, 163n2, 179
Mele, A., 19
Menzel, H., 19, 21, 139
Merriam, S., 114
Michotte, A. E., 39
Miles, M. B., 4, 6, 11, 16, 37, 39–40, 46,
    78, 88, 90, 95, 111, 114, 117–119,
    123–125, 131, 144–145
Milgram, S., 45
Mill, J. S., 34
Miller, A., 3
Miller, B.
Miller, B. A., 69, 120
Miller, M., 119, 134, 139–140
Miller, P., 127–128, 137
Mishler, E. G., 114, 116–117,
    130–131, 143
Mittapalli, K., 13, 43, 179
Mohr, L. B., 34, 36, 146
Morgan, D. L., 21, 93
Morrison, K., 36
Morse, J. M., 38
Mulaik, S. A., 9, 35, 103
Murdock, G. P., 153n1, 154–156, 160
Murnane, R. J., 9, 35
Murphy, R. F., 28, 161–162

Nadel, L., 111
Neumann, A., 60
New, C., 10
Newton, R. R., 78
Niiniluoto, I., 3, 128
Nisbet, R. A., 55, 63
Norrie, A., 4
Norris, C., 12
Norris, S. P., 8, 90, 128, 130
Novak, J. D., 88
Nyberg, L., 111

Oppenheim, P., 34

Palys, T., 94–95
Parsons, T., 22–24, 27, 63
Pattee, H. H., 24
Patton, M. Q., 95, 104, 115, 142, 144
Pawson, R., 4n1, 11, 36, 40, 141, 147,
    149, 164
Pelto, G., 28, 31, 49
Pelto, P., 28, 31, 49
Perkins, D., 29
Peshkin, A., 82–84, 97–99
Pfaffenberger, B., 113, 123
Phillips, D. C., 3, 8, 129
Platt, J. R., 42, 131, 144
Poggie, J. J. Jr., 31
Popper, K., 42
Porter, S., 11, 130
Portmann, A., 18
Pratt, M. L., 29
Preissle, J., 78, 99, 113
Premack, A. J., 39
Premack, D., 39
Putnam, H., 3–5, 8–9, 11, 16–17,
    19, 24, 133

Rabinow, P., 101
Radcliffe-Brown, A. R., 154
Ragin, C. C., 36
Rappaport, R., 28
Regan-Smith, M. G., 46–47
Reichardt, C. S.
Resnick, L. B., 29–30
Rey, G., 18
Rice, S., 52–53
Richards, L., 123
Robb, D., 19
Robson, C., 75, 78
Rorty, R., 52, 133n2, 136
Rosch, E., 134
Rosenau, P. M., 50–51, 66–67
Rosenthal, J-L., 45
Rossman, G., 76
Rousseau, J., 175
Rudestam, K. E., 78
Runciman, W. G., 133–135, 137, 140
Russell, B., 8
Ryle, G., 18

Salmon, W. C., 3–4, 8, 33–35,
    38n3, 147
Sandlow, L. J., 45
Sanjek, R., 28
Sankoff, G., 28, 31, 66
Sapir, E., 9
Saussure, F. de, 53–54
Sayer, A., 1, 4, 11, 19, 21, 24, 27, 36–37,
    40, 42, 45, 54, 147
Scheffler, H. W., 168
Schmid, M., 27, 63
Schneider, D. M., 26, 31, 157, 160,
    168, 176
Schoen, D. A., 139
Schumacher, S., 111–112
Schwandt, T. A., 3, 6, 21, 34, 145
Schwartz, P., 74
Scott, D., 12
Scriven, M., 38, 42, 47, 136, 145
Seale, C., 11, 13, 129–130, 132, 134,
    137, 145
Seidman, I. E., 101, 110, 115–116, 118
Service, E. R., 154, 160
Shadish, W. R., 5, 46, 75n1, 130
Shaffer, C., 59
Shakespeare, W., 18, 135
Shanks, D., 39
Shavelson, R., 35
Sheldon, R. C., 27
Shepard, L. A., 113
Shettleworth, S., 18, 111
Shore, B., 28, 30
Shubin, N., 77
Shulman, L., 65
Silverstein, M., 171
Simon, H., 24
Singer, J., 34
Smith, J. K., 12, 131
Smith, K. K., 98, 113
Smith, L., 110
Smith, M. L., 12
Spencer, R., 122
Sperber, D., 39
Stake, R., 93, 114
Stanley, J., 130
Staples, M., 60
Starnes, B., 94n1
Stawson, 34n1

Steele, D. J., 45
Steiger, J. H., 103
Steward, J., 153
Strauss, A. L., 76, 87, 94, 103, 111–112,
    118–120, 142
Strauss, C., 64
Strawson, G., 8, 34
Strike, K., 52
Suppe, F., 3
Swartz, M. J., 28
Sypnowich, C., 28

Tambiah, S., 161
Tappan, M., 98
Tarrow, S., 37
Teasley, S. D., 29
Tesch, R., 113–114, 124
Tetzlaff, M., 18
Tilley, N., 4, 11, 36, 40, 141, 149
Tilly, C., 13, 36–37
Tinbergen, N., 18
Toennies, F., 57
Tolman, D. L., 96, 98, 101–102
Toulmin, S., 24
Towne, L., 35
Trend, M., 45
Tulving, E., 110–111
Tuval-Mashiach, R., 44
Tylko, S. J., 38
Tyson, D., 77

Urban, G., 28, 30

Varenne, H., 30
Verba, S., 41
Voget, F., 157

Wahl, B., 91
Waletzky, J., 116
Wallace, A. F. C., 28–29, 179
Watson, J. D., 82
Wax, R., 102
Webb, R. B., 113
Weber, M., 42
Weinberg, M. C., 122
Weingast, B. R., 45
Weisner, T. S., 45
Weiss, R. S., 37, 95, 107

Weitzman, E. A., 123–124

Welch, S. D., 63

Wheeler, M. A., 111

Wieviorka, M., 117

Willett, J. B., 9, 34–35, 60

Williams, B., 57

Willis, P., 28

Wimsatt, W., 4, 166

Wolcott, H. F., 133, 135, 138

Wolf, M., 66

Yanagisako, S., 31

Yin, R. K., 93–94, 114, 141, 162

Young, I. M., 52, 61–62, 67

Zilber, T., 44

Subject Index

Abstraction, 26–27
Account, 138–140
    cultural, 26
    descriptive validity of, 137
    validity of, 133–134
Action, 19, 179–180
Affirmative postmodernism, 50–51, 67
Agential realism, 4
Alternative hypothesis, 144
American Kinship: A Cultural Account
    (Schneider), 157
Analytic generalization, 94
Analytic narrative, 45
Analytic strategy. *See also* Categorizing
    strategy; Connecting strategy
    for categorization, 117
    contiguity of, 109, 116
    data analysis of, 110
    of similarity and contiguity, 109
    types of, 109
Animal mind, 18
Aphasia, 123
Arbitrary causal judgment, 39
Association, 53
Associative relationship, 55

Behaviorism, 17–18, 26, 158, 168–170
Belief, 19–20, 72, 86
Bias, 82
    methodological, 64–66
    in qualitative research, 64
    in quantitative research, 64

of subjectivity, 97
subjectivity as, 97–98
systematic, 106
uniformist, 66
Big Sort: How the Clustering of
    Like-Minded America Is Tearing
    Us Apart, The (Bishop), 58
Biological organism, 22–24
Black box approach to causation, 34-37,
    146, 181
Blackfeet kinship, 158–159

Case-focused analysis, 110
Case study, 114
Categories, 111–113
    functional, 117
    organizational, 111–112
    substantive, 112, 117
    theoretical, 112–113
    types of, 111–113
Categorization, 44
    connecting strategy and, 118–123
    dangers of, 115
    in qualitative research, 44
    in quantitative research, 44
Categorizing strategy, 109 ff.
Causal claim, 35, 42
Causal cognition, 39
Causal explanation, 11, 16, 19, 33 ff.,
    90, 149, 156, 161–164. *See also*
    Causation
    constructivism and, 34

context-dependence of , 40, 114
development of, 42–43
positivist view of, 34
process of, 36–37
realist view of, 34
regularity theory of, 34, 37
validity of, 164
variance-theory model of, 34, 37
Causal inference, 46
Causal judgment, arbitrary, 39
Causal knowledge, 39
Causal maps, 39, 40, 42
Causal mechanism, 40, 43
Causal narrative, 42
Causal pluralism, 47
Causal process, 36, 38–39, 47
Causal research, 35, 129
Causal validity, 140
Causality, local, 37, 40, 44, 90.
    See also Causal explanation
Causation
    analysis of, 34
    causal/mechanical view of,
        35comparison and, 46–47
    concept of, 2, 32, 35, 41, 128, 181
    connecting analysis and, 44–45
    contextualization and, 40
    covering law approach to, 34
    deductive-nomological theory of, 34
    evidence for, 41–42
    Humean view of, 36–37
    intervention and, 45–46long-term
        involvement and, 43–44
    meaning and, 20, 40–43
    modus operandi strategy for, 47
    and narrative analysis, 44–45
    observation of, 38–39, 43-44
    process of, 36–37, 41
    realist view of, 35, 38, 41, 47
    regularity theory of, 9, 34–36,
        34n1, 114, 128
    rich data and, 43–44
    in single case studies, 38–39
    social, 36–37
    secessionist theory of, 34
    theory of, 8–9, 147–148
    thick description and, 43–44
Cause, 8, 19, 34, 47

Cause explanation, 41
Change
    causal process of, 158–159
    in kinship, 152–153
    social, 152–153, 159
Children, treatment of, 173–176
Claim, 42, 145–147
Coding, 111–114
    categories of, 111, 121
    concept and, contrast
        between, 110
    of data, 121
    defined, 119
    in narrative, 117, 122
    open, 119
    strategies for, 118
Cognition, 29–30, 39
Cognitive consistency, 60
Coherence, 67
Collective consciousness, 63
Common ties in community, 62
Communal relationship, 55
Communication, personal, 105
Community
    common ties in, 62
    contiguity in, 55–59
    difference and, 60, 62
    homogeneous, 58
    linguistics of, 29
    loss of, 55
    postmodernism and, 51–53
    realism and, 51–53
    similarity and contiguity in, 52–53,
        59, 61
    social interaction in, 62
    solidarity in, 55–59
Comparability, 94
Comparison, 46–47, 156
Complementarity, 60–61, 63, 123
Complexity, 24, 63
Composite sequence analysis, 119
Computers, 123–125
Concept mapping, 88
Concepts, 18, 72, 110
Conceptual framework, 77–78
    alternative theories for, 86
    defined, 85–86
    evaluating, 86

heuristics for, 86
sources for, 87–88
theoretical modules for, 86
Conceptualization, 167, 170, 178
Conclusion, 97, 131–132, 148
Conditional path, 119
Conflict theory, 65
Connectedness, 60, 62
Connecting strategies, 44–45. 109 ff.
    categorizing and, 118–123
    of display, 117–118
    overview of, 115
Connection, 119, 170
Consensus theory, 65, 140–141
Consistency, cognitive, 60
Constant conjunction of events, 34
Construct validity, 137, 140
Constructive realism, 4
Constructivism, 20, 33, 41, 151
    on causal explanation, 34
    epistemological, 6, 10
    paradigm of, 127–128
    and trustworthiness, 128
    and validity, 128
Constructivist epistemology, 180
Contact, linguistics of, 29
Contextual analysis, 117
    causation and, 40
    of evidence, 146
Contextual relations, 115, 118–119, 164
Contiguity. *See also* Similarity and
        contiguity
    as source of coherence, 67
    in community, 55–59
    complementarity and , 123
    connection and, 119
    in contemporary society, 59–60
    of data, 111
    difference and, relationship
        between, 54
    display of, 117–118
    integration and, 67
    interdependence and, 54
    loss of, 56
    relationship and, 53, 109
    solidarity and, sources of, 54–59, 62,
        64, 110–111
    theoretical analysis of, 109

Western social theory and, 59
Contiguity disorder, 123
Control group, 45
Controlled comparison, 46, 156
Convenience sampling, 95
Covering law approach, 34
Credibility, 148
Critical ethnography, 65
Critical humility, 66
Critical realism, 4n1, 5n2, 8–10, 12, 30,
        160–164
    dialectical, 4
    postmodernism and, 49–50, 67
Critical validity, 140, 143
Cultural account, 26
Cultural diversity, 59
Cultural phenomenon, 54, 66
Cultural system. *See* Culture
Cultural theory, 27
Culture, 27
    as abstraction, 26–27
    concept of, 1–2, 15, 21–25, 28–29,
        31, 161, 177
    defined, 21–22, 26
    distributional view of, 31
    diversity within, 29, 66
    ideological approaches to, 28, 30
    Inuit, 177–180
    levels conception of, 27
    as mental, 161
    mind and, 21–32
    nonreflectionist view of, 28
    psychological useful concept of, 22
    realist concept of, 15, 25, 30–31,
        161, 177
    replication of uniformity approach
        to, 29
    as shared concepts, 28–32, 179–180
    traditional concept of, 15, 22, 29
    uniformist view of, 49

Darwinian revolution, 49
Data
    coding of, 121
    contiguity of, 111
    direct analysis of, 118
    as evidence, 103
    fracturing the, 111

observable, 90
rich, 43–44
sense, 97
validity of, 133–134
Data analysis, 109 ff.
Data collection, 103–107
  observation and, 106–107
  research questions and, 104–106
  strategies for, 106
  triangulation and, 106–107
Decontextualizing, 113, 115
Deductive-nomological theory,
  33–34
Deforming power of established
  theory, 153–154, 155
Descriptive validity, 134–137
  of account, 137
  characteristics of, 135–136
  observation and, 135
  overview of, 134–135
  positivism and, 136–137
  primary, 135
  reliability of, 137
  secondary, 135
Design map, 80–81
Dialectical critical realism, 4
Difference, 52
  as basis for solidarity, 52–53
  community and, 60, 62
  politics of, 62
Direct analysis of data, 118
Displays, 117–118
Distributed intelligence, 29
Distributional view of culture, 31
Diversity
  of conceptualization, 178
  cultural, 29, 59, 66
  intracultural, 31, 49
  in Inuit culture, 177–180
  irreducible, 66
  of meaning, 177–180
  methodology and, 64–66
  postmodernism and, 51–53,
    66–67
  within qualitative research, 64–65
  real phenomenon of, 49 ff., 90
  unity and, 52
Division of labor, 29

Dualism, 15–17

Ecological self, 59
Emergent realism, 4
Emic category, 112
Empiricism, 20, 33–34
Environment for research design, 80
Episodic memory, 110
Epistemic fallacy, 12–13
Epistemological collapse, 12
Epistemological constructivism, 6, 10
Epistemology, 12–13, 128–129
  constructivist, 180
  evolutionary, 5n2
  of solidarity, 63
Espoused theory, 139
Essentialism, 49
Established theory, 153–155
Ethical issues in research relationship, 101
Ethnographic microanalysis, 44, 116, 119
Ethnography, critical, 65
Etic category, 113
Evaluative validity, 143–144
Evidence
  for causation, 41–42
  claim and, 145–147
  concept of, 127, 145, 148
  contextualization of, 146
  data collection as, 103
  defined, 145
  property of, 145–146
  in qualitative research, 146, 148
  in quantitative research, 146
Evidence-based research, 128–129
Evolutionary epistemology, 5n2
Evolutionary theory, 49
Exemplars, as approach to validity,
  130–131
Experiential realism, 4, 30
Experimental design, 75n1
Experimental intervention, 45
Explanation, 140
  cause, 41
  credible, 182
  process, 36, 44
  reason, 41
  variance-theory model of, 34
Explanatory theory, 41

External generalizability, 142–143
External reality, 128
External validity, 128, 134. *See also*
    Generalizability
External world, knowledge of, 72

Facts, as evidence, 146-147
Fallacy, epistemic, 12–13
Fixed research designs, 75
Fracturing the data, 111
Functional categorization, 117

Genealogical connection, 170
Generalizability, 141–143
Generalization, 90, 94, 127, 162
Generalized elimination model,
    144–145
Goals
    change in, 82
    defined, 81–82
    intellectual, 84–85
    practical, 84–85
    as real properties of researcher , 82
"God's eye view" of phenomenon, 133
Grounded theory research, 103, 119–120,
    120n1
Group solidarity, 157

Habitus, 64
*Handbook of North American
    Indians*, 162
Handicraft production, 125
Hegemony, 67, 86
Heterogeneity, 60
Heuristics, 86
Homogeneity, 29, 52
Homogeneous community, 58
Human Relations Area Files
    (HRAF), 153
Humean view of causation, 36–37
Hypertext program, 125
Hypothesis, 42, 144
Hypothesis testing, 103
Hypothetical question, 85

Idea, 53
Idealism, 10
Ideational phenomena, 21

Identity, 61, 72
Ideological distortion, 28
Ideological hegemony, 86
Ila, 168–173
Image, 18
Immaculate perception, 97
Impostor syndrome, 82
Imprisonment in story, 117
Individualism, liberal, 52
Inference
    causal, 46
    interpretive validity of, 138–139
    validity of, 133
Innocent realism, 4
Inquiry-guided research, 130
Instrumentalism, 8, 90, 128–129, 133
Integration, 67
Intellectual goal, 84–85
Intelligence, distributed, 29
Intended research design, 73
Intention, 18–19
Interaction, 77
    ethnographic microanalysis of,
        44, 116
    of procedures and phenomena, 132
    social, 62
    symbolic, 19
Interconnectedness of meaning and
    world, 180
Interdependence, 54
Internal generalizability, 142–143
Internal validity, 128, 140
Interpretation
    contradictory, 107
    credibility of, 148
    of data collection, 103
    divergent, 107
    process of, 36
Interpretive claim, 146
Interpretive qualitative research, 96–97
Interpretive research, 18n3
Interpretive understanding, 21, 41
Interpretive validity, 137–139
Interpretivism, 6, 20, 151, 156–160.
    See also Interpretation
Intervention, 45–46
Interview/interviewing, 167
    analysis of, 110

data collection, process for, 104–107
generalizability of, 143
Intracultural diversity, 31, 49
Introspection, 18
Inuit culture, 177–180
Inuit kinship, 176–177
Invalidity, 131
Irreducible diversity, 66
Isomorphism, 133
Issue-focused analysis, 110

Judgment, 39, 128

Kin terminology, 159–162, 171–176
Kinship
    Blackfeet, 158–159
    change in, theories of, 152–153
    defined, 171–173
    Inuit, 176–177
Knowledge, 39, 72, 131"Law of the
    Instrument, The," 123–124

Level of organization, 24
Levels conception of culture, 27
Liberal individualism, 52
Linguistics, 29, 53–54
Listening guide strategy, 122–123
Literature review, 87
Local causality, 37, 40, 44, 90
Logic-in-use, 71–72, 74, 145, 164
Logic of identity, 61
Logical positivism, 33, 128
Logico-scientific thought, 54
Long-term involvement, 43–44
Longitudinal comparison, 46
Loss, shared experience of, 55–56

Manipulation, experimental, 45
Map/mapping
    causal, 39, 40, 42
    concept, 88
    design, 80–81
    research design, 80–81
Marxism, 21
Material phenomenon, 21
Matrix , 118, 121–122
Meaning and mind
    behaviorism and, 158

causation and, 20, 40–43
consequence of, 19
critical realist approach to, 15–21
interconnectedness of, 180
nature of, 15
nonmaterial entities, 18
Meaningful phenomena, 21, 24
Mechanical causation, 35
Mechanical solidarity, 63
Mechanism, 39, 164
    causal, 40, 43
    concept of, 9
Memetics, 163
Memo
    reflective, 102–103
    research identity, 72, 82, 99
Memory, 110
Mental phenomena , 15–16, 20, 41, 103
Method
    and question, relationship between, 106
    as component of research design, 77–78
    scientific, 131
    and validity, 128-132
Methodological bias, 64–66
Mind, 15–21. See also Meaning and mind
    animal, study of, 18
    culture and, 21–32 (See also Culture)
    nature of, 15
Mind-body problem, 15
Moderate postmodernism, 50–51
"Modus operandi" strategy, 47
Mood, 18
Morality, 56
Multi-perspectival realism, 5
Multilinear evolution, 153
Multiple realities, 9
Myth, 53

Nagli, 176
Naïve realism, 5–6
Narratives, 116, 118–119
    analysis of, 110, 117
    analytic, 45
    causal, 42, 44–45
    coding and, 117, 122
    matrices and, 122
    types of, 110
Narrative thought, 54

Natural causal perception, 39
Natural realism, 4
Natural sciences, 153n1
Naturalism, 17
Network, 118
New World Encyclopedia, 153
Nonreflectionist view of culture, 28
Norm, 56

Objectively knowable reality, 127
Objectivism, 5, 128, 131
Observable action, 179
Observation
    of causation, 38–39, 47
    data collection and, 106–107
    descriptive validity and, 135
    participant, 167
Omission, 137
Ontological collapse, 12
Ontological realism, 5–6, 8, 10-13, 107
Ontology, 12–13, 89, 128–129
Open coding, 119
Operational definition, 128
Operationalism, 104, 128
Organic solidarity, 55, 58, 62–63
Organism, biological, 22–24
Organization, 24, 29
Organizational category, 111–112

Paradigm, social research, 151
Paradigmatic relationship, 53, 133n2
Paradigmatic thought, 54
Participant observation, 167
Participatory qualitative research,
    96–97
Pathological metonym, 125
Perception, 39, 97
Personal relationship, 96
Personality, 22–24, 27
Perspective, 106, 109
Phenomena
    biological, 24, 27
    cultural, 54, 66
    "God's eye view" of, 133
    ideational, 21
    linguistic, 54
    local, 90
    material, 21

meaningful, 21, 24
mental, 15–16, 20, 103
physical, 20, 40
physical-behavioral, 24
separate, 20
single complex, 107
social, 20, 40, 54, 66, 139
sociocultural, 24
symbolic, 32
Philosophic realism, 3
Philosophical debate over realism, 3–4
Philosophical diversity, 31
Physical-behavioral phenomena , 24
Physical phenomenon, 20, 40
Physical process, 43
Physical science, 38n3
Physical world, 180
Physicalism, 15–16
Pluralism, 47, 63
Political issues in research
    relationship, 101
Population thinking, 49
Positivism/positivist, 8, 20, 26, 151,
    152–156
    approaches to validity, 128, 133
    assumptions of, 141
    causal explanation and, 34
    descriptive validity and, 136–137
    logical, 33, 128
    rejection of, 156–160
Postmodernism, 9–10
    affirmative, 50–51, 67
    characteristics of, 66
    critical realism and, 67
    diversity and, 51–53, 66–67
    moderate, 50–51
    skeptical, 67
Postpositivism, 151
Practical goal, 84–85
Primary descriptive validity, 135
Primary understanding, 135
Probability sampling, 93–94, 95
Procedural validity, 129–130,
    129n1, 131
Process, 37, 103, 146
    analysis of, 39
    approach to causation, 36–39, 41, 47
    of interpretation, 36

physical, 43
   social, 42–43
Process explanation, 36, 44
Process theory, 90
Process tracing, 45
Profiles, 110, 116
Psychophysical correlation, 16
Purposeful sampling, 94, 95, 142
Purposive selection, 95

Qualitative data analysis. *See also*
   Categorizing strategy; Connecting
   strategy
   computers and, 123–125
   grounded theory method for, 119
   realist perspective on, 109
Qualitative research, 10, 127
   analysis in, 65
   bias in, 64
   categorization in, 44, 109n1
   causal explanation to, 41
   critical approach to, 21
   data collection in, 65
   diversity within, 64–65
   evidence in, 146, 148
   explicit comparison in, 46
   generalizability in, 141–142
   generalization of, 94, 162
   grounded theory approach to, 103
   interpretive, 96–97
   participatory, 96–97
   philosophical diversity within, 31
   quality of, 132
   quantitative research and, 66
   realist ontology for, 13
   sampling in, 93
   subjectivity, as constituent for
      understanding, 98
   trustworthiness of, 129
   validity of, 129, 133–145
Qualitative research design, 76–77
*Qualitative Research Design: An
   Interactive Approach* (Maxwell),
   91, 145
Quality
   of conclusions, 131
   constructivism and, 128
   positivism and, 128

of qualitative research, 132
   realism and, 148
Quantification, 45
Quantitative research
   bias in, 64
   categorization in, 44
   causal, 35
   evidence in, 146
   explicit comparison in, 46
   qualitative research, combination
      of, 66
   sampling in, 93
Quantitative research design, 76
Quasi-foundationalist, realism as, 11–12
Quasi-statistics, 137
Question. *See also* Research questions
   real, 105

Random sampling, 94, 142, 142n1
Randomized controlled trial (RCT), 129
Rapport, 101
Real phenomenon/phenomena, 13,
      20–22, 85, 90, 107, 131, 161, 163-164
   causality as, 8-9
   contiguity as, 67
   diversity as, 2, 49 ff., 90, 102
   goals as, 69
   meaning as, 168, 177, 179, 181
   reasons as, 41
   research designs as, 71-72
   research relationships as, 97, 100
Real question, 105
Real world, 127–128
Realism, 17, 33–34, 151
   agential, 4
   of causation, 35, 38, 41, 47
   constructive, 4
   of credibility, 148
   critical, 4, 4n1, 5n2, 8–10, 12, 20–21,
      30, 49–50, 164
   culture and, concept of, 25, 30–31
   of diversity, 51–53, 64, 66
   emergent, 4
   experiential, 4, 30
   of goal, 82–84
   innocent, 4
   of interpretive validity, 139
   of knowledge, 72

for mental phenomenon, 41
multi-perspectival, 5
naïve, 5–6
natural, 4
objections and, 5
ontological, 5–6, 10
philosophical, 3–4
for qualitative research, 11, 13,
    22, 166
of quality, 148
quasi-foundationalist, 11–12
realist view of, 5–6
of research design, 71, 73–74, 97
scientific, 3–4
of subjectivity, 98
subtle, 4, 11, 132
of trustworthiness, 148
of validity, 130–132, 133, 148
Realist culture, 15, 161, 177
Realist ontology, 13, 89
Realist perspective, 109
Realist theory, 176–177
Realist understanding, 51–53
Realist view of realism, 5–6
Reality/realities
    of diversity, 66
    external, 128
    multiple, 9
    nature of, 127
    objectively knowable, 127
Reason explanation, 41
Reconstructed logic, 71–72, 74,
    145, 164
Recontextualization, 113
Reductionism, 17
Reductionist physicalism, 16
Reflective memo, 102–103
Reflexivity, 96
Regularity theory
    of causal explanation, 37
    of causation, 9, 34–36, 34n1, 114, 128
Relationship. See also Research
    relationship
    associative, 55
    communal, 55
    contiguity and, 53, 109
    paradigmatic, 53, 133n2
    between similarity and contiguity, 53

syntagmatic, 53, 133n2
    virtual, 109
Relatives, 168
Relativism, 20, 110
Reliability, 128, 137
Replication of uniformity, 29
Reportage, 135
Representativeness, 93–94
Research. See also Qualitative research;
    Quantitative research
    causal, 129
    on diversity, 51
    evidence-based, 128–129
    grounded theory, 103, 119–120, 120n1
    inquiry-guided, 130
    interpretive, 18n3
    science-based, 41, 128–129
    social, 19, 41, 151
    subjectivity and, 97
Research conclusion, 97
Research design, 45, 77–78
    components of, 77–81, 91
        (See also Individual components)
    conceptual framework for, 75, 76,
        85–88
    conduct of, 71
    contextualization of, 80–81
    defined, 75, 76
    environment of, 80
    fixed, 75
    flexible, 75
    intended, 73
    interactive model of, 77–80
    mapping of, 80–81
    products of, 80
    qualitative, 76–77
    quantitative, 76
    as real entity, 71
    research question and, 88–91
    sequential concept of, 76
    systemic model of, 77
    typological concept of, 75–76
Researcher identity memo, 72, 82
Research questions
    assumptions of, risk of, 89
    data collection and, 104–106
    and interview questions, distinction
        between, 104–105

operationalizing, 104
process theory for, 90
purpose of, 88–89
research design and, 88–91
types of, 89–90
Research relationship
conceptualization of, 100, 101, 167
establishing, 96
ethical issues in, 101
personal subjectivity and, 96
political issues in, 101
process for creating, 101
and rapport, 101
real phenomenon of, 102
revisionist view of, 100
sampling and, 93–96
Researcher subjectivity, 96–103
    See also Subjectivity
Researcher identity, 72
Researcher identity memo, 72, 99
Resemblance, 53, 54
Rich data, 43–44
Rival hypothesis, 42

SAGE Dictionary of Qualitative Inquiry
    (Schwandt), 21–22
SAGE Encyclopedia of Qualitative
    Research Methods (Given), 21, 35
SAGE Handbook of Qualitative Research
    (Denzin and Lincoln), 26, 30
Sampling, 79
    convenience, 95
    guiding principles for, 94
    probability, 93–94, 95
    purposeful, 94, 95, 142
    in qualitative research, 93
    in quantitative research, 93
    random, 94, 94n1, 142
    representativeness of, 93
    selection strategy for, 95–96
    survey, 93
    theoretical, 94, 142
Schefflerian analysis, 175–177, 180
Science-based research, 41,
    128–129
Scientific concept, 90
Scientific investigation, 129
Scientific method, 131

Scientific objectivism, 5
Scientific realism, 3–4
Secondary descriptive validity, 135
Segmented causal network, 118
Selecting settings and participants.
    See Sampling
Selection, 95–96. See also Sampling
Semantic memory, 110
Semiology, 54
Sense data, 97, 141
Separate phenomenon, 20
Sequential research design, 76
Shared concept of culture, 28–32,
    179–180
Shared value, 56
Signature of cause, 47
Similarity and contiguity
    coherence, as fundamental
        source of, 67
    in community, 52–53, 59, 61
    complementarity of, 61, 123
    distinction between, 59, 61–64,
        110–111
    ideologies of, 58, 61
    integration of, 67
    relationship between, 53
    solidarity and, 52–55, 61–64
    theoretical analysis of, 109
    as virtual relationship, 109
    Western emphasis on, 62
Similarity disorder, 123
Situated relativity, 110
Skeptical postmodernism, 67
Social action, 180
Social causation, 36–37
Social change, 159
Social diversity, 59
Social interaction, 62
Social metaphysics, 177
Social order, 65
Social phenomena, 20, 40, 54, 66, 139
Social process, 42–43
Social research, 19, 41, 151
Social solidarity, 51, 54
Social Structure (Murdock), 153
Social system, 22–25, 27, 152–153
Social theory, 59
Socially distributed cognition, 29

Socially shared cognition, 30
Socially situated cognition, 29
Society theory, 42
Sociocultural phenomena, 24
Solidarity. *See also* Similarity and
    contiguity
  complementarity and, 63
  contiguity and, 54, 55–59, 62, 64
  difference, as basis for, 52–53
  diffuse enduring, 176
  epistemology of, 63
  group, 157
  heterogeneity and, 60
  ideology of, 61–64
  loss of, 55
  mechanical, 63
  organic, 55, 58, 62–63
  politics of, 52
  social, 51, 54
  source of, 53–55
Solidarity theory, 157
Statistical generalization, 93–94
Story/storytelling, 45, 110, 117, 119
Structural equation model, 35
Structuralist linguistics, 53
Subjectivism, 18. *See also* Subjectivity
Subjectivity, 97–98
Subjectivity statement, 99
Substantive categories, 112, 117
Subtle realism, 4, 11, 132
Successionist theory of causation, 34
Survey sampling, 93
Symbolic interactionism, 19
Symbolic phenomena, 21, 24
Systematic bias, 106
Systemic model of research design, 77
Syntagmatic relationship, 53, 133n2

Thematic classification, 114
Theoretical analysis, 109
Theoretical categories, 112–113
Theoretical instrumentalism, 8
Theoretical module for conceptual
    framework of research design, 86
Theoretical sampling, 94, 142
Theoretical understanding, 139–140
Theoretical validity, 139–140, 139–141
Theory-building program, 124–125

Theory-in-use, 134, 139
Thick description, 43–44, 179
Theory-free knowledge, 131
Thought, 54
Time-ordered matrix, 118
Totalizing metanarrative, 51, 66, 180
Traditional society, 153
Treatise of Human Nature, A (Hume), 53
Triangulation, 106–107
Trustworthiness, 128–129, 131, 148
Truth, 12, 67, 133

Unconscious belief, 72
Unconscious concept, 72
Uniformism, 65–66
Uniformist bias, 66
Uniformist view of culture, 49
Uniformity, 29
Unity, 52, 67
University of Chicago, 156

Validation, 130
Validity, 107
  of account, 133–134
  causal, 140
  of causal explanation, 164
  concept of, 127–128, 130, 133
  of conclusion, 131–132, 133
  constructivism and, 128, 137, 140
  critical, 140, 143
  of data, 133–134
  descriptive, 134–137
  evaluative, 143–144
  evidence and, 145
  exemplar as basis for, 131
  external, 128, 134 (*See also*
      Generalizability)
  generalizability and, 141–143
  of inference, 133
  instrumentalism and, 133
  internal, 128, 140
  interpretive, 137–139
  objectivism and, 131
  positivism and, 128, 133
  procedural approach to, 129–130,
      129n1, 131
  of qualitative research, 129, 133–145
  of quantitative research, 128

realism and, 130–132, 133, 148
rejection of, 130
as component of research design,
   77–78
secondary descriptive, 135
theoretical, 139–141
typology of, 133, 134
Validity threat, 27, 131, 147
Value, 20, 56
Variability, 66
Variable analysis, 36
Variance theory, 37n2
  black box of, 146

of causal explanation, 34, 37
and process theory, 36, 94, 146
question, 90
Verbal behavior, 18, 26
Vignettes, 110
Violence, gang, 39
Virtual relationship, 109

Western emphasis on similarity as
   basis for solidarity, 61–62
Western social theory, 59
Writing for Social Scientists
   (Becker), 72